Die Reihe „Weltwirtschaft und internationale Zusammenarbeit" wird herausgegeben von

Prof. (em.) Dr. Hartmut Sangmeister, Universität Heidelberg
Prof. Dr. Aurel Croissant, Universität Heidelberg
Prof. Dr. Detlef Nolte, GIGA Institut für Lateinamerika-Studien Hamburg

Band 21

Richard Scholz

Industrializing Africa

Understanding the Uniqueness of the Manufacturing Sector

Nomos

Der Druck der wissenschaftlichen Ausgabe wurde gefördert von:

WifOR
WIRTSCHAFTSFORSCHUNG

The Deutsche Nationalbibliothek lists this publication in the Deutsche Nationalbibliografie; detailed bibliographic data are available on the Internet at http://dnb.d-nb.de

a.t.: Leipzig, Univ., Diss., 2018

ISBN 978-3-8487-5180-8 (Print)
978-3-8452-9376-9 (ePDF)

British Library Cataloguing-in-Publication Data
A catalogue record for this book is available from the British Library.

ISBN 978-3-8487-5180-8 (Print)
978-3-8452-9376-9 (ePDF)

Library of Congress Cataloging-in-Publication Data
Scholz, Richard
Industrializing Africa
Understanding the Uniqueness of the Manufacturing Sector
Richard Scholz
280 p.
Includes bibliographic references.

ISBN 978-3-8487-5180-8 (Print)
978-3-8452-9376-9 (ePDF)

1st Edition 2018

Acknowledgments

First and foremost, I would like to express my sincere gratitude to my advisor Doz. Dr. Georg Quaas but also Prof. Dr. Friedrun Quaas for their continuous support of my dissertation. Their guidance, patience, motivation, and expertise helped me at all times of research and writing. I could not have imagined having better support for my doctoral thesis.

I am also thankful to my great colleagues in the Forschungsseminar Politik und Wirtschaft for a range of critical, valuable, and professional advice and discussions.

I am profoundly thankful to Prof. Dr. Robert Kappel for valuable advices and the assessment of my dissertation.

This thesis would not have been accomplished without financial support. Thus, I gratefully acknowledge the funding but also the valuable non-material support received from the Foundation of German Business (SDW). I also thank the FAZIT-Stiftung for its completion scholarship.

My sincere thanks are given to Helmut Asche, Trudi Hartzenberg, Anthony Black, Surajit Mazumdar, Ute Rietdorf, and Fabian Scholtes for always finding time for me as well as for their inspiring discussion and fruitful advices.

I would like to offer my special thanks to Jens Sommer-Ulrich who helped me especially during the time of writing my exposé. I also like to express my gratitude to Prof. Dr. Ullrich Heilemann and Prof. Dr. Udo Ludwig for their useful suggestions and letters of recommendations.

I owe a particular debt for precious critique and proof-reading to Martin Bull, Lucas Wotzka, Thomas Krause, Mischa Stratenwerth, Philipp Sack, Felix Arglist, Tabea Braun, Louisa Künstler, Martin Winkler, Theo Schöppenthau, Lasse Hansen, David Detterer, and Pascal Poss. Special thanks goes to Dr. Anne Hamker for language editing and proofreading.

Finally, I am indebted to my family and friends for providing wholehearted support and comfort whenever needed. A heartfelt thank goes out to my girlfriend Jenny for all her love, support, encouragement, and patience.

Leipzig, 21 May 2018 *Richard Scholz*

Content

List of figures

List of tables

Abbreviations

AfDB	African Development Bank
AGR	agriculture, hunting, forestry, and fishing
AMU	Arab Maghreb Union
APRM	African Peer Review Mechanism
AU	African Union
BII	backward integration index
BLH	Hirschman's backward linkage
BPI	backward participation index
COMESA	Common Market for Eastern and Southern Africa
CON	construction
DBL	domestic backward linkage
DFL	domestic forward linkage
e.g.	exempli gratia (for example)
EAC	East African Community
EC	European Commission
ECA	Economic Commission for Africa
ECCAS	Economic Community for Central African States
ECLAC	Economic Commission for Latin America and the Caribbean
EU	European Union
FII	forward integration index
FIRE	finance, insurance, real estate, and business services
FLH	Hirschman's forward linkage
FPI	forward participation index
GCC	global commodity chain
GCSPS	community, social, personal, and government services

GDP	gross domestic product
GGDC	Groningen Growth and Development Center
GTAP	Global Trade and Analysis Project
GVC	Global Value Chain
i.e.	id est (that is to say)
IBL	international backward linkages
IFL	international forward linkages
IMF	International Monetary Fund
ISIC	International Standard Industrial Classification
MAN	manufacturing
MENA	Middle East and North Africa
MIN	mining and quarrying
MITI	Ministry of International Trade and Industry
MRIO	multiregional input-output table
NACE	Nomenclature Générale des Activités Économiques dans les Communautés Européennes
NDE	New Development Economics
nec.	not elsewhere classified
NEPAD	New Partnership for Africa's Development
NIC	Newly Industrializing Countries
OAU	Organisation of African Unity
OECD	Organisation for Economic Co-Operation and Development
PI	total participation index
PPP	Purchasing Power Parity
PRIM	primary sectors
PU	public utilities (electricity, gas, and water)
RCA	revealed comparative advantage
REC	regional economic community
SADC	Southern African Development Community

SAP	structural adjustment programs
SER	services
SIC	Standard Industrial Classification
SITC	Standard International Trade Classification
SNA	system of national accounts
SUM	economy-wide (sum of all sectors)
TiVA	trade in value added
TSC	transport, storage, and communications
UN	United Nations
UNCTAD	United Nations Commission for Trade and Development
UNDP	United Nation Development Program
UNIDO	United Nations Industrial Development Organization
US	United States
USD	United States Dollar
UTI	utilities
WBL	world backward linkage
WDR	World Development Report
WFL	world forward linkage
WRT	wholesale and retail trade, hotels, and restaurants
WTO	World Trade Organisation

1 Introduction

The historical evidence for the importance of industrialization is overwhelming. Leading scientist advocating a structural perspective on economic development and mostly recommending some sort of industrial policy argue that each developed country has gone through a process of industrialization (UNIDO 2011: 104, 2009: 4; United Nations Department of Economic and Social Affairs 2007: 7; Szirmai 2009: 35; Syrquin 2007: 208; Chenery et al. 1979: 70).1 Undoubtedly, there are some examples of economies which manage to develop without a significant share of the manufacturing sector. However, these economies are either extraordinarily small or resource-rich or both. For all other economies industrialization still seems to be an inevitable process they need to undergo.

Most of the African states reached political independence in the 1960s and started to promote industrialization via import substitution. Besides the hopes for a fast economic development, the economic independence was a declared objective of these policies. The heavy oil shocks and the structural debt crisis lead to a preliminary consensus suggesting that these policies have not been successful. Spurred by the neoliberal resurgence in the Western States, the World Bank and the IMF imposed the Washington Consensus which promoted structural adjustment including privatization and deregulation as well as specialization according to Africa's comparative advantages (Soludo & Ogbu 2004). The policies of structural adjustment finally resulted in the lost development decades in sub-Sahara Africa 1980–2000 (e.g., Easterly 2001). At the same time, the Newly Industrializing Countries (NIC) in South East Asia experienced an unprecedented growth which can be attributed to the export-oriented industrial policy of the government and a strong role of the government (Wade 1990; Evans 1995; Lall 1994; Jomo 2001). The influence of the East Asian Develop-

1 Some authors admit exceptions for very small states and resource-rich countries. However, it seems necessary to conduct such a hypothesis testing since Hong Kong is often stated as a counterexample which is misguiding and shows the lack of knowledge of concrete data. According to the Groningen Growth and Development Center (GGDC) 10-sector database, Hong Kong had an employment share of 45 percent in manufacturing in the year 1976.

ment Model spurred a renewed commitment to industrialization in Africa (UNIDO 2011).

The objective of this thesis is, therefore, to question the importance of industrialization and manufacturing for economic development in African economies. The purpose is to explore the role of structural change for economic development. If industrialization is not only a by-product but the engine of economic growth, what are the special characteristics of the manufacturing sector? Does manufacturing yield specific benefits and, if so, why? Is the service-led growth model paving the way for African economies?

1.1 History of industrialization

Even though historians question the revolutionary character of the "industrial revolution" (Mokyr 1993; Maddison 2001), the subsequent industrialization process, which started during the second half of the 18th century, spurred an unprecedented growth in Western Europe, the so-called Western Offshoots2, and Japan. Stearns (1993: 5) characterizes the industrial revolution as "one of those rare occasions in world history when human species altered its framework of existence", and Hobsbawm (1990: 13) denominates the Industrial Revolution as the "most fundamental transformation of human life in the history of the world recorded in written documents". In economic terms the notion "industrial revolution" captures the radical change of production technologies, which fundamentally affect the system of production (Naudé & Szirmai 2012: 5).3 Besides these widespread definitions, industrialization describes a relatively wide-ranging process of change accompanied by increased economic growth. Indeed, the period from 1820 onwards seems to be the most dynamic one in the last two millenniums. Following Maddison (2001), world per capita in-

2 The "Western Offshoots" consist of the United States, Canada, Australia, and New Zealand.

3 Actually, the notions "industrial revolution" and "industrialization" is often used interchangeable. While both notions were sometimes used as synonyms, a common use nowadays is to constrain the process of "industrial revolution" to a short and regional concentrated period, whereas the term "industrialization" is employed for the long-term progressive process. Some authors, in contrast, contest the revolutionary quality of the "industrial revolution" and most often emphasize the evolutionary character. Hahn (2011: 51 ff.) provides a good overview of the discussion.

come increased more than eightfold and population more than fivefold. While the income ratio between the industrializers (Western Europe, Western Offshoots, and Japan) and the rest of the world was 2:1 in 1820, the income gap rose to 7:1 in 1998 (Maddison 2001: 27).

Industrialization describes a transformation from an economy based on agriculture to industry and commerce (Hopkins 2000: 2). The most often cited categorization of economic sectors is the division of Kuznets (1967) between agriculture, industry, and services, which was introduced by Clark (1957) as primary, secondary, and tertiary sectors. Such a division is meanwhile part of the International Standard Industrial Classification (ISIC). Regarding ISIC, "industry" can be used to reflect all kinds of economic activities. To narrow this definition, economic activities are usually classified into three broad divisions: agriculture, industry, and services. Industry in this narrower meaning refers to "activities where inputs are transformed into different form of product, so that value is created at different stages of the production process" (Weiss 2010: 1), which is also called manufacturing industry and is hence represented by the sector D (Manufacturing) in the ISIC rev. 4. However, in some definitions industry comprises not only manufacturing but also mining, construction as well as utilities including electricity, water, and gas (Weiss 2010: 2). Industrialization thus emerges once the manufacturing sector (or industry) takes a leading role in the economy.4

The first phase of industrialization started at the end of the 18th century in Great Britain, which became the technological leader for a long time (Naudé & Szirmai 2012: 5). Between 1820 and 1913 the British GDP per capita grew faster than ever before (Maddison 2001: 21). Britain became the forerunner in industrialization and role model for lots of other countries (e.g., Rostow [1960] 1997). Subsequently, "manufacturing became the main engine of accelerating economic growth in the nineteenth century. A global race for industrialization had begun" (Naudé & Szirmai 2012: 5). The first industrial successors were the European countries of France, Belgium, and Switzerland. Between 1850 and 1900 the industrial development spread to Germany and the United States, altering the economic balance between the West and the rest of the world (Stearns 1993: 52).

4 Since most economic theories about the importance of industrialization consider the manufacturing sector as essential (see theory chapter 4), the definition should also refer to this sector and not only to the industry sector as a whole.

Following Stearns (1993), the second phase of industrial development started at the end of the 19th century, while Germany and the United States were still completing their industrial transformation, and ended in 1950. Several other new major players—including Russia and Japan being the first non-Western nations—started to industrialize. Despite neither of these countries matched the economic power of the West, they achieved higher growth rates (like Germany and the United States before) than the established industrial powers. The catch-up of newcomers became a key feature of this second phase of industrialization, but the involvement of the two non-Western states was the most striking element (Stearns 1993: 90 ff.). Taking the end of the colonial system in the late 1940s and 1950s and the subsequent creation of new independent states into account, the question arises, why some states managed to industrialize and others not. The end of the cold war and the rising inequality between industrialized countries and the rest of the world thus is the starting point for scholars and policy-makers to study the development process. Further, it subsequently marks the beginning of development economics as a separate subdiscipline of economics (Meier 2005: 53).

For a short period of time after the Second World War it seemed that only the economy of the United States was capable to further industrialize, whereas Japan and Europe suffered huge losses. However, the third phase of industrialization started in 1950. With the help of the United States aid, Japan and Europe were able to rebuild their industrial strength surprisingly fast. Decolonization spurred hopes in Africa and in the other newly independent states for quick economic development, but those states did not manage to generate industrialization. Therefore, vast economic inequalities persisted. Despite, there were a number of new industrializing states at the Pacific Rim, which became known as the Tiger States5. By 1990 some major economies including India and China had followed and in 2000 over half of the world was effectively industrial for the first time; still, regional inequality remained the most severe problem (Stearns 1993: 202 ff.).

Until today, the history of industrialization has bypassed the continent of Africa. While the manufacturing share in GDP of developing African economies rose from 6.3 percent in 1970 to 15.3 percent in 1990 (UNIDO 2011: 15), it started to decline again afterward reaching 10 percent in

5 Tiger States: Singapore, Hong Kong, South Korea, and Taiwan first; Indonesia, Thailand, Malaysia, and the Philippines followed.

2012. Thus, in 2012 Africa accounted for a very low share of 1.9 percent of global manufacturing. Global manufacturing in 2013 was still divided between Europe (26.3 percent), North America (18.2 percent), and Asia (46.5 percent) (UNIDO 2016).

1.2 The entity of analysis

Writing a thesis with a title including the term "Africa" evokes the question whether the continent can be viewed as a single unit. It is often stated that "Africa is too large and diverse a region to be treated as a single aggregate" (Collier 2008: 3) and that there is no one-size-fits-its-all policy recommendation (Sender et al. 2005). However, these are general statements which apply to every regional entity and not only to the continent of Africa. According to Alesina et al. (2011) eighty percent of African borders do not coincide to ethnic, religious, or linguistic groups.6 Many African states may thus be described as artificial states which are often associated with political and economic failures and hence are the origin for the African growth tragedy (Easterly & Levine 1997; Englebert et al. 2002).

Even though the borders were mainly drawn by former colonial rulers, the charter of the Organisation of African Unity (OAU) (OAU 1963) had a strong commitment to the sovereignty and territorial integrity of each state. The decision was mainly made to avoid conflicts among the African states and connected with a strong common desire for more coherence within the African continent. However, there was disagreement on how this should be achieved. The debate was led by Kwame Nkrumah, the president of Ghana (Casablanca Group), arguing for immediate continental unity, whereas the opposing group (Monrovia Group) proposed a gradual approach through consolidation of independent nation states and economic cooperation, which prevailed in the establishment of OAU (Bujra 2004: 2–3). In response to the Berg report (World Bank 1981), the OAU initiated, among others, the Lagos Plan of Action (OAU 1980) with the ambition to unite Africa and develop the continent through import substitution industrialization. Implementing the idea of a gradual regional integration, the continent was divided into three regional economic communities (RECs): the Economic Community of West African States (ECO-

6 In the decolonization process, the African states kept the borders drawn by former colonial rulers to avoid conflicts.

WAS); the Common Market for Eastern and Southern Africa (COMESA), and the Economic Community for Central African States (ECCAS), and later, the Arab Maghreb Union (AMU). Additionally, the Southern African Development Coordinating Conference (SADCC) was established in 1980, which became the Southern African Development Community (SADC) in 1992 and was joined by South Africa in 1994. The RECs are perceived as the building blocks of a united Africa. "In short, the RECs were and continue to be the glue that will cement African unity" (Melo & Tsikata 2015: 224).

In 2000, all African countries, except of Morocco, signed the constitutive act of the African Union (AU), which is oriented towards the idea of the European Union (EU) and includes commitments, such as to "achieve greater unity and solidarity between African countries and the peoples of Africa" (AU 2000: 5). The establishment of the AU replaced the OAU and is accompanied by the development program New Partnership for Africa's Development (NEPAD) as well as the African Peer Review Mechanism (APRM). The African continent has a long history of regional integration, which does not mean that regional integration was and is always straightforward and successful (Hartzenberg 2011). Critics argue that the institution never developed major political impact but was widely derided as a bureaucratic "talking shop" with little power (Thomson 2016: 280). The most recent development is the aim to establish the Tripartite Free Trade Agreement which was negotiated in 2008 by the three RECs: COMESA, SADC, and the EAC7 (Hartzenberg 2011: 19 ff.).

Up to the present, the AU is far from being a political union. However, most African countries have common characteristics and share a long history of regional integration with the ambition to achieve greater solidarity and unity amongst the African countries. In this thesis the African continent will be treated as a region with common characteristics comparable to other world regions, such as Latin America, Europe, or East Asia. The critical examination aims to identify common characteristics without obliterating the diversity between single African economies.

---

7 The East African Community (EAC) was established in 1999 between Kenya, Tanzania, and Uganda. The current EAC is a revival of an earlier East African Community which was established in 1967 and disbanded in 1977. A customs union protocol was signed in March 2004, a customs union was launched in 2005, and a common market protocol was signed in June 2010. Meanwhile Burundi, Rwanda and also South Sudan have acceded to the EAC. In 2013, the EAC outlined a plan for creating a monetary union within ten years.

1.3 African growth perceptions and the renewed interest in industrial policy

For a long time until the early 2000s, the African continent had predominantly been associated with crisis, wars, and catastrophes. The perspective was reproduced by *The Economist* which titled its issue "The hopeless continent" in 2000. Additionally, the academic debate concentrated on the "African growth tragedy" (Easterly & Levine 1997, 1995; Artadi & Sala-i-Martin 2003) and the quest for the African dummy (Englebert 2000; Block 2001) which represented the unexplained failure of growth in African economies. The continent Africa was the distant counterpart of the East Asian miracle.

Figure 1: GDP per capita in Purchasing Power Parity (PPP in constant 2005 international Dollar) for Africa from 1960 to 2011

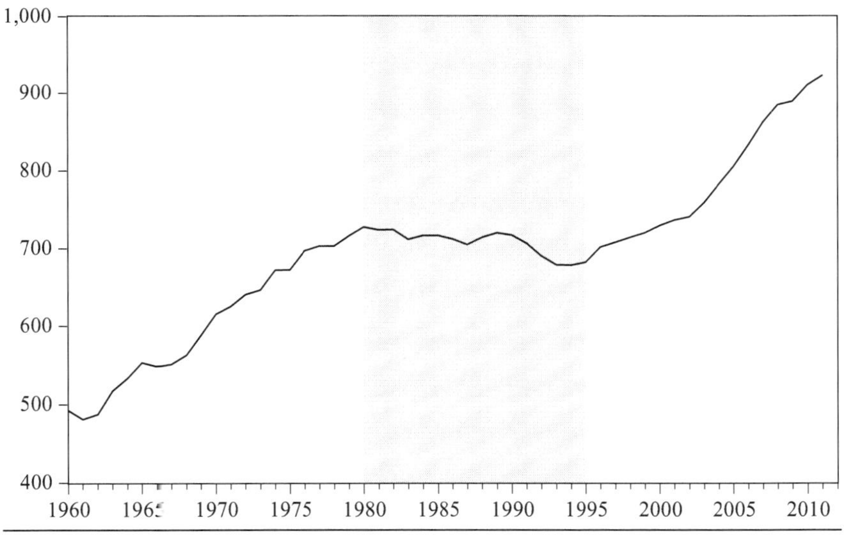

Source: African Development Indicators, World Bank

Only ten years later, in 2010, the picture had completely changed. The McKinsey Global Institute's title read "Lions on the Move: The progress and potential of African economies" (Roxburgh et al. 2010), and also The Economist promised "Africa Rising" (The Economist 2011). Indeed, the African growth experience had changed since 1995. Figure 1 shows a steady rise of GDP per capita since 1995 as well as a constant growth rec-

ord in Africa from 1960 to 1980. It seems that the African growth tragedy can only be attributed to the period between 1980 and 1995.
The exaggerated euphoria of the media has weakened since declining resource prices hampered economic growth in several Africa economies in recent years (IMF 2015a, 2015b). In 2016, the International Monetary Fund (IMF) even announced the "time for a policy reset" (IMF 2016). However, the growth performance differs across countries and the regions medium-term prospects remain favorable. It seems that a third stage of perceptions within the last 15 years has emerged which, considering the diversity of African economies, is characterized by a cautious optimistic but realistic expectation (Kappel 2014; Asche 2015a).

While the economic growth record of African economies is continually reported in the media, the demographic projections, which were neglected for a long time, just recently attracted attention in the light of the current refugee crisis in Europe. According to the newest UN Population prospects (UNDESA 2015), the total fertility rate (children per woman) in sub-Saharan Africa is still above five, whereas the world average is only 2.5. The population prospects in the medium variant (including an anticipated slight reduction in the fertility rate) predict that population in Africa, which reached 1.2 billion in 2016, will more than double until 2050 to 2.5 billion, meaning that more than 25 percent of world population will live in Africa. The projection for 2100 is that population in Africa will even reach 4.4 billion. Notwithstanding the accuracy of these figures, they provide a vague map of challenges lying ahead. One of the most urgent problems is and will be to provide jobs for the huge amount of young people (Woellert & Klingholz 2016).

Encountering this problem led to a renewed interest in industrialization and industrial policy, not only in academic literature, but especially in policy papers. The Economic Commission for Africa (ECA) dedicated its last four flagship publications to industrialization: The Economic Report on Africa (ECA 2013, 2014, 2015, 2016). The Economic Development in Africa Report of the United Nations Commission for Trade and Development (UNCTAD) in 2011 and 2012 dealt with industrial development and structural transformation.8 Furthermore, the African Economic Outlook9

8 Interestingly, the report in 2015 is on the potential of services (UNCTAD 2015b).

9 The African Economic Outlook is compiled as a collaborative venture of the African Development Bank (AfDB), the Organization for Economic Co-

2013 and 2014 (AfDB et al. 2014; AfDB et al. 2013) reported an analysis of Africa's industrialization and transformation. Additionally, the Industrial Development Report of the United Nations Industrial Development Organization (UNIDO) has its subject in industrial development already by declaration.

Besides the fact that industrialization and industrial policy became a dominant issue for the African continent again, there also seemed to be a new commitment to industrial policy in the developed economies (Rodrik 2008). Especially after the global crisis of 2007–09, industrial policy issues increased again. The European Commission (EC) has launched several communication papers since 2010 (EC 2010, 2012, 2013, 2014) to call on EU countries "to recognize the central importance of industry for boosting competitiveness and sustainable growth" (EC 2014: 22). Indeed, the goal of industrialization is even implemented in the new United Nation Sustainable Development Goals. Goal nine states: "Build resilient infrastructure, promote inclusive and sustainable industrialization and foster innovation". This is further specified in Goal 9.2: "Promote inclusive and sustainable industrialization and, by 2030, significantly raise industry's share of employment and gross domestic product, in line with national circumstances, and double its share in least developed countries".

1.4 Prospects for industrializing Africa

Despite the overwhelming historical record of the industrialization process in recent literature, the relationship between development and the growth of the manufacturing sector is seen with doubt (Szirmai & Verspagen 2015). Meanwhile, services account for nearly three quarter of value added and 70 percent of employment in high income countries.10 The share of services in developing countries steadily increased to meanwhile more than 55 percent in 2014. Thus, it seems that the manufacturing share of value added and employment is steadily decreasing, making industrialization increasingly difficult for developing economies. Furthermore, latecomer economies from Africa need to compete with newly industrialized

operation and Development (OECD), and the United Nation Development Program (UNDP).

10 According to the World Development Indicators of the World Bank, services account for 70.6 percent of employment and 73.9 percent of value added in high income countries.

countries of East Asia, especially China, and have fewer opportunities in exploiting new markets.

Despite these general concerns, it is argued that several African economies face specific challenges which make industrialization even more complicated. Especially small, landlocked and political fragile economies have not been able to establish competitive industries. Besides the larger economies South Africa, Kenya, Ethiopia, and Nigeria, only some economies could establish small industrial clusters and achieved a significant industrial growth (Döver & Kappel 2015).

The most prominent factors inhibiting industrial development in Africa are geographical impediments, infrastructure, and energy bottlenecks as well as institutional capacity problems. Some of those factors will be discussed in the following.

1.4.1 Institutional capacity

The renewed interest in industrialization is accompanied by a changing perception of the world history. In the 1990s, free trade was mainly seen as the road to economic welfare and it seemed undeniable that protectionism hurts the economy that imposes it (Bhagwati 1993). Since new millennium the historical relationship between industrialization and industrial policy has (again) been documented the other way around, especially by Ha-Joon Chang (2006) and Erik S. Reinert (2008). Both argue that the industrialization process, particularly in latecomer economies, has always been accompanied by a variety of industrial policies. However, the question of protectionism versus free trade is as old as economic theory. Along the conflicting views on economic history, the theoretical arguments for and against such policies are manifold. The typical textbook solution is that of a familiar perfect competitive market in absence of externalities and coordination failure so that free trade is the global Pareto-optimal solution. The most prominent argument in favor of industrial policy is the infant industry argument next to various types of market failure, such as externalities and coordination failure. None of those arguments should be questioned in general. However, the optimal intervention to either eliminate or cope with distortions is not always clear. The most prominent argument against government intervention roots in the negative implications of the economics of rent-seeking provided by Anne Krueger (1974). Rent-seeking in form of bribery, corruption, black markets, and smuggling is especially attributed to African economies. Politics in most African countries are characterized as neopatrimonial. Neopatrimonialism, which is seen as the all-purpose explanation for poor economic performance, is to some respect the African counterpart to the East Asian developmental state. It provides "the 'common denominator' for a range of practices that are highly characteristic of politics in Africa, namely: nepotism, clannish behaviour, so-called 'tribalism', regionalism, patronage, 'cronyism', 'prebedalsim', corruption, predation, factionalism etc." (Bach 2012: 221).11 It is hence questioned whether such circumstances in the political economy of African countries make the effective implementation of industrial policy feasible (Page 2012; Chang 2015; Altenburg 2013).

Responses to the question of implementation remain controversial but reveal a positive tendency: Chang (2006: 67–123) argues that today's advanced economies perform much worse in terms of corruption, bureaucracy, property rights and other institutions than today's African economies but nonetheless managed to industrialize. The problem of bureaucratic capabilities should not be overestimated. There is no presumption that industrial policy is more demanding than any other policy. Bureaucratic capabilities can be enhanced during the industrialization process by learning by doing (Chang 2013: 14).

Altenburg (2013) provides a more in-depth analysis. Using case studies of seven African economies, he explores the effectiveness of industrial policy under the neopatrimonial rule. He concludes that selective industrial policy is often used for patronage and clientelism, but is also implemented successfully and effectively in the cases of Tunisia and Ethiopia.

1.4.2 Infrastructure

One of the most frequently mentioned barriers to greater competitiveness, either on the firm or on the aggregate level, are the deficiencies in infrastructure. Indeed, sub-Saharan Africa lags behind all other regions in just about every aspect of infrastructure despite the density of cellphones and internet connections, outscoring South Asia (Yepes et al. 2009: 6). The largest gaps are found in the availability of rural roads and the provision of electricity.

11 The original citation in French is from Médard (1991: 300). See also Mkandawire (2015) for a critical evaluation of the concept.

Despite Africa's enormous fossil as well as renewable resources, it faces severe problems in energy provision. According to the Africa Energy Outlook (International Energy Agency 2014), more than 620 million people in sub-Saharan Africa remain without access to electricity, and the numbers are still increasing due to the population growth. 80 percent live in rural areas. Additionally, electricity prices in parts of sub-Saharan Africa are among the highest in the world (International Energy Agency 2014: 42). Energy prices are an important factor for international competitiveness, especially in energy intensive sectors (International Energy Agency 2013: 261). Since industrial sectors are by far the most energy intensive sectors, energy problems are an exceptional impediment for industrialization. In African economies the average energy intensity12 of the industrial sector is with a ratio of 3.6 nearly twice as high as in the agricultural sector (1.6) and more than seven times as high as in the service sector (0.48).13 These ratios are also relatively stable for high income countries.

1.4.3 Geographic location

Another aspect concerning the underdeveloped infrastructure as one of the major structural impediments for African industrialization, is the geographic location. Despite the historical trend for declining transport cost (Hummels 2007), geographic position and transport cost still pose a significant barrier for development in Africa. Africa's distance to the main manufacturing hubs in Europe, East Asia, and North America thus poses a severe dilemma for its integration into the world economy. Another geographic characteristic imposing economic burdens is the missing access to coastlines. According to Faye et al. (2004), nine of the twelve economies with the lowest Human Development Index are landlocked. All of them are sub-Saharan African economies. In total, 16 of 48 landlocked economies are in sub-Saharan Africa. A study of UNCTAD (2015a: 55) shows that the average transport cost in developing African economies is with 11.4 percent nearly twice as high as the world average of 6.8 percent.

---

12 Energy intensity is a ratio between energy consumption and value added measured at purchasing power parity. Energy intensity is an indication of how much energy is used to produce one unit of economic output. A lower ratio indicates that less energy is used to produce one unit of output.

13 The average is calculated from 21 available economies in the Sustainable Energy for all (SE4ALL) database from the World Bank.

Radelet & Sachs (1998) show that geographic isolation and higher shipping cost make it more difficult, if not impossible, for developing economies to promote manufacturing exports and thereby follow the East Asian export-led industrialization model. These conclusions are especially true for export goods with high import content and small profit margins, such as electronics (Radelet & Sachs 1998: 12). However, Chang (2015: 35) argues that being landlocked or being in a bad neighborhood "may not be as disadvantageous as it may seem". India, for instance, managed to show high growth rates in the last decades despite being in the poorest region of the world. Chang argues that the lack of investments in the infrastructure, e.g., the river transport system, rather than geographic location itself is the problem.

Chang (2015) surprisingly uses India as an example for successful development by arguing that industrial policy is feasible for Africa. However, he (deliberately or not) misses the point that India growth experience was based on the service-led growth model rather than the industrialization experience.

In contrast to agricultural, mineral and manufacturing goods, transport costs do not matter for most services: Either they are non-tradable, because they are bound to proximity and time (e.g., restaurants, hotels), or they are only tradable if embedded in other goods (this issue will be discussed in chapter 5) or their transport cost are only dependent on the availability of information and telecommunication technology.

1.5 Leapfrogging

It seems to be useful, especially for remote countries, to directly jump into the service sector and specialize on tradable services. The most prominent example for a service-led growth model is presented by India (Dasgupta & Singh 2005). Some authors even argue (e.g., Ghani & O'Connell 2014) that India could be a role model, in particular for low income countries in sub-Sahara Africa. They argue that the service-led growth model provides an alternative growth model beyond the manufacturing based growth model which prevailed since the initial industrial revolution in Great Britain.

The question whether a service-led growth might be realistic became increasingly popular in the context of climate change and the concern to what extent industrialization may no longer be a viable strategy for developing economies (Zhang 2011). The recent global environmental change may provide the unique opportunity for the "leapfrog continent" Africa (The Economist 2015) to jump directly into the service sector. Indeed, several promising examples of leapfrogging can already be found on the continent. Recent infrastructure shortcomings may be seen as a chance to move forward in energizing Africa without repeating the previous developmental stages, such as installing large size power plants (Szabó et al. 2013: 508). The analysis of Szabó et al. (2013) identifies sustainable electrification opportunities also for rural areas which cannot be reached by existing grid without excessive extension cost. However, the most striking example of leapfrogging experience is telephony. "Africa was the first region in the world where cellphones overtook the number of fixed line telephones" (Wright 2004). This is seen as an example on how Africa's infrastructure problem (in this case the lack of fixed telephone lines) can assist innovative technology.14 The most recent example for leapfrogging technologies is the rise of mobile money especially in Kenya (e.g., Jack & Suri 2014).

Against the background of those developments, this thesis will give insights into the considerations whether Africa can directly jump into the service sector without a considerable increase of the manufacturing sector. Indeed, there are already several doubts as to whether the service-led growth model is a sustainable strategy (Singh 2012).

1.6 Structure of the thesis

The renewed interest in industrialization is associated with a contemporary revival of the ideas of early development theorists. The thesis thus draws heavily on those theoretical contributions.

The methodological groundwork for testing the empirical relationship between structural change and economic development was developed by Kuznets and Chenery. The theoretical arguments in favor of the manufacturing sector mainly rely on the methodological and theoretical contributions of the modernization theorists. The structural bonus hypothesis is based on the famous dual sector model by Arthur Lewis (1954). The theory of increasing returns to scale is as old as the economic discipline, but the emphasize on the manufacturing sector was put forward by the big

14 See James (2009) for a more critical evaluation of the leapfrogging experience in cellphone market.

push theories of Rosenstein-Rodan (1943) and Leibenstein (1957). The hypothesis that the manufacturing sector shows stronger linkages than the primary sector and services was incorporated into the theory of unbalanced growth by Hirschman (1958). The theory of global value chains (GVCs)—discussed in chapter 5—stands in the footsteps of dependency theorists which arose from criticism of modernization theories.

Besides taking these theoretical approaches into account, the thesis's main purpose is to question the arguments in favor of the manufacturing sector. By employing data from African economies the present study empirically investigates the characteristics of the manufacturing sector.

Whether African economies can and should industrialize, is a complex topic which proves to be impossible to cover at this point. The identification of key sectors and the corresponding trade and industrial policy strategies is a country specific task that goes beyond the scope of this thesis.

The **second chapter** provides a short economic history of the African continent. It especially focuses on the role of international development paradigm, which had major influence on the economic performance. While most of the economic literature start in the 1960s, when the majority of African countries reached political independence, in this thesis, the record of African economies before 1960 is not ignored. By reviewing the imperial influence before and during the colonial system in sub-Saharan Africa, certain continuities can be emphasized. Most of the African states reached political independence in the 1960s and started promoting industrialization via import substitution. Besides the hopes for a quick economic development, economic independence was the declared objective of these policies. After the heavy oil shocks and the structural debt crisis, the preliminary consensus suggests that these policies have not been successful. Spurred by the neoliberal resurgence in the Western world, the World Bank and the IMF imposed the Washington Consensus which promoted structural adjustment including privatization and deregulation as well as specialization according to Africa's comparative advantages (Soludo & Ogbu 2004). Industrialization and structural change only play a minor role in modern development economics, often associated with the neoclassical and new growth theory. Instead, it is mainly concerned with the country's factor endowments[15] (Lin 2011: 202) and consequently rejects the role of

15 The most popular endowment is physical capital, but as theory evolves, human capital, social capital as well as institutions play a role and hence can contrib-

the government and industrial policy. The policies of structural adjustment finally resulted in the lost development decades in sub-Saharan Africa 1980– 1995 (e.g., Easterly 2001). Since 2010, the influence of the East Asian Development Model spurred a renewed commitment to industrialization in Africa (UNIDO 2011).

The **third chapter** uses the Chenery Hypothesis to gives an empirical record of the industrial development in selected African economies.

Since the work of Kuznets and Chenery (Kuznets 1967; Chenery 1960; Chenery & Syrquin 1975; Chenery 1982; Syrquin & Chenery 1989) structural change can be regarded as one of the stylized facts of economic development. The stylized facts of this earlier work are: The share of agriculture falls as economies grow richer, the share of industry rises but falls later in the development process, and the share of services rises unambiguously as economies grow rich. The idea of general patterns between sectoral change and per-capita GDP became to be known as the Chenery Hypothesis. Recent studies (Dabla-Norris et al. 2013; Rodrik 2015) argue that these regularities have changed over time. According to them, the inverted-u-shape relationship between income and manufacturing output or employment has shifted downwards and peaks earlier in the developmental process. The 10-Sector-Database from the Groningen Growth and Development Center (GGDC) is used to measure the relationship between GDP per capita income and the employment shares of the individual economic sectors. The measured relationship will be used to represent the normal development path on the assumption that economic development follows regularities which do not change between countries. Using differing time periods and analyzing the time series effects of the panel regression allows to test whether these regularities have changed over time. In a second step, I benchmark African economies within this framework. The analysis allows tracing back individual country pathways in an historic and international perspective. The structural deviation index is calculated to measure to what extend African economies deviate from the general pattern of development.

Chapter four focuses on the theoretical arguments in favor of the manufacturing sector. In general, three strands of theories can be distinguished for explaining the relationship between structural change and economic development. Chenery and Kuznets explain this relationship with differing

ute to the countries endowment structure. These endowments determine the development status of the country and can change over time.

income elasticities of demand. With regard to the neoclassical approach, the specialization of production according to the existing supply of production factors determines the structure of an economy. In both strands structural change plays a relatively subordinated role for economic development. The structure of the economy is either determined by demand or the production endowments available. The level of development thus determines the structure of the economy. As to the structuralist approach, causality runs the other way around: Structural change and especially the manufacturing sector are seen as the engine of economic growth. The literature in this strand of theory mainly draws on three arguments:

Firstly, the structural bonus hypothesis suggests that labor productivity in the agricultural sector is much lower than in industry. Thus, a shift of production from agriculture to industry as proposed in the Chenery Hypothesis would automatically enhance labor productivity. McMillan et al. (2014) as well as Timmer et al. (2016) apply this method for the African economies using the GGDC 10-Sector Database. The analysis is replicated and results for African economies are presented.

Secondly, the manufacturing sector is supposed to exhibit increasing returns to scale, whereas the agricultural sector and the service sector are prone to decreasing returns to scale. The section uses the GGDC 10-Sector Database to analyze the returns to scale of the manufacturing sector in African economies.

Thirdly, the manufacturing sector is supposed to show the strongest inter- and intra-sectoral back and forward linkages The argument is mainly based on the modernization theorist Albert Hirschman (1958) and is strongly associated with the idea of complementarity, which could lead to a massive coordination failure. He argued that, due to these linkages, particular industries can spur economic growth in the whole economy. Thus, the role of linkages has especially attracted attention to identifying economic key sectors. The purpose of this section is to test whether the manufacturing sector shows stronger production linkages than other economic sectors. I use input-output tables from the Africa Database of the Global Trade and Analysis Project (GTAP) to analyze the backward and forward linkages across sectors in African economies.

In the **5th chapter** the inevitable challenges of globalization and their role for Africa's industrialization are discussed. The failure of early import substitution industrialization efforts in sub-Saharan Africa are often attributed to the negligence of technology and knowledge transfer via international trade. In the current international environment, a main part of the global trade and production are organized in global value chains (GVCs).

Integration into GVCs seems to be a necessary condition for benefiting from technology and knowledge transfer. In this chapter, data from international input-output tables is employed to assess Africa's position in the international economic system. I give insight into particular sectors of African economies that entered GVCs.

Chapter six summarizes the discussed issues.

1.7 Data situation

In echo of the dramatically changing perceptions within only few years, doubts about the reliability of African statistics emerged. Several authors ask why and how economic estimates can be so wrong (Devarajan 2013; Jerven 2014; Young 2012). One general problem, which has specific relevance for the economies in Africa, is the quality of the data.

Indeed, in the last few years, several major economic countries in Africa had to make extensive recalculation within its national accounts. Just after Ghana needed to correct its gross domestic product (GDP) and added 60 percent in 2010, other major African economies recalculated their GDP with substantial upward revisions in 2014: Nigeria (89 percent), Kenya (25 percent), Uganda (13 percent), Tanzania (32 percent), and Zambia (25 percent).

These recalculations support, among others, the critique of Young (2012) who indicates that international datasets heavily underestimate the economic growth rate in sub-Saharan Africa.

In reaction to the upcoming distrust in African statistics, the African Development Bank carried out two methodological surveys to evaluate especially the African GDP statistics (AfDB 2013, 2014). With exception of Eritrea, Libya, and Somalia, all African economies participated in the AfDB questionnaires, which may be regarded as a general commitment to the statistical capacity building initiative, initiated by the ECA and AfDB with support of the World Bank and the Partnership in Statistics for Development in the 21st Century (PARIS21) (ECA & AfDB 2006).

In order to prevent confusion: The sources and methods used by African countries are similar to those in other countries and are based on the internationally agreed system of national accounts (SNA 1993 or 2008). The only difference is that African statistics rely on a much smaller amount of basic data from administrative sources as well as statistical surveys. The required surveys are sometimes so infrequent that due to new surveys previous estimates need to be substantially revised (AfDB 2014: 6).

In the case of Ghana, the major GDP revision was caused by outdated base price year which is necessary to construct constant price estimates. According to international statistical standards, the use of annual chain indices is recommended (SNA 1993 and SNA 2008). However, according to the SNA 1993, if alternative measures are used, constant price series should be not allowed to run for more than five (or at most 10 years), otherwise the price of the base year becomes increasingly irrelevant (UN 1993: 493). The Ghana statistical service published constant GDP series in 1993 prices until the year 2010 (Jerven 2014: 4). These problems are of special relevance for this thesis as the revisions do not affect all economic activities in the same way. The old estimates did not pick up the large growth in the communication sector (e.g., cellphones), thus, 72 percent of the revision originated from the service sector.

Ghana is not an individual case. According to the survey of the AfDB (2013: 11), 19 of 34 countries use base years which are at least 10 years old, and 8 countries use base years which are even more than 20 years old. However, five other major economies rebased their GDP in 2014 with substantial revises on the size and the structure of the economies (Sy 2015). There are similar problems with employment statistics because the standard periodicity of the population censuses is about 10 years (Devarajan 2013: 11).

Analyzing the structure of African economies, I do not only face the problem of data availability, but also need to take into account the quality of the given data. A general indicator to assess the quality of statistics is the statistical capacity indicator provided by the World Bank (see table 1). It shows that the overall level of statistical capacity in African countries in general is as low as in average low income countries. However, there are huge differences between economies. Especially large economies show relatively high statistical capacities.

A more refined analysis of the quality of African national account statistics is provided by the AfDB (2014) but gives no comparison to other lower or middle income countries. The African Development Bank (AfDB) concludes that, despite all the doubts on African statistics, there is no reason assuming that "levels or growth rates are deliberately falsified" (AfDB 2014: 2).

I conclude that African statistics are possibly more prone to severe revision and consequently should be used even more cautiously than official statistics from e.g., European economies. However, there is no indication that African statistics in general are less reliable than those from other low respectively middle income countries. A general disregard of accessible information is seen to be no alternative for analyzing African economies.

Table 1: Overall level of statistical capacity[16] *(scale 0 - 100) in 2004 and 2015*

Country	2004	2015	Country	2004	2015	Country	2004	2015
MIC	69	71	Cabo Verde		67	Burundi	43	56
LIC	52	60	Chad	60	66	Kenya	64	54
Africa (avr.)	56	60	Lesotho	71	66	Algeria	54	53
Mauritius	70	93	Gambia	63	66	Guinea	67	53
Morocco	80	81	Ghana	51	66	CAF	40	52
South Africa	87	81	Sao Tome		66	Liberia	17	51
Tunisia	72	77	Togo	52	66	Sudan	36	51
Tanzania	68	76	Seychelles		66	Congo, R.	42	50
Malawi	68	76	Sierra Leone	30	63	Namibia	59	48
Senegal	79	76	Suriname		62	Angola	41	48
Rwanda	61	73	Zimbabwe	58	62	Botswana	72	46
Uganda	60	72	Zambia	66	60	Guinea-B.	38	44
Mozambique	68	72	Cote d'Ivoire	80	59	Eq. Guinea		42
Niger	64	71	Madagascar	63	59	Gabon	44	40
Nigeria	44	71	Swaziland	66	59	South Sudan		34
Ethiopia	67	69	Congo, D.	32	58	Eritrea	38	28
Burkina Faso	68	68	St. Kitts		57	Libya	29	22
Mauritania	56	67	Trin.&Tob.	63	57	Somalia	22	20

Source: Bulletin Board on Statistical Capacity, World Development Indicators; MIC: middle income countries, LIC: low income countries

The main data sources used in this thesis is the 10-Sector Database of the Groningen Growth and Development Center (GGDC) which provides value added and employment data for 11 sub-Saharan African economies plus the two North African states Morocco and Egypt. The above mentioned revision for Ghana but also for Nigeria, Tanzania and Zambia were incorporated in September 2014. Unfortunately, it does not include the rebased GDP figures from 2014 for Kenya (up to now: June 7, 2016). The

16 The statistical capacity indicator is a composite score assessing the capacity of a country's statistical system. It is based on a diagnostic framework assessing the following areas: methodology, data sources, and periodicity and timeliness. Countries are scored against 25 criteria in these areas, using publicly available information and/or country input. The overall statistical capacity score is then calculated as a simple average of all three area scores on a scale from 0 (very low) to 100 (very high).

second major source is the Africa Database from the Global Trade and Analysis project (GTAP) based on the GTAP 8 Database. Other data sources and detailed discussions on the data used are provided in the corresponding chapters.

2 A short economic history of Africa

Most of the economic literature (e.g., the famous Berg-Report of the World Bank 1981) starts its analysis in the 1960s, when most African countries gained political independence. It implicitly assumes that the record of African economies before 1960 could be safely ignored in terms of economic policy (Manning 1987: 50). This cut-off in African economic history has been widely criticized. In Wallerstein's (1976) historiography of modern Africa, decolonization is not even regarded as a major turning point. On the contrary, he regards the time period between 1900 and 1975 as one of intensifying integration of Africa into the capitalist world economy (Wallerstein 1976: 39–48). In contrast to the emphasis on the newly independent political regimes, he stresses the continuities or even reinforcements of the imperial economic system. In the same way, Austen (1987: 197) treated decolonization rather as a chronological marker for long-term changes than as an event creating a new economic situation. Accordingly, key features of the colonial economies during the mid-20th century such as a dominant position of the state, a weak role of indigenous entrepreneurs as well as a heavy dependence upon external markets of the colonial economies remained the same (Austen 1987: 224).

Firstly, an interpretation of why modern economists see political independence as a major turning point in the economic history of Africa can be traced back to a lack of research about the economic history as such. The last author who tried to deal with the economic history of Africa as a whole was Ralph Austen in 1987. As Hopkins (2009: 155) points out:

> "By the close of the 1980s [...] economic history was in failing health; in the 1990s its public appearances were limited; today, it seems to have died, unlamented, from that most mortifying of scholarly ailments – neglect."

Secondly, there was a shift to methodological nationalism which attributes national economic success to internal factors rather than analyzing national trends within a global economic context (Gore 1996: 78ff.). Thirdly, today's economic analysis rely mainly on national accounts established after 1950. Several attempts to introduce national accounts retrospectively were made in the early years of independence but were generally abandoned (Manning 1987: 51). Thus, empirical economists face the problem of divergent datasets: one colonial, one national.17 Manning (1987: 52) even concludes that the division of labor between economists doing research on the period after 1960 and historians working on the period before 1960 resulted in the elimination of communication and reference between both groups of scientists.18 The data for the years just after independence used in this chapter are derived from an ECA publication, respectively from a compilation of those data by Roider (1971). For the period after 1970, data from UNCTADStat is used which draws mainly on the National Accounts Main Aggregates Database of the United Nations (UN). Due to its scope, it provides a good overview of the manufacturing record of African economies and makes it very suitable to use in this chapter. It is, however, not very reliable. A more detailed evaluation using the dataset from the Groningen Growth and Development Center (GGDC) is provided in chapter three. The following section, a retrospect of the African economies, will neither start with the period after independence nor with the colonial conquest or the European discovery of Africa. Each of those starting points would create a totally different impression of the African economic history and would intensify the Eurocentric view on Africa. Therefore, the chapter starts in the era before the arrival of the Europeans.

17 An exceptional example is South Africa, where the distinction between colonial and national has been sufficiently resolved and a continuous set of national accounts going back to the early twentieth century exists (e.g., South Africa - Bureau of Census and Statistics 1960; Houghton 1976).

18 In recent years, international economists have put renewed emphasis on the importance of economic history. The probably most influential example is the reversal of the fortune thesis (Acemoglu et al. 2001, 2002). In short, econometric methods are used to measure the impact of European settlers on the distribution of income today. It is argued that European colonizers were more likely to introduce institutions encouraging investments and economic growth in regions which had been poor before. Poor regions were sparsely populated, which enabled the settlers to easily establish their growth-enhancing institutions, while in densely populated regions, extractive forms of colonization were more profitable. In turn, colonization reversed income distribution such that parts of the world which were poor before 1500 became rich in present-day. However, an elaborated critique concerning the implications of the theory for sub-Saharan Africa is provided by Austin (2008). Besides data problems, several methodological issues, and theoretical shortcomings, he emphasizes the importance of combining econometric approaches with context-specific studies and other forms of global historical comparisons.

2.1 Africa from the 11th to the 16th century: kingdoms and Islamic influence

In the period between the 11th and the 16th century, the first independent states developed their own culture but assimilated external, especially Islamic, influences. This era preceded the European control of the seas and world trade. Africa was characterized by the development of kingdoms, empires, and cities. Especially in the northern part of the continent, the spread of the Islam brought political and religious change.19

One of the main prosperous regions was the Sudanic Zone20 in West Africa which "appears to be an ideal center for the emergence of long-distance trade and commercial production" (Austen 1987: 31). The insularity between the desert in the north and the forests in the south provided the pressure for the emergence of early agriculture and encouraged long-distance trades to other regions of Africa. In this area, several empires such as Ghana, Mali, and Songhai in West Sudan or Kanem and Borno in Central Sudan were established between the 9th and the 16th century. In contrast to the Sudanic Zone, where long-distance trade was realized via caravans through the Sahara, the East African regions were much more dependent upon external influences, such as migration of people and foreign technology, due to its connection to the Indian Ocean.21

2.1.1 Islam and Trade

As indicated above, the Muslims dominated the commercial world in this period. In contrast to Christianization, Islam's success was based on a

---

19 Subsequently, economic history in this time span predominantly draws on Arabic texts. Concerning those parts of Africa which has been beyond the range of Islamic influence, especially south of the Sahara, history is more dependent on the descriptions of the first Portuguese seafarers. However, for many areas in this period, the best source is archaeology (Oliver 1977: 3). Niane (1984a: 684) for this reason also stresses the relevance of linguistics, anthropology, and especially oral traditions.

20 The Sudan region in West Africa is ranging south of the Sahara from today's Senegal to Lake Chad and should not be confused with the Republic of the Sudan.

21 The economic importance of the Indian Ocean reached its peak in medieval times and can be compared to the contemporary Mediterranean (Austen 1987: 56).

slow and peaceful spread without establishing clergy or missionary bases. Islam did not destroy traditional structures in Africa but rather took a distinctly African form (Niane 1984b: 3).

Furthermore, Africa was a hub for inter-regional trade relations. Especially the northern part played an important role for trade between the Mediterranean and the Indian Ocean, which was arguably the most important center for international trade and commerce at this time (Devisse 1984). Even though, south of the Sahara, the Islamic influence was not as large; centers for future expansion had been established. In fact, Muslim merchants nearly held a monopoly in long-distance trade in Africa at this time (Oliver 1977: 2). The main exports from the Sudanic empires were gold, of which about one ton per year was transported to the Mediterranean, and African slaves, of which about six million had been token to the Islamic world between 650 and 1600 (Austen 1987: 36). Immense caravans numbering from 6 000 to 12 000 camels carried products of all kinds from north of the Sahara through the forest regions farther south. Niane (1984b: 4) further proposes that even the "fundamental cultural unity of the African continent may be explained by the exchanges that took place between regions during this period." However, except for the evidence for Islamic long-distance trade, the domain of economic development until the arrival of the first Portuguese was largely internal (Oliver 1977: 3).

2.1.2 Modes of production

As already noted, gold, copper, and ivory had been the most important trade items between Africa and the rest of the world. Therefore, the group of merchants, which Niane (1984a: 680) regards as a "bourgeoisie in embryo", was an important factor. These merchants fostered relations between different regions and people. Also, accumulation of capital began in this group. The merchants and nobles together formed a comparatively small aristocracy. However, agriculture remained the most important economic sector, especially south of the Sahara. According to Duignan & Gann (1975: 35), tilling as well as hunting and fishing, wherever possible, were the main modes of pre-colonial production in sub-Saharan Africa. It should be noted that, in contrast to Europe, land in Africa was considered to be an indivisible property of the community. Peasants, for instance, needed to pay fixed rents per family (Niane 1984a: 680–682).

Large West-African states like Ashanti, Dahomey, Benin, or Nupe had more complex systems of production with serfs and slaves but also special artisans and craftsmen producing a variety of goods. There is also evidence for slave trade, especially from Sudan to the Maghreb and Egypt. In some regions, slaves even played important roles in military and civil services. In this period, however, slavery did not take the form of mass exploitation comparable to the Atlantic slave trade, and the share of slaves in the population never exceeded that of peasants (Niane 1984a: 680–684).

Generally speaking, the kingdoms and empires of Africa reached a high level of development. In contrast to popular beliefs, Africa was far from being an unpopulated continent: It was densely populated, especially south of the Sahara. Mali alone accounted for more than 400 towns or centers of population. Niane (1984a: 683) estimates a total African population of at least 200 million in the 14th century of which ten percent lived in urban centers. Hence, Africa was a comparatively densely populated continent (the distribution was not even due to geographical barriers) and dependent on extensive agricultural production.

2.2 Africa from the 16th century: integration into the world capitalist economy

The 15th and 16th centuries, when the Europeans took control over the seas and, thus, world trade, mark a turning point in African history. They established a new Atlantic-oriented geo-economic system with a triangular trading pattern between Europe, America, and Africa. With the discoveries of the Indian Ocean by Portuguese and Spanish Christians, the Muslims lost their predominant role in international trade (Niane 1984a: 673). The opening of the Atlantic sea route in West Africa challenged the commercial role of the Sahara and Sudan. Also, the 17th and 18th centuries were a time of demographic and economic stagnation and decline for the Islamic Middle East, negatively affecting trans-Saharan trade (Austen 1987: 37). The European superiority in the transport system22 superseded nearly all other commercial links and established the Atlantic trade route as the primary and regular link to the outside world (Austen 1987: 81).

Soon after the arrival of the Portuguese, the French, British, and Dutch arrived and competed for the most important and profitable trading bases,

22 At the end of the sailing area, one man was needed to carry about 9-14 tons which exceeded the transport capacity of the trans-Saharan caravans 15 to 30 times and the Indian Ocean dhows 2-3 times (Austen 1987: 82).

mainly on the West Coast of Africa. East Africa, on the other hand, was of relatively little interest for the Europeans (Malowist 1992: 10ff.). African States located directly at the coast were the important commercial partners of European merchants. These commercial partnerships provided the basis for the later colonization of the interior. However, the varying intensity of European presence in Africa depended on political competition among Europeans rather than upon trade volume or composition. In most cases, the greatest quantities were associated with minimal European presence (Austen 1987: 85).

These developments should be regarded in the light of the history of thought. From the 16th until the late 18th century, the economic thought of the dominant Western European nations was dominated by what Adam Smith called the *commercial or mercantile system* (Smith 2008 [1776]: 407–430). The mercantile era promoted the discovery of the New World as well as the East Indies at the close of the 15th century. Adam Smith's idea of mercantilism is often criticized for confusing money with wealth.23

The main principle of mercantilism was to achieve a "favorable" balance of trade, i.e., a country had to export more than to import, leading to a net inflow of silver and gold. There was no coherent system of thought and practice across time and different countries (Magnusson 2015: 217). What held them together, though, was the question of how to acquire, especially military, power (Magnusson 2015: 220).

According to this general principle, several interventionist policies were employed which tried to increase the productive powers of the nation. Special importance was, therefore, given to the manufacturing sector, since manufactured goods had a much higher trade value than the raw materials with which they had been produced. A side effect was that manufacturing requires a lot more labor than agriculture (Vaggi & Groenewegen 2006: 18). The import of cheap raw materials thus increased the trade surplus while also improving the competitiveness of manufactured export goods. International trade was seen as a zero-sum game. Accordingly, the establishment of monopolies, especially in colonial markets, had

---

23 This popular assertion has been strongly criticized. According to Schumpeter & Schumpeter (2009: 341), no proposition in the mercantilist writings could be found that cannot be explained without assuming the confusion of wealth with money or bullions.

the purpose of obtaining cheap raw materials and selling manufactured goods.

When the Portuguese arrived at the west coast of Africa, they first sought gold and spices rather than men. African exports included ivory, dyewoods, hardwoods as well as gum and wax. African trade had in most phases been dominated by one single good. At the beginning of the European trade, it was gold. However, the plantations of the New World created a large market for slave labor which was supplied by African potentates in exchange for European manufactures (Duignan & Gann 1975: 40–44). The Portuguese soon discovered the slaves as a second "product"24. Initially, slaves were mainly exported to Arab countries from the Sudan. Inikori (1992: 82) estimated that during the Atlantic slave trade about 15.4 million people were exported as slaves. Adding the slave trade across the Sahara, the Red Sea, and the Indian Ocean, about 22 million Africans in total were exported from Africa between 1500 and 1890.

Undoubtedly, the transatlantic triangular trade between America, Africa, and Europe played an important role and was a critical factor for growth for the labor abundant economic system in the American colonies. In fact, it was the first historical example of international factor mobility, albeit enforced (Hopkins 1980: 117). It was a highly profitable business and thus has been regarded as a major contribution to the industrial take-off (Hopkins 1980: 117). This view has been challenged by authors arguing that slave trades were a highly risky business and played only a minor role in the early industrialization of Great Britain (Inikori 1992: 82; O'Brien 1982: 9–15)25. Austen (1987: 111) concedes that slave trade and British capitalism may have grown together. However, he dismisses the importance of slavery for economic development in Britain based on the fact that the abolition of slavery in the early 19th century did not threaten its growth.

The economic effects of slave trade on Africa cannot be neglected. According to Ajayi (1989a: 5) it not only significantly reduced the population, especially in west and central-west Africa, but also traumatized those

24 Europeans wiped away their moral concerns of the slave trade arguing that it enabled them salvation while, as non-Christians, they would have been damn to perdition. Furthermore, it was argued that blacks descended from Ham (a son of Noah) and are thus in any case condemned to slavery (Malcwist 1992: 7).

25 See also the answer of Wallerstein (1983).

left behind. He sees slave trade as the main reason for the economic and political fragility of 19th century Africa.26

Diagne (1992) emphasizes the introduction of feudal structures in either pure or distorted forms into African societies, referring to the introduction of land-ownership and new social orders, in particular. These developments can often be attributed to external influences but in some cases need to be explained by internal developments (Diagne 1992: 27ff.). He identifies three major economic structures of the time. The *craft economy and caste system* of production in Western Sudan, the Niger-Chad region, and the Sahara developed various crafting, manufacturing, and industrial processes and products. A *predatory economy* emerged in the areas bordering on the Mediterranean, the Indian Ocean, and the Nile when Spanish and Portuguese expansionism expelled large colonies of Jews and Muslims. The demise of the trans-Saharan long-distance trade, which had enriched the medieval centers of trade and commerce, led to the disruption of ports and market towns which had been established before the 15th century (Diagne 1992: 34ff.). North African states mostly continued to preserve their political independence but depended heavily on tribute, duties, and piracy rather than on trade or industry (Diagne 1992: 36). Most West African states, in contrast, depended largely on the *entrepôt* or *trading post economy,* supplying the Europeans with gold, ivory, and slaves in exchange for cheap manufacturing products, such as yarn or iron and copper bars, which often had been incorporated into local artisanal activities.

Due to the high cost of interior transportation, European goods such as clothes, metal vessels, blades, guns, jewelry, and alcohol only reached consumers in coastal regions (Austen 1987: 99). Local craftsmen about 150 kilometers away from the Atlantic coast still enjoyed a cost advantage in addition to their ability to easily adapt to specific and varying local demand. Austen (1987: 100) thus assumes that artisanal activity increased in

26 It is often argued that slavery was nothing new when Europeans arrived in Africa. That is especially true for the appearance of Muslim traders, who used slaves mostly for domestic services, even for civil services and military purposes. Even before the arrival of Muslim traders, especially in West Sudan and the Niger-Chad region, there had been a form of slavery also called the *jonya* system. However, Jons (a Mande word meaning "captives") were mostly captured during battles, were not transferable, owned a part of what they produced and belonged to a socio-political category with a minimum of political influence. Hence, the *jonya* system can hardly be compared with western forms of slavery (Diagne 1992: 24).

this time. However, the African economy could not profit from European advanced technology. On the contrary, Africa suffered from European competition in textile or iron manufacturing, which hampered African technological development (Austen 1987: 100; Diagne 1992: 42). However, as Malowist (1992: 22) concludes, Africa has probably been underestimated as a market for manufacturing and industrial products in the 16th and 17th century.

2.3 Africa at the eve of the European conquest

During the late 18th century, when Africa supplied early industrial Europe with slaves for sugar plantations in the British Caribbean colonies, the first phase of industrialization started in Great Britain, which remained the technological leader for a long time (Naudé & Szirmai 2012: 5). Between 1820 and 1913, the British GDP per capita grew faster than any time before (Maddison 2001: 21). Britain became the frontrunner in industrialization and set an example for many other countries (Rostow [1960] 1997). Subsequently, "manufacturing became the main engine of accelerating economic growth in the nineteenth century. A global race for industrialization had begun" (Naudé & Szirmai 2012: 5). The first industrial successors were France, Belgium, and Switzerland. Between 1850 and 1900, the spread of industrial development to Germany and the United States altered the economic balance between the West and the rest of the world (Stearns 1993: 52).

The first phase of industrialization in Africa was characterized by the "informal empire" of Great Britain.27 Mostly coastal regions were integrated into the capitalist world system, but local political sovereignty remained. The internal political and economic developments on the eve of European conquest were characterized by major transformations.

27 The term "informal empire" was coined by Charles R. Fay in an article for the Cambridge History of the British Empire (1940: 399). In the 18th century slave exports had dominated Africa's export structure, but during the 19th century it shifted towards non-human exports, such as palm-oil, palm-kernels, coffee, and ground-nuts (Duignan & Gann 1975: 62). The volume of African-European trade as well as the terms of trade for African exports (e.g., palm oil, see Hopkins (1980: 133)) increased heavily until 1860 (Austen 1987: 112). The African societies were able to adapt to the changes of trade structure from slaves to non-human exports.

The tropical commerce of Europeans in Africa was characterized by several forms of monopolistic restrictions and, generally, by a mercantilist view of international trade. When Britain had become the industrial leader of Europe, it sought to utilize its initial advantage and lobbied for a free trade system (Austen 1987: 110).28 Economic Theory played a crucial role in the campaigns for free trade since classical economics, favoring a market system and free trade, had replaced the mercantilist view on trade.29 The "Wealth of Nations", in which Adam Smith criticizes the mercantile system, is usually considered the beginning of 'liberal economics'.30

The new economic approach had its roots in the libertarian movement, beginning with the abolition of absolutism and the philosophical movement of the Enlightenment. The failure of mercantilist colonial policies and the independence of the colonies New England paved the way for the new paradigm (Ott & Winkel 1985: 50–52).

In the "Wonderful World of Adam Smith" (Schefold & Carstensen 2014: 69), markets were assumed to regulate themselves, and the division of labor became the superior explanation for economic growth. Furthermore, the theory of absolute cost advantage (Adam Smith) as well as the theory of comparative advantage (David Ricardo) predicts gains from trade for all trade partners. In contrast to the mercantile system, the proposed economic policy therefore sought to create a free market system and to stop protectionism and monopolies.

Britain's fight for a free trade system coincided with the abolition of slave trade31 which had been the driving factor of the economic transfor-

28 It is important to mention that Britain's technological lead at this time, which enabled the shift to more free trade, was based upon a system of high and long-lasting trade barriers. Already at the beginning of the 19th century, when Britain was losing ground on Germany and the United States in several branches, the reintroduction of protectionist measures was discussed (Chang 2006: 24).

29 Especially in France, the mercantile economic thinking was replaced by the physiocrats.

30 There are several definitions of classical economics. According to Marx, classical economics starts with Petty and ends with Ricardo. According to the definition of Keynes, the school starts with Ricardo and ends with Pigou.

31 Austen (1987: 113) claims that the abolition of slave trade was not for free for the industrialization in Europe. However, since several African rulers and merchants benefited from African slave trade, not only European powers resisted the abolition movement (Malowist 1992: 20). It is thus difficult to point to economic motives for abolitionism which made historians return to *moral* motivations. To Europeans, being opposed to slavery primarily meant taking a

mation of Africa in the second half of the 18th century. With the effective end of the Atlantic slave trade and a changing export structure, the demand for captives to produce and transport these goods increased. However, African trade decreased in relative terms because the world economy was growing much faster than African commerce. According to Austen (1987: 117), this was the time in which Africa fully entered into European periphery. Industrialization in the Western economies led to several technological advancements in transport, medicine, and firearms, which made the further exploration of Africa possible. Steam ships augmented the already established coastal hegemony, and the development of firearms and medicine enabled Europeans to further exploit the land (Austen 1987: 113–114).

African societies faced the expansion of chartered companies with the aim of colonial conquest, fueled by laissez-faire capitalism and intensified competition among the European powers (Duignan & Gann 1975: 63). Economic imperialism in Africa led to an increasing commercialization of nearly all aspects of economic life. The number of merchants and their importance increased. In some areas, a merchant middle class, widely influenced by Christianity, established itself and began to pursue power and influence (Ajayi 1989b: 784).32

2.4 Colonialism in Africa

The growing competition among Germany, France, and the United States during the second phase of industrialization led to an increasing imbalance between European powers and African states. Italy and Germany in particular expected to be more involved in the competition for African resources. Those claims finally led to the 1884 Berlin Conference which regulated European colonization and trade in Africa and can be regarded as the starting point of the "scramble for Africa" (Wallerstein 1976: 38).

Even though Africa had been integrated into the capitalist world economy to some degree before, colonization can be regarded as the most fun-

critical stance on industrial capitalism, but slavery also contradicted some core values of modern society, such as individual liberty and the sanctity of the nuclear family.

32 Another major turning point of the European expansion was the introduction of private property which included the increasing commercialization of land (Ajayi 1989a: 11).

damental change in African history (Boahen 1985a: 1). In the late 1880s, only very few regions had been under direct European rule. Between 1890 and 1910, the imperial powers conquered nearly all of Africa (Boahen 1985a: 1). Figure 2 shows the new geopolitical map of Africa in 1914.

Yet, what actually happened during the colonial period of less than a hundred years, ranging roughly from 1880 to 1960?

Figure 2: Africa in 1914

Source: Own depiction using QGIS, based on Ajayi (1969: 503)

From a conservative point of view, colonialism went hand in hand with a transition from a "primitive", subsistence-based system to modern market-oriented economies in Africa. Even though research has shown that this view cannot be sustained, since the previous African economic system cannot be described as primitive and subsistence-based, the colonial period did bring economic modernization. Gann & Duignan (1969: 22) exhibit a very liberal view and do not equate colonialism or profits with exploitation. European imperialism in Africa is seen as political domination but also as an engine of modernization, especially in terms of education, technological, and economic development (Gann & Duignan 1969 23) Especially theorists of development and underdevelopment are in strong opposition to this view and claim that colonialism was not beneficial at all. Guyanese historian Walter Rodney, for instance, rejects the proposition that there were good hands of colonialism: "Colonialism had only one hand – it was a one-armed bandit" (Rodney 1980: 123).

Even accepting that colonial governments in neither case did not serve the interests of Africans and positive effects were not deliberately calculated, Rodney's perspective is probably too extreme. It is unlikely that no positive effects at all emerged, but rather accidentally or as a by-product of the capitalist system. It is important to notice that the author neither shares the view that colonialism had a positive nor a balanced record; it is portrayed as a disaster on various levels.

However, colonialism did have some positive effects, such as the provision of infrastructure (even though they were only connecting the interior with the coastal market places), commercialization, or the introduction of a monetary economy (Boahen 1985b: 790). Probably the most important economic impact of colonialism was the deliberate neglect of industrialization33 and the discouragement or even destruction of already existing manufacturing industries with products like soap, beads, iron tools, pottery, and cloth (Boahen 1985b: 792). Instead, cash crops and other export commodities were prioritized by the Europeans, which had a disastrous effect on the internal agricultural sector producing for subsistence. Food thus often needed to be imported, mostly at high prices (Boahen 1985b: 793).

As the following examination will demonstrate, progress in industrialization in Africa depended heavily on the balance between national and international actors. Describing the economic developments during colonial rule, Austen (1987: 122–196) distinguishes between the *Étatist-Peasant Regimes* dominating West Africa from Senegal to Nigeria and the *Regimes of Competitive Exploitation* including the regions of Southern, Central, and East Africa.

33 According to Fieldhouse (1981: 68) no colonial government had established a department of industry until 1945.

2.4.1 Étatist-Peasant Regimes

At the beginning of the colonial movement, when commercial organization indicated a movement towards an open market, a growing number of African and European private firms were established along the coasts of East and West Africa. Meanwhile, European inland trade often followed the colonial conquerors and the railways.

Once established, these firms quickly displaced the African middlemen, and by the late 19th century, nearly all European and African merchants had vanished. The market was dominated by three commercial conglomerates: the French *Compagnie Francaise de l'Afrique Occidentale*, the *Société Commerciale de l'Ouest Africain*, and the British *United Africa Company* (Austen 1987: 130). Despite the success of these large European trading enterprises and the increasing demand for manufacturing goods, investments into large-scale manufacturing remained scarce.

The focus on import-export investments rather than on local manufacturing can be explained by market instability and risk. After price fluctuations in African commodities, merchant firms became even more cautious than before. Investment shifted from fixed assets in manufacturing to capital that could be liquidated easily. Additionally, colonial governments still saw themselves as representatives of their European economies and therefore inhibited manufacturing, under the condition that they were in competition rather than in complementation with the European industrial base (Brett 1973: 266–282).

Agricultural modes of production in colonial territories under African control exhibited small and self-owned (no rent payments and no threat of displacement) units of production which were only partly integrated into the rest of the national economies (Austen 1987: 138). The commercial output, mainly designated for remote markets, mostly consisted of palm oil and kernels, peanuts, coffee, cocoa, and cotton. To the surprise and consternation of European regimes, Africans dominated these markets and adapted very well to new market situations. The output of such agricultural production expanded very quickly in the early periods, which can be at least partly traced back to the European recovery from the Great Depression between the 1870s and 1890s; afterward it grew rather slowly (Austen 1987: 138–140).

A great controversy amongst liberal market and structuralist scholars has been about the inadequate development in the agricultural sector. In short, structuralists often interpret the interventionist policies of colonial governments as measures to preserve traditional modes of production in agriculture and, thus, European dominance over Africans (Brett 1973: 165 ff.). Liberals, in contrast, point out the advantages of small scale and labor-intensive production (Hopkins 1980: 210). European technologies sometimes simply did not offer effective gains for African farming. As a result, only some cheap new forms of technology especially designed for African conditions, such as light ploughs or hand-operated oil presses, were available to African farmers at the end of 1920s (Austen 1987: 145).

Industrialization hardly occurred in *Étatist-Peasant Regimes*. At the turn of the century, there was almost no manufacturing in the African colonies. When manufacturing finally started growing at the beginning of the 20th century, it was driven by the processing of primary products and later shifted to products for the domestic market, such as processed food, light consumer goods, and construction materials (Kilby 1975: 518). Only in some countries, especially the Belgian Congo, Kenya, Southern Rhodesia, and South Africa, more sophisticated manufacturing was established (Kilby 1975: 479–482). The drop of imports during World War II acted as a stimulant for those local industries.

2.4.2 Regimes of competitive exploitation

In contrast to the *Étatist-Peasant Regimes*, which allowed Africans to easily adapt to the new structures, Europeans forced the indigenous workers either to submit to the terms of employment or to compete with the new system of production.

The most compelling example of this kind of regime is South Africa. Between 1865 and 1900, South Africa became the world's leading supplier of diamonds and gold. Soon after, similar developments took place in Rhodesia and the Belgian Congo. The mineral revolution was accompanied by the expansion of European political control and large scale mining investments by monopolistic capitalist firms, such as *De Beers Consolidated Mines* in South Africa or *Rhode's British South Africa Company* in Rhodesia (Austen 1987: 162–163). These private mining enterprises also characterize the forms of labor. The employment was divided into well-paid skilled Europeans, temporally employed, unskilled, and low-paid Africans as well as skilled Africans which were paid at intermediate wages (Austen 1987: 165).

The transformation of society depended on whether mines were economically isolated without significant linkages to other parts of the economy or whether advanced technology in the mining industries induced industrial manufacturing. The development of such sectors in turn relied on the existence of a capitalist agricultural sector influencing government policy (Austen 1987: 168).

The capitalist agricultural sector was characterized by competition for land between Africans and Europeans, which had the effect of marginalizing many African farmers to proletariat. However, it contributed to the emergence of entrepreneurs among African landowners. The existence of such a capitalistic agricultural sector depended on three factors: The strategic imperative of servicing trade routes, climate and soil conditions allowing for European-type agriculture, and the non-existence of local African agriculture capable of serving the demands of international markets (Austen 1987: 168).

How did this regime provide the necessary conditions for successful industrialization? Firstly, some profitable mines and plantations introduced modern technologies and systems of production, but more importantly, they provided capital to finance needed infrastructure, for instance. The economy thus grew more independent of the state sector which typically served the interest of the European commercial centers. Austen (1987: 181 ff.) stresses the distinction between domestic and international orientations among economic actors.

International actors fearing potential colonial competition in fact focused on their mission to supply their respective European centers with cheap raw materials and, on the other hand, to open markets for their manufactured products (Austen 1987: 181; Brett 1973: 273). This clashed with the interest of domestic economic actors, such as small-scale merchants favoring local manufacturing with less exposure to international price fluctuations or European wage laborers generally favoring the expansion of employment and increasing wages. Examples of colonial industrialization show that the political influence of mostly white settler-farmers had a positive impact on industrialization.34

Hence, Africa's first experiences with industrialization started in the 1920s under colonial rule in the *Regimes of Competitive Exploitation,* especially in South Africa but also in the Belgian Congo, Southern Rhodesia, and Kenya. The colonial performance of the manufacturing sector in

34 Belgian Congo is a counter-example which experienced an exceptional degree of industrialization driven by the international sector. Austen (1987: 183) suggests that the Belgian economy was too small and advanced to benefit from the African primary good export and consumer import dependence economy.

these economies (see figure 2) provided the starting point for further industrialization of the newly independent nation states after decolonization.

However, these achievements obviously came at the price of political and social repression of the non-white majority (Austen 1987: 186). The crisis of the European powers during and after World War II contributed to and finally initiated decolonization. The new superpowers, the United States and the Soviet Union, pressured the European colonizers to grant sub-Saharan states independence (Young 1970: 453). Economically, though, the rising demand for African commodities led to deepening economic ties to Africa. The United States at first could be easily convinced that strengthening the Western European powers should be prioritized over political concerns in Africa (Austen 1987: 204–205). The Soviet Union and the People's Republic of China remained the only powers who maintained, at least vocally, opposition to colonialism in Africa. Furthermore, World War II brought colonialism in Asia to an end, which in turn inspired the emergence of nationalism in African states (Young 1970: 453–455).

Even though the emerging opposition towards colonialism did not directly lead to decolonization, it at least induced large increases in public expenditure. The new policy began with the *British Colonial Development and Welfare Act* (CDW) in 1940 and the *Fonds d'Investissements pour le Developpement Économique et Social* (FIDES) in 1947. Governmental efforts and public investments in infrastructure, health and education were supposed to fuel social and economic development in the colonies. These investments were also partly directed to private enterprises, but mainly to those which supplied cheap agricultural products and raw materials to France and Britain. Industrial policy and manufacturing remained the exception in British and French colonies (Kipré 1993: 358–360).

By the mid-1950s, it turned out that large agricultural projects failed in most of the African colonies due to miscalculations and overestimations of large-scale technological innovations under African environmental conditions. Commodity prices were falling and European economies had been recovering from supply shortages and trade deficits (Austen 1987: 208). Economists have recognized that there were no substantial economic reasons35 for efforts against the political momentum of decolonization (Austen 1987: 210). The formation of nationalist movements in Africa finally

35 See for example Bauer (1954: 34, 205–210 and 242).

provided a major impetus for decolonization (Wallerstein 1976: 48).36 1960 became the *Year of Africa* in which 18 former African colonies reached political independence.

In 1958, the average African income was about $111, twenty-one times lower than the income of an average American. However, it exceeded the average income in South and Southeast Asia, which was approximately $101 (ECA 1968: 20). Figure 3 compares the distribution of economic activities of large world regions. Africa already had its first industrial bases, especially in South Africa and Rhodesia. Its agricultural share of value added was comparatively high, whereas the manufacturing share was relatively small in international comparison, but about the same as in East and Southeast Asia.

Figure 3: Sector shares in world regions 1960

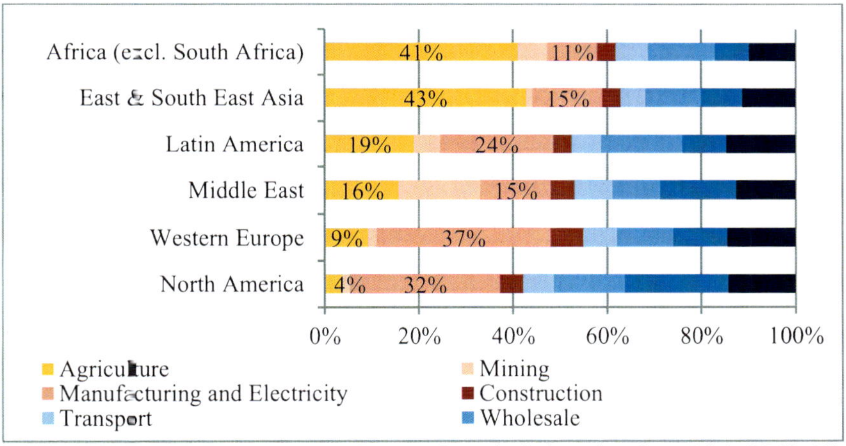

Source: Own depiction, data from ECA (1968: 27)

Due to the different historical paths, the manufacturing share of value added was distributed unevenly among the African economies (see figure 3). South Africa was the only economy with a manufacturing share of value added above twenty percent. It was followed by Zimbabwe (19.4 percent), Congo-Kinshasa (15.7 percent), and Tunisia (15.6 percent). According to the ECA (1968: 95), the contribution of heavy industries was

36 Young (1970: 462) points out that in retrospect, African nationalism in the 1950s and 1960s was not strong enough to withstand ruthless colonizers. However, it was a major trigger for decolonization in 1960.

only 32 percent, much lower than in the industrialized economies (55 percent). Manufacturing value added accounted for only two percent of employment in manufacturing, which can be attributed to the fact that wage earners only accounted for 16 percent of the total labor force in Africa (ECA 1968: 96).

Figure 4: Share of manufacturing of total value added in African countries in 1960

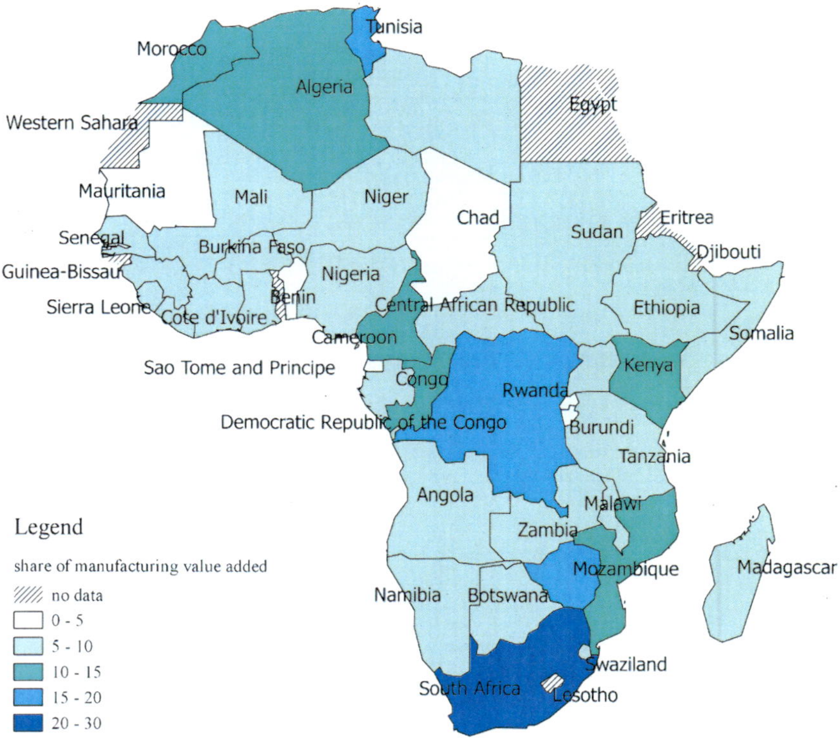

Source: Own depiction using QGIS, data from Roider (1971: 43)

2.5 Import substitution industrialization

After decolonization and political independence, the newly established governments started to think about economic independence from their former colonial masters. Especially the quest for industrial self-sufficiency became apparent since the former colonies had been serving as markets for industrial goods and exported mainly raw materials and food. Greater economic strength accompanied by military strength was to be achieved through rapid industrialization, which, in turn, facilitated the preference for economic planning and public control as well as hostility towards foreign direct investment.

2.5.1 International world order: capitalist vs. socialist

When Patrice Lumumba, the first elected prime minister of the Democratic Republic of the Congo, contacted Moscow for help with the Belgian occupation forces after independence on July 14th, 1960, the cold war became a new scramble for Africa (van Reybrouck 2013: 354).

African Socialism became a vision and ideology for restoring the traditional African way of life. At least the African culture was seen to lay a good foundation for the implementation of socialist political programs (Rosberg & Callaghy 1979: 3). The first wave of *African Socialism*, which Young (1982) called the *populist socialist pathway*, was especially represented by the Nkrumah in Ghana (from 1960 to 1966) but also by President Nyerere in Tanzania (since 1967). African societies were seen as relatively free of class divisions with a traditional ethos of communitarianism, in contrast to the capitalistic penchant for individualism (Young 1982: 98). Young's (1982) *populist socialist* group includes Algeria, Egypt, Ghana, Guinea, Mali, and Tanzania (Hughes (1992: 9) adds Zambia). Since most of the populist socialist experiments had experienced deep trouble, scientific socialism with a focus on Marxism and Leninism became the second wave of socialist experiments represented by Angola, Benin (1974), Congo-Brazzaville, Ethiopia (1976), Madagascar (1975), Mozambique, Sao Tome, and Somalia. The second wave was characterized by coercion and Marxist-Leninist vanguard parties instead of building on local conditions or some forms of African Socialism. Table 2 provides a list of countries which have been characterized as socialist.

Some other states officially declared following a capitalistic pattern of development. Capitalistic regimes can also be regarded as a residual for those countries which did not commit to any alternative. Popular examples are Cameroon, Ivory Coast, Kenya, Nigeria, Malawi, Senegal, and Zaire (Young 1982; Austen 1987: 234).

Despite the immense influence of the Cold War and the question of economic systems, the issue of African socialism seems not to be regarded as relevant for African history. The Cambridge History of Africa does not even have a catchword entry for either socialism or communism. Socialism, in fact, had been stuck in ideological phrases rather than converted into real economic systems. The ideological alignment to either socialism or capitalism did not necessarily influence economic policy at all (Austen 1987: 234). The comparisons of economic performances in socialist and capitalist regimes thus remained inconclusive (Young 1982: 324–326). According to Austen's (1987: 238) comparison between the socialist examples Ghana and Tanzania and the capitalist countries Ivory Coast and Kenya, the capitalist regimes performed much better in terms of production. However, if regimes were defined by the size of the state sector, nearly all African countries in the 1970s would need to be classified as socialist (Austen 1987: 236). The next section will therefore exclude the distinction between socialist and capitalist ideologies. Instead, a more influential aspect of political economy in Africa becomes apparent. The emergence of development economics and the ensuing political recommendations characterize the first period of economic policy in Africa.

Table 2: Socialist Countries in Africa after independence

African Socialism	Source	Marxist-Leninist Socialism	Source
Algeria	Young (1982)	Angola	Young (1982)
Egypt	Young (1982)	Benin	Young (1982)
Ghana	Young (1982)	Congo (Rep.)	Young (1982)
Guinea	Young (1982)	Ethiopia	Young (1982)
Mali	Young (1982)	Madagascar	Young (1982)
Tanzania	Young (1982)	Mozambique	Young (1982)
Zambia	Hughes (1992, 9)	Somalia	Young (1982)
Cape Verde	Hughes (1992, 12)	Burkina Faso	Hughes (1992, 11)
Guinea-Bissau	Hughes (1992, 12)	Zimbabwe	Hughes (1992, 12)
Sao Tome	Hughes (1992, 12)	Guinea-Bissau	Rosberg (1979, 9)
		Sao Tome	Young (1982)

Source: Own compilation

2.5.2 Early development economics

The challenges of decolonization and the accompanying problems of late industrialization gave birth to development economics. Without doubt, problems of development had been part of economic theory before (Szentes 2005: 156; Jomo & Reinert 2005). According to Srinivasan (2000: 171), economics had been development economics until the advent of neoclassical economics. Since the second half of the twentieth century, only few studies on growth and development have been published.37 The emergence of development economics as a sub-discipline was driven by the assumption that much of economic theory is bounded by special conditions and preconceptions of the advanced industrialized countries which cannot be applied to developing economies. The best example is Albert Hirschman (1981), who distanced himself from what he calls "monoeconomics", i.e., applying the same type of economics to developed and less developed countries.

Economic theory after World War II was dominated by the rejection of the *laissez faire* doctrine which had failed spectacularly during the interwar period. Thus, development economists were widely influenced by Keynesianism, which, in contrast to the neoclassical view, suggests that governments should intervene to allow for economic development (Chang 2002: 539). There were two main strands of development theories at the time: modernization and dependency theories. Despite the obvious differences between these theories, they exhibit a close historical and theoretical relationship.

Several authors such as Srinivasan (2000: 191) or Gore (2000) argue that there was a paradigm of development economics in the Kuhnian sense in the 1950s and 1960s, corresponding to the Keynesian Revolution which replaced the former neoclassical view of economics. The paradigmatic dominance of early development economics was not only exhibited in scientific writings but also manifested itself in the relevant institutions. Development programs and national planning boards, complemented by the already established Bretton Woods institutions, including the IMF and the World Bank, as well as aid agencies in the already industrialized countries provided the framework for underdeveloped countries at this time. According to Krugman (1993: 15), these early and glory days of development economics were marked by "great intellectual prestige and substantial real-world influence".

---

37 According to Srinivasan (2000: 171), there are only two important exceptions: Allyn Young (1876–1929) and Joseph Alois Schumpeter (1883-1950).

2.5.2.1 Modernization theories

In the beginning, the development discourse was dominated by modernization theories.[38] Economic growth became the main policy objective, which was held to be achievable via massive investments in *modern* activities like manufacturing. Many theorists saw industrialization as the main engine of economic growth. The industrial, not the agricultural sector was assigned to the dynamic role with high productivity growth pulling the economy forward. Probably the most famous modernization theory is the theory of the "Stages of Economic Growth" by Walt Whitman Rostow ([1960] 1997). He assumed that countries go through five stages of economic growth: the traditional society, preconditions for take-off, the take-off, the drive to maturity, and, lastly, the age of high mass consumption. The most important stage is the "take off" in which dynamic growth through rationalizing and economies of scale in the manufacturing sector accelerates the shift from the agrarian to the secondary sector. Another proponent of the linear stage theory was formulated by Alexander Gerschenkron (1966).**39** His theory implies that latecomer economies can benefit in their industrial development from using advanced technologies from already developed economies, enabling them—due to their "advantage of backwardness"—to grow faster and catch up with already developed countries. Concerning the question why some countries manage to industrialize and others do not, Paul Rosenstein-Rodan (1943) developed the theory of the "big push", which was absorbed by the similar "critical minimal effort" thesis of Leibenstein (1957). Rosenstein-Rodan and Nurkse (1953) further postulated the concept of *balanced growth* which is in contradiction with the theory of *unbalanced growth* by Hirschman (1958). Another major characteristic feature of modernization theories was the analytical framework of dualism, provided by Arthur Lewis (1954). He de-

---

38 Modernization theories assume that the least developed societies can—via economic growth and modernization per se—be transformed in the same manner as already developed countries. While dualism and inequalities can be eliminated, trade-offs are neglected and thus different kinds of development goals like wealth, equity, stability, democracy, and autonomy can be achieved simultaneously. They are complementary to economic growth (Weiner & Huntington 1994: 6–11).

39 Gerschenkron is not a typical modernization theorist. He rather emphasizes the differences in the development processes, especially between forerunner and latecomer economies. He thereby includes external factors to economic development, whereas modernization theorists mostly focus on internal policy.

veloped a two-sector model differentiating between the low-productivity subsistence sector with diminishing returns to scale due to limited amount of land and the capital-accumulating capitalist (industrial) sector.40

2.5.2.2 Structuralism and dependency theories

Modernization theories assume that economic development is a systemic process including similar stages of development through which all nations go when implementing the right economic policy. Structuralism and dependency theories arose from criticism of modernization theories. While the primary object of investigation of modernization theories is the nation state and its economic policy, these theories reject the idea of the sovereign state as an entity of analysis (especially in the case of Africa) and explain changes as a consequence of evolution and interaction within the world system (Wallerstein 1974: 7). Originating mainly from two papers by Hans Singer (1950) and Raúl Prebisch (1950), a component of these theories is that development is dependent on the structure of the international economic system, which can be divided into the poor "periphery" and the rich "core". The theory is based on observations that imply a negative trend of the terms of trade[41] for primary commodity exporters.

The differentiation between structuralism and dependency theories is not always obvious, since both strands of theory have a close theoretical and historical relationship. However, there is a fundamental difference: While structuralist theories assume that economic development is possible in the periphery by import substitution industrialization, dependency theories are more pessimistic, arguing that capitalism systematically puts the periphery at a disadvantage and that only a change in the world system (to global socialism, for instance) can help development economies escape from underdevelopment (Saad-Filho 2005: 128).

---

40 Arthur Lewis draws on Boeke (1942) who originally created the concept of the dual economy. However, the Lewis-Model is probably the most famous one, providing the underlying framework and giving rise to a whole series of dual sector models. Examples can be found in: Fei & Ranis (1963), Jorgenson (1961), Zarembka (1970), Harris & Todaro (1970), and Dixit (1973).

41 Terms of Trade describes the quantity of imports that can be purchased through a fixed amount of exports. It can be calculated in dividing the price of exported goods by the price of imported goods. The development of terms of trade is sometimes interpreted as an indicator for economic wealth.

In addition to the analytical differentiation between sovereign nation states and the world system, dependency theorists do not start their analysis with the establishment of sovereign nation states after decolonization in 1960 (as modernization theory often does). Instead, they emphasize colonial continuities and, hence, start their analysis either with the arrival of Europeans in Africa (Rodney 1980) or with the mercantilist slave trade (Amin 1972), thus the integration of Africa into the world economy. The most famous African authors in this line of theory are Kwame Nkrumah, the first president of Ghana (1960-1966), and the Egyptian economist and advocate of Pan-Africanism, Samir Amin.

2.5.3 Import substitution industrialization

As shown in the previous section, all theories either implicitly or explicitly stress the importance of the manufacturing sector, in which imperfect competition, economies of scale, or external effects prevail. Accordingly, early development economists did not endorse free trade and specialization but were export-pessimistic and recommended policies of import substitution industrialization (ISI). ISI—heavily drawing on the infant-industry argument[42]—in its ideal type is based on the promotion of a domestic industrial sector protected with the help of tariffs or other import controls, and a reduction of import-dependency for manufactured goods (Kiely 1998: 79). In other words, it is each kind of government intervention that encourages domestic industrial production with the goal of replacing imports.

ISI typically commences with the domestic production of non-durable consumer goods (e.g., food and textiles) and later diversifies into more complex, durable products (household applications, car parts, simple chemical products, oil refining) and finishes with the complete manufacturing structure producing technologically advanced capital goods (machinery, aircraft, electronic instruments) (Saad-Filho 2005: 129). However, the production level heavily relies on intermediate and capital goods, which made ISI dependent on the import of these goods.

42 The infant industry argument was first articulated by Alexander Hamilton (1790) and later picked up by Friedrich List (1841). It states that new industries, in which a country has a comparative advantage, need to be protected during an initial period until firms reach international competitiveness due to economies of scale or by adopting new technologies (Meier 2005: 144).

The practical problem was how to go beyond the immature development plans deriving from colonialism, which consisted mainly of an incoherent list of possible investment projects (Toye 2006: 26). Tools and techniques relied on available data. The absence of reliable data, however, promoted a tendency towards planning without facts on the basis of doctrinaire assumptions (Toye 2006: 26).

Despite the lack of internationally comparable data for African sectoral value added, there is a widespread consensus that the industrial share rose substantially from 1960 until the late 1970s (UNIDO 2011: 15; Wangwe & Semboja 2003: 163; Page 2011: 11). It was expected that if the industrialization process proceeded, linkage effects would help expand the production of intermediate and capital goods as well, thus enhance self-reliance and prevent balance-of-payments problems (UNIDO 2011: 10). At the end of the 1970s, expectations were under threat, as linkages between the industries remained minimal and only few industries became competitive (Wangwe & Semboja 2003: 163). Africa had produced industries with low efficiency, low returns, and low labor productivity.

The African industrial sector rose substantially: from 29.4 percent in 1970 up to 36.7 percent in 1980. This increase, however, can be attributed to a large extent to the mining sector rather than to the manufacturing sector. Indeed, assessing the performance of the African manufacturing sector between 1960 and 1980 is difficult. Internationally comparable data before 1970 is rare, and the data sources for the time between 1970 and 1980 are contradictory. According to the ECA (1971: 27), the manufacturing sector (including energy) in developing Africa (excluding South Africa) rose from 10.7 to 12.6 percent of total value added, meaning an average growth rate of 6.1 percent, whereas the average growth rate of the total economy was only 4.4 percent.

For the time period between 1970 and 1980, UNCTAD & UNIDO (2011: 15) reports an increase in the size of the manufacturing sector in developing Africa from 6.3 to 11.9 percent, whereas UNCTADstat reports an increase from 12.0 to 12.6 percent. I report the publicly accessible data from UNCTADstat in figure 5 and table 5.

In general, the outcomes of industrialization remain negligible. The African share in world manufacturing was negligible at 2.3 percent in 1980. However several economies such as Congo-Kinshasa, Kenya, Malawi, Zambia, Zimbabwe, Swaziland, and Mauritius managed to increase their manufacturing share considerably.

Figure 5: Share of manufacturing of total value added in African countries in 1980

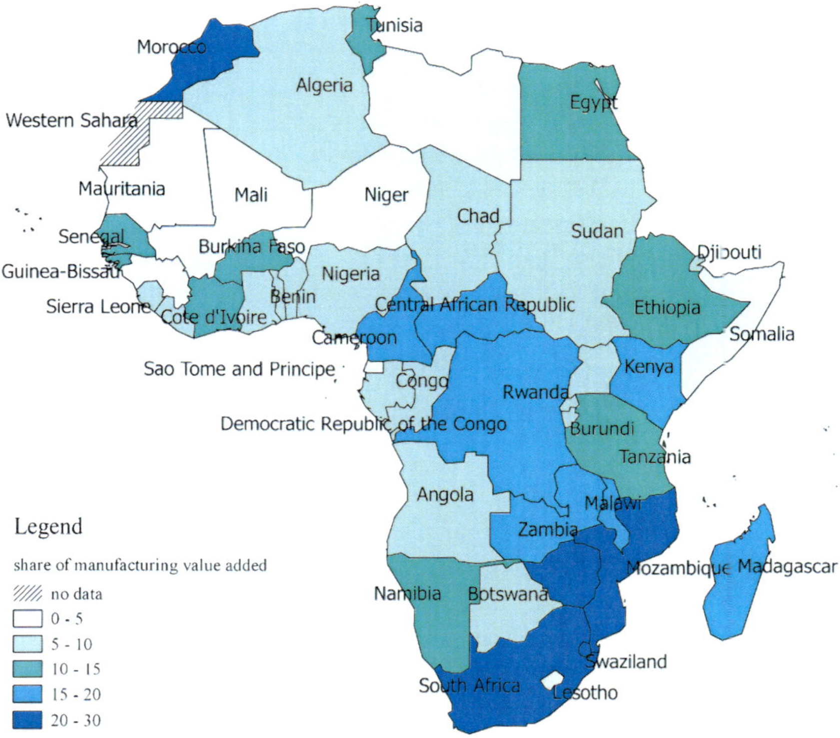

Source: Own depiction using QGIS, data from UNCTADstat

2.6 Structural adjustment

African countries experienced a disastrous crisis at the beginning of the 1980s. Even though Africa could not be perceived as "developed" by then, its growth rates had been relatively high between 1960 and 1970. While GDP per capita in sub-Saharan Africa experienced a moderate growth of 3.3 percent from 1965 to 1973, it decreased by 0.3 percent from 1973 to 1980 and 1.1 percent from 1980 to 1989 (Tarp 1994: 12) (see also figure 1). Besides, African countries experienced falling export volumes contributing to severe balance-of-payments deficits as well as increased external long-term debt, which diminished the capacity to import intermediate and capital goods needed for economic growth (Sender & Smith 1985: 126).

In addition, African countries suffered from domestic problems: The political scenery was characterized by coups d'état, ethnic fragmentation, and civil strife. Political stability was rare in sub-Saharan Africa (Owusu 2003: 1657).

There have been two kinds of explanations for this economic crisis in Africa. The structuralists, especially academics with Marxist orientations such as Amin (1974), Lawrence (1986), or Sutcliffe (1986), saw the crisis as a result of long-term underdevelopment. Quite similar, the *United Nations Economic Commission for Africa* (ECA 1989: 1) explained the African crisis with the underlying structures of the African economy in production, consumption, technology, employment, and socio-political organization. As Fole (2003: 79) points out, both explanations of the crisis focus on historically formed structures.43

Additionally, the structuralist approach assumes that the world trade system had a major impact on African development. Structurally decreasing prices for agricultural goods, the world depression, and protectionist agricultural policies in developed countries finally caused the decreasing share of exports. The following deficit in the balance of payments, the increased interest rates as a consequence of the global depression, and the oil crises of 1973 and 1979 eventually resulted in increasing government debts (Lensink 1996: 41).

The neoclassical explanation of the African crisis also focuses on government debts, but sees them as a result of high state consumption, corruption, and inefficient allocation. Import substitution policies and development plans, including the promotion of the industrial sector, were evaluated as a neglect of the beneficial effects of market incentives. The recommendations of privatization, deregulation, and liberalization thus gained supremacy in the important development institutions for the following decades.

2.6.1 Washington Consensus

In 1990, John Williamson (1990) coined the term "Washington Consensus" to describe the neoclassical standard economic policy of the World Bank or the IMF for developing countries, starting in 1981. While the ear-

43 For further reading concerning the African crisis in the 1980s, see Bienefeld (1988)

ly development thinkers mainly focused on market failure due to information or coordination externalities, the economists of the 80s and 90s stressed government failures and pointed to excessive government consumption, misallocation of resources as well as inadequate macroeconomic policy or corruption (Tarp 1994: 14 ff.). The neoclassical market price system with a minimalist government and a balance-of-payments as well as fiscal deficit equilibrium became the main feature of the new development paradigm of the 1980s and 1990s (Thorbecke 2007: 16). Along with Béla Balassa and Jagdish Bhagwati, Anne Krüger became the famous advocate of this school of thought.

With the revival of neoclassical economics in the Western industrialized countries and the rise to power of Margaret Thatcher and Ronald Reagan, neoclassical orthodox economists regained massive influence in the World Bank and the other Bretton Woods institutions. As Meier (2005: 83) puts it: "Reagan's 'magic of the market' and Thatcher's minimization of government provided a congenial intellectual environment for the neoclassical resurgence." In 1980, World Bank president Robert McNamara was followed by A.W. Clausen with a different ideological focus. He replaced the former chief economist Hollis B. Chenery by Anne O. Krüger, an institutional reflection of the neoclassical takeover.44

The following two decades were characterized by the second generation of development economists criticizing the former policies for ignoring fundamental neoclassical principles (Meier 2005: 85). Economic theory in the following years became synonymous with privatization, deregulation, and liberalization as driven by the Bretton Woods institutions IMF and World Bank, which became more and more dominant while African economies suffered from severe debt problems.45

---

44 While Chenery emphasized the role of structural change for economic development, Krueger was a strong believer in neoclassicism, pointing out the failures of import substitution policies. In her article "The Political Economy of the Rent-Seeking Society" (1974) she showed how rent-seeking economies produce deadweight losses.

45 The hegemonic power of the World Bank in development economics was also underscored by a range of World Bank studies and the annually published World Development Reports. The WDR is the flagship publication by the Research Department led by the World Bank chief economist. The 1997 World Development Report cost $3 million, and the report was translated into various languages and printed about 150.000 times. Almost half of the copies were distributed as free copies to libraries and universities in developing countries (Menzel 2000, 208). About eight of the World Bank's best and most senior re-

Due to the severe debt crisis in developing countries in the 70s, the World Bank initiated structural adjustment programs (SAP) in 1980, which made loans conditional on the implementation of economic policies in line with the new "Washington Consensus". The IMF and the World Bank made 958 adjustment loans to developing countries between 1980 and 1998, thus became the most dominant players in the economic policy of African states (Easterly 2001: 136).

2.6.2 Methodological issues

The World Bank's famous "Berg Report" (World Bank 1981) attributed most of the growth failure in sub-Saharan Africa to the false perception that development is equivalent to industrial growth. It argues that the overoptimistic interventionist import substitution industrialization policies had led to a huge unproductive administrative public sector marked by corruption, delays, and an underutilization of capacities (Sender & Smith 1985: 126).

The central argument of the report and the upcoming economists at this time was that individuals react to incentives. The inefficient use of resources and the debt-ridden public sector could thus be traced back to wrong institutional incentive structures. While the early development economists focused on structure rather than individuals, methodological individualism and physical metaphors, which already had been prominent during the marginal revolution in 1870, became popular again (Hodgson 2012: 503).

Development economics, in consequence, distanced itself from development studies and the incorporation of interdisciplinary elements (Fine 2010a: 69). The historical analysis of modernization, progress, and industrialization, which was accompanied by an interdisciplinary exchange with development studies, was abandoned in favor of the analysis of individual agents, incentive structures, and the assessment of performance in perfectly working markets (Gore 2000: 794). Development economics in the following years reverted back to being an applied field of "normal" econom-

searchers are working on a WDR report at any time, which represents about 10 percent of the World Bank's total research effort in terms of man-hours (Deaton 2009: 107).

ics, in which the same tools of labor economics, agricultural economics as well as international economics were used (Krueger 1986: 62–63).

When the principles of marginalist economics had been extended to macroeconomics (Fine 2010b: 63), the rise of neoclassical thinking was accompanied by the rise of modern growth theory in which human capital becomes one of the prime movers of economic development. Furthermore, the role of knowledge, technology, and innovations were important additions to the understanding of development (Lucas 1988; Romer 1990). Interestingly, these endogenous models could be equally applied to development economics and industrialized countries, revealing the neglect of structural issues in these models. Gore (2000) further emphasizes that the explanatory framework of development in the Washington Consensus was national, whereas the structuralist approach (especially dependency economists but also modernization theorists) had a global framework for explaining development and underdevelopment. The changing perspective explains why development economics was simply seen as an applied field of normal economics and why economic policy gained primacy in explaining differentials between the performances of economies. However, the framework dismisses the impact of global developments as well as historically grown path-dependencies.

According to the national framework of explaining economic growth, the neoclassical analysis is underlined by empirical growth regressions in which around 60 variables were found to be significant for economic growth (Sala-I-Martin 1997: 178). Dualism and structural change have been nearly completely absent from empirical growth research. On the contrary, "much of that research proceeds as if structural change can be ignored" (Temple & Wößmann 2006: 188).

An influential study by Little et al. (1970) showed that import substitution policies had been much more costly than expected and that the export-led policies of the Newly Industrializing Countries (NIC) in East-Asia had been much more successful. Instead of import substitution industrialization, an externally-oriented trade policy was seen as a key ingredient for economic growth and development (Krueger 1997: 1). The theory provided indications that protectionist policies encourage rent-seeking involving corruption, smuggling, and black markets (Meier 2005: 85). Simultaneously, dynamic trade theory (Helpman & Krugman 2002; Jensen & Wong 1997) helped the comparative advantage theory to celebrate its comeback and to become prominent again. The use of tariffs or any other type of import-restrictions was in consequence deemed hampering for economic development.

2.6.3 Structural adjustment policies

According to the Washington Consensus, the main aspects of these adjustment programs had been a) the devaluation of the currency, b) the reduction of tariffs and other import restrictions, c) stimulating agricultural production, and d) restructuring the public sector, i.e., the reduction of subsidies and the number of civil servants as well as the privatization of public enterprises (Lensink 1996: 77–93).

According to the World Bank (1992), Africa received 117 of a total of 258 adjustment loans between 1980 and 1991, which account for $10,025 million or 24 percent of all adjustment loans (World Bank 1992: 69). The survey shows that 14 out of the group of 27 *intensive adjustment* lending countries and 18 out of the group of 30 *other adjustment* lending countries were African. Only Botswana, Egypt, Ethiopia, Lesotho, Liberia, and Rwanda did not receive any adjustment loans (see table 3). Adjustment policies in African economies were implemented fully in 73 percent and substantially in 87 percent (World Bank 1995: 84).

Table 3: Adjustment lending countries in Africa

Intensive-adjustment lending countries [a]	**Other adjustment lending countries** [b]	**Non-adjustment lending countries**
Côte d'Ivoire	Algeria	Botswana
Ghana	Benin	Egypt
Guinea-Bissau	Burkina Faso	Ethiopia
Kenya	Burundi	Lesotho
Madagascar	Cameroon	Liberia
Malawi	Central African Republic	Rwanda
Mauritania	Congo (Brazzaville)	
Mauritius	Congo (Kinshasa)	
Morocco	Gabon	
Nigeria	Gambia	
Senegal	Mali	
Tanzania	Niger	
Togo	Sierra Leone	
Zambia	Somalia	
	Sudan	
	Trinidad and Tobago	
	Tunisia	
	Zimbabwe	

Source: World Bank (1995: 15); a) countries which received two or more adjustment loans effective in June 1990, with the first adjustment loan effective before June 1986, b) other countries that received at least one adjustment loan effective by 1990.

The effects of the adjustment policies are noticeable but unclear. Most of the studies, especially those by the World Bank or the IMF, suggest that they had a positive effect on economic growth (World Bank 1992, 1994). Concerning exports, investments, and savings, even the estimates of the IMF and the World Bank are inconclusive (Lensink 1996: 107). However, the World Bank assessments were harshly criticized by several authors. Most of the evaluation studies, except for the studies by the implementation institutions themselves, conclude that there has not been any positive impact of adjustment policies on economic growth (Mosley et al. 1995; Wangwe & Semboja 2003; Easterly 2005).

Apart from the modest economic outcomes of structural adjustment, its critics stress the high environmental and social costs of the policies (Lensink 1996: 125) as well as the political consequences. Since adjustment policies had been entirely external to the governments and driven by donor concerns, they reduced the accountability and transparency of national decision-making. Furthermore, large capital flows yielded to increased aid dependency and, thus, dependency to international financial donors (Van de Walle 2008: 228–229). Shrinking legitimacy and public impatience up to social unrest against western domination were the results. Herbst (1990) emphasizes that politicians faced an even more risky political environment when adopting more decentralized forms of government. Adjustment loans limited the direct financial flows from political leaders to their old network, which, in turn, broke down and thus weakened the central state apparatus. Van de Walle (2008: 14) concludes that adjustment lending had a negative impact on state capacity and even facilitated the emergence of neo-patrimonial systems.

Due to the overall decline of growth rates in sub-Saharan Africa during the 80s until the mid-90s, this period time came to be known as the "lost development decades" (Easterly 2001). The decline is mysterious, since growth regressions that had been successful in explaining cross-country variations in economic growth predicted an upward trend of overall economic growth due to country characteristics, such as school-enrollment, financial depth, or telephone density (Easterly 2001: 137). The typical growth regression over-predicted economic growth in the 80s and 90s. According to Easterly this overall decline must probably be attributed to worldwide factors, such as the terms of trade (commodity prices), interest rates, or the overall growth slowdown of industrial economies.

Figure 6: Share of manufacturing of total value added in African countries in 1995

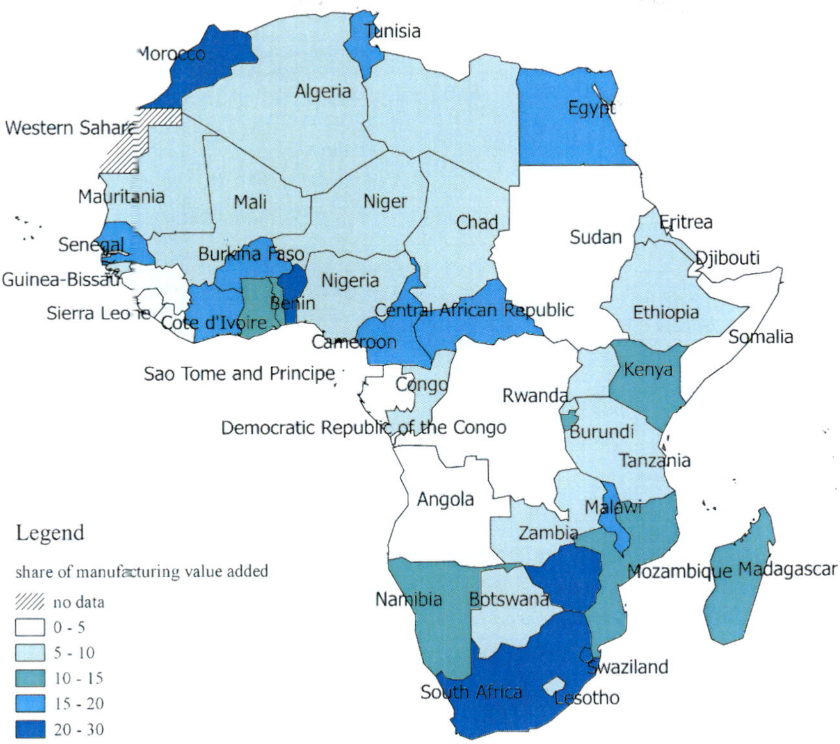

Source: Own depiction using QGIS, data from UNCTADstat

Considering the manufacturing share of African economies, the results during this period are very diverse (see figure 6). While the manufacturing share in all of Africa rose from 11.5 to 14.8 percent, the same share in developing Africa fell from 12.6 percent in 1980 to 8.2 percent in 1995. The share of manufacturing rose substantially in several economies during this time, for example in Swaziland, Benin, Côte d'Ivoire, Burkina Faso, Mali, Mauretania, but also in Libya and Tunisia. However, it shrunk in Angola, Congo-Kinshasa, Djibouti, Liberia, Kenya, Mozambique, and Zambia.

2.7 Post Washington Consensus Consensus

As most of the developing countries needed to go through a painful adjustment process, it became clear that the overall situation had become one of stagnation. While in the time span 1960–1980, the average per capita growth was 2 percent, in the period 1980–1995, the average per capita growth was negative at -0.43 percent, and even -1.7 percent in sub-Saharan Africa (see table 4). The period between 1980 and 1995 became the "lost decades" for development economics (e.g., Easterly 2001). Only the Newly Industrializing Countries (NIC) in East Asia[46] managed to sustain their growth during this time. Botswana and Mauritius are two African outliers which also experienced high growth in this period.

Table 4: Average GDP per capita (constant 2010 USD) growth in percent

	1960-1980	**1980-1995**	**1995-2011**
Africa	1.97%	-0.43%	1.91%
World	2.65%	1.11%	1.73%
North America	2.68%	1.91%	1.47%
Latin America & Caribbean	3.16%	0.16%	1.82%
Europe & Central Asia	-	1.27%	1.91%
East Asia & Pacific	4.23%	3.39%	3.22%
Sub-Saharan Africa	1.59%	-1.72%	2.08%

Source: World Development Indicators

The success of the NIC on the one hand implied the demise of dependency theory, which was not able to explain this phenomenon, but also challenged the neoclassical view on development policy. Several authors emphasized the Japanese development experience in contrast to the structural adjustment conditions. The first one was Chalmer Johnson who used the term "miracle" in his book "MITI and the Japanese Miracle". Further milestones were: Cumings (1984), Evans et al. (1999), Amsden (1989), Wade (1990), and Aoki et al. (1997). All authors focused on the role of government and institutions as well as industrial policy and henceforth

46 The NIC are sometimes called the four "Tigers": Hong Kong, Singapore, South Korea, and Taiwan. Later a second generation joined the "Tiger Club": Indonesia, Malaysia, the Philippines, and Thailand.

heavily challenged the neoclassical interpretation of the "The East Asian Miracle" (World Bank 1994).47

The Japanese government itself supported adjustment loans until 1991 due to concerns about the bilateral relationship with the United States (Stein 1998: 40). After the collapse of the Soviet Union followed by a shift in Japanese-American relations, it started to voice its criticism (Stein 1998: 41). Japan's increasing influence as a donor and investor thus challenged the Washington consensus in 1991. The result of this process was the World Development Report (WDR) 1991 (World Bank 1991), which represented a market-friendly view, in contrast to the radical liberal one of 1987. According to the Japanese Ministry of Finance and the Japanese directors of the World Bank, the WDR still proved unacceptable because too little attention was paid to the role of bureaucracy and the developmental state. However, the WDR can be seen as a first small shift away from orthodox neoliberalism (Menzel 2000: 209).

The report recognized that generally strong states managed to stabilize their economies and to introduce market-friendly reforms. Against the backdrop of the democratic experiences, especially in Africa, it stresses the relationship between the state and the market. It acknowledged the principal faults in the dichotomy of laissez-faire and intervention and advocates a consensus for a market-friendly approach (World Bank 1991: 1–2). The role of the state was to limit its activities and public services to a minimum (Yusuf 2009: 33). Scarce state capability still was to be addressed by reducing unnecessary government involvement. State fragility was attributed to authoritarian and predatory governments, working in opposition to market forces. In general, democracy was seen as complementary to market forces, and the successful authoritarian governments in the NIC were seen as an exception rather than the rule (World Bank 1991: 133).

With the end of the Cold War and the subsequent change of the world order, development economics changed dramatically. The Post Washing-

47 The World Bank (1994) tried to explain the "East Asian Miracle" with the help of the neoclassical export-oriented economic policy. The fast development was attributed to the pace of human and physical capital accumulation. Macroeconomic stability for optimal allocation of production functions was seen as the key to achieve long-lasting economic growth. Furthermore, the World Bank admitted that most East Asian countries conducted industrial policies. However, the interpretation was that the NICs achieved a high growth rate and industrialization despite relying on industrial policies.

ton Consensus Consensus, which is still dominated by the World Bank, refuses its former SAPs. *New Development Economics*, mainly coined by Joseph Stiglitz, is the new paradigm within the World Bank. However, Gore (2000: 795) proposes that besides the western-dominated paradigm of development economics, there is a Southern Consensus of *Latin American Neostructuralism*, mainly articulated by United Nations Economic Commission for Latin America and the Caribbean (ECLAC), and the *East Asian Development Models*, described by United Nations Economic and Social Commission for Asia and the Pacific (1990).

2.7.1 New Development Economics

The World Bank's 50th anniversary was accompanied by massive public protest against the Bretton-Woods institutions. The International Monetary Fund's annual meeting in Madrid was hemmed by the critic's slogan "50 years is enough"48 (Yusuf 2009: 34). President James Wolfensohn, appointed in June 1995, responded to the critics with the attempt to convince civil society of the bank's relevance. His appointment marked the next change in international development politics. Wolfensohn was supported by two Nobel laureates: Amartya Sen, who is famous for his many-sided view of development and welfare (his suggestions heavily influenced the Human Development Index introduced by the UN in 1990), and Douglass North, famous for his work on institutions.

In Wolfensohn's proposal for a comprehensive development framework, he challenged the World Bank and the IMF not to focus only on structural adjustment but to respect the structural, social and human dimensions as the other side of the coin (Wolfensohn 1999: 7). Unlike in the phase of SAP, the focus shifted from macroeconomic stability and economic growth to poverty and inequality reduction as well as human development including education and health (Owusu 2003: 1661). Nonetheless, the World Bank still believes that the best way to reduce poverty is economic growth (Dollar & Kraay 2002).

The turning point for a new consensus within the World Bank after the failures and criticism of the Washington Consensus was pushed forward by the Japanese view on development. Its influence was felt in the WDR

48 The slogan became the header of a collective volume bringing together the critique on the World Bank and the IMF (see Danaher 1994).

1997, "The State in a Changing World" (World Bank 1997), in which the World Bank acknowledged the role of the state for economic development at least in principle "as partner, catalyst and facilitator" (Menzel 2000: 210).

The policy shift in the important development institutions was accompanied by advances in development economics differing from traditional neoclassic economics. Joseph Stiglitz calls it "New Development Economics" (NDE) (Stiglitz 1986). One of the main features of this new brand of economics is the departure from excessive beliefs in market fundamentalism. The role of the government, apart from assuring property rights and macroeconomic stability, was strengthened due to several reasons. The traditional neoclassical paradigm admits that markets are imperfect in certain cases when external economies or public goods are considered. Stiglitz (1986) established the "Imperfect Information Paradigm" assuming that, as information is imperfect in virtually all cases, markets lead to efficient allocation only under exceptional circumstances. Thus, market failures are the rule rather than the exception. New development economics focuses on information, learning, incentives as well as incomplete or missing markets.

According to Stiglitz (2008: 3), NDE provides the theoretical underpinning for the belief that in early stages of development, markets will not lead to efficient outcomes. The ascension of NDE was accompanied by the comeback and resurgence of ideas and concepts deriving from high development theory. The theories of poverty traps were subsequently illustrated by models including multiple equilibria. The big push is modeled by the existence of coordination failure, economies of scale, and imperfect tradability (Rodrik 1996). Ray (2000) also stresses the role of interindustry links and demands complementarities in a Hirschmanian tradition. Ros (2001) further attempts to reintegrate the ideas of early development economists such as Rosenstein-Rodan, Nurkse or Lewis into the new growth theory and shows a wide range of theoretical congruence between them.

Already in the 1980s, new trade theories based on economies of scale as well as imperfect information suggested selective and country-specific interventionist industrial policies (Deraniyagala 2003: 87). NDE is neither in favor of a strong overarching role of the state, as most modernization theories are, nor does it conform to a minimalist state, as proposed by the Washington Consensus. On the contrary, NDE aims to exploit the complementarities between the state and the market (Ndulu 2007: 322).

A shift from market-liberalism to a more moderate view can thus be interpreted as a convergence towards the East Asian model of development. While the policy implications may converge, the market remains the starting point of analysis for the NDE. East Asian models, on the other hand, interpret the market as a tool which can be helpful for achieving economic growth.

2.7.2 East Asian model of development

The emergence of the NIC in East Asia prompted the question why these economies had been so successful, whereas others had not. In spite of their regional concentration, the East Asian economies differed widely concerning size, political regime, resource endowments as well as their socio-cultural and ethnic structures. Several authors therefore proposed the presence of a typical form of state as the most important factor in generating high and sustainable economic growth. Chalmer Johnson (1982) invoked the concept of the "developmental state" in characterizing the Japanese economic bureaucracy, especially the Ministry of International Trade and Industry (MITI), and its role for the extraordinary Japanese post-war development. The policies of MITI became the role model for the NIC, especially for South Korea, Taiwan, Hong Kong, and Singapore. China also adopted the institutions of the model during the 1990s (Johnson 1999: 40). Several other authors stressed the role of the state in the development process in East Asia, such as Alice Amsden (1989), Robert Wade (1990), Peter Evans (1995), and Adrian Leftwich (1995), thus established the "developmental state" model as a paradigm.

Since several authors focused on the political economy of the developmental state and analyzed the relationship between the state and the economy, Amsden (1989) examined the economic policy of South Korea in detail. The government took a strategic role in selecting and developing industries which had been critical for the productive transformation of the economy. According to Öniş (1991: 124), the industrial policy of the developmental state is characterized by three features which distinguish them from economic policies proposed by neoclassical economists or even associates of the New Development Economics. Firstly, the process of development and thus the building up of infrastructure, education, and research has the priority over direct ownership and control of industrial production. Secondly, the state plays a key role in the promotion of cooperative labor-management relations. And thirdly, the state assumes responsibility for the creation of comparative advantages (Leftwich 1995: 402).49

In contrast to the neoclassical postulations of profit maximization and conforming to comparative advantages, the state in the East Asian model is supposed to heavily intervene and create price distortions by subsidizing and directing capital to strategic industries before cautiously exposing them to international competition. Again, even though the East Asian Model conforms to New Development Economics in the aspect that competition is deemed useful, its starting point of analysis is not the market but rather the state and the question of how to achieve economic transformation. The market is therefore seen as an instrument for industrial policy, which is employed to expose carefully identified industries to international competitive pressure (Öniş 1991: 124).

2.7.3 Latin American Neostructuralism

Latin American Neostructuralism is a collection of policy orientations and proposals, mainly put forward by the *United Nations Economic Commission for Latin America and the Caribbean* (ECLAC), rather than an academic theoretical framework. However, Leiva (2008b) suggests that it meets the criteria of a paradigm as listed by Fine (2002).[50] Neostructuralism emerged in reaction to the neoclassical experience of the 1980s and invokes the traditional Latin American thinkers of structuralism in the 70s. One of the main thinkers is Fernando Fajnzylber who coined the term and laid the foundation in two publications: "Changing production patterns

---

49 Since the Flying Geese model had been adopted by the New Development Economics, it came to be known as the idea of *dynamic comparative advantages*. A discussion emerged whether industrial policy should defy or conform to comparative advantages (Lin & Chang 2009). Since the idea of dynamic comparative advantages allows for market failures, there can even be a need for selective industrial policy. However, from a theoretical point of view, the difference lies within the framework of new development economics in which the comparative advantages (even though they are dynamic) are given or determined by the market and need to be identified. A methodology as to how identifying the dynamic comparative advantage is presented in Lin & Monga (2010). According to the East Asian Model of development, comparative advantages are not given but need to be created.

50 Leiva (2008b: 4–5) identifies and compares three development paradigms: the old Latin American Structuralism, Neoliberalism, and Neostructuralism.

with social equity" (ECLAC 1990) and "Sustainable development: changing production patterns, social equity and the environment" (ECLAC 1991). Neostructuralism is seen as a structuralist reaction and Latin American answer to the historical conditions after the Washington Consensus. The term "neo" signifies the adoption of export-led oriented policies, but the analytical basis remains structural, at least according to Bielschowsky (2009: 182).

Leiva (2008a: 3) states that neostructuralism distinguishes itself from the neoliberal framework. He concludes from the SAPs that the focus on economic development itself is not sufficient and that such policy reforms are not possible as long as political legitimacy is not ensured. He thus emphasizes the interplay of economic development and participatory processes, democratic governance as well as social cohesion and equality. In the end, however, the aim of his brand of neostructuralism is still to increase the society's capacity and to achieve international competitiveness (Leiva 2008b: 11). It needs to be distinguished from the idea of comparative advantages, in which the international competitiveness of commodities is the key for economic development.

In contrast, ECLAC (1990) developed the notion of *systematic competitiveness*, incorporating the entire social system, competing on a world scale. Technical progress and increases in productivity are determined by institutional, political, and cultural factors. Economic policy, according to this theory, must account for the entire system and cannot merely focus on allocation, optimization, efficiency, and externalities. The need for interdisciplinarity is the most distinguishing aspect between neostructuralism and New Development Economics. In the publication of 2007, the approach of social cohesion and its importance for economic policy, especially in developing countries confronting an economic transformation process, is elaborated (ECLAC 2007). The approach aggregates the Latin American historical legacies as well as cultural peculiarities into an economic framework to provide policy recommendations (ECLAC 2007: 19–32). Its analysis in this aspect totally differs from NDE, which uses categories like social capital. Neostructuralism further distinguishes itself from NDE in the sense that it neglects the idea of 'one model fits it all'. A general blueprint for economic development thus cannot be developed but is dependent on historical legacies, local peculiarities, as well as the technological circumstances and the international context.

Still, the neostructuralists agree with the idea of an export-led growth model. Even though the mode of integration into the world economy must be purposeful and cannot be left to the market alone, neostructuralists assume that joining the globalized economy is necessary for economic development and could be attained relatively easy. Active industrial policies which encourage more sophisticated manufacturing exports, including a higher degree of value added, are thus supported (Leiva 2008a: 8).

It should be mentioned that in contrast to NDE, neostructuralism assumes that there is a dichotomy between *spurious* economic growth, denoting a catching-up of the economy via the exploitation of cheap labor, and *genuine* or innovation-based growth, which is due to increased productivity and the incorporation of technical innovations. Competitiveness in international markets should be reached by means of research and development, integrating into global value chains, rapidly adapting to new technologies, products as well as service technologies, and the establishment of production networks and clusters. The active promotion of private-public partnerships as well as state-civil alliances consequently increase the society's capacity to innovate and, thus, to increase productivity. Additionally, neostructuralists promote an open regionalism and therefore campaign for making the WTO regime compatible with regionally-based initiatives.

2.8 Interim conclusion: an African development paradigm?

In contrast to the conventional wisdom that African countries are characterized by traditional economies without external relations, the continent was integrated into the international system, especially via the Islamic trade, and was characterized by influential kingdoms long before the arrival of the European imperial powers, which marked a major turning point in African economic history. Large parts of Africa became involved in the European and the world capitalist system. Since then African economies have been heavily influenced by their external trade relations and hence by the major economic paradigms.

The first industrial experiences on the continent are to be found in the regimes of competitive exploitation (South Africa and Rhodesia) during the colonial period. The general record of colonization, however, is disastrous on many levels, and the main economic activities remained traditional agriculture and the production of cheap raw materials for export. Despite the early industrialization efforts and the gain of political independence of most countries in the 1960s, Africa never managed to become economically independent. The SAPs during the 1980s provided the basis for the "lost development decades" in Africa.

In the period after the Washington Consensus, starting in 1995, the African economic growth rate has been as high as in the time of import substitution industrialization. Sub-Saharan Africa even outscored these growth rates. However, the growth was not associated with an increasing share of manufacturing value added. The share fell from 14.8 percent in 1995 to 10.4 percent in 2010. The loss of manufacturing capacity seems to be a general problem. No African economy managed to increase its manufacturing share considerably during this period. The largest gains can be noted in Chad (from 7.3 to 11.5 percent) and in Nigeria (6.6 to 9.6 percent). Even in South Africa, the largest economy in Africa and a former manufacturing hub, the manufacturing share of value added steadily decreased to 13.2 percent in 2014.

Table 5: Sectoral contribution to GDP and world share of manufacturing

Africa	**1970**	**1980**	**1995**	**2010**	**2014**
Agriculture, forestry, fishing	22.3	17.2	16.5	15.5	15.7
Industry	29.4	36.7	31.5	34.5	33.0
Manufacturing	13.0	11.5	14.8	10.4	10.4
Services	48.3	46.0	52.0	50.1	51.3
LDCs: Africa					
Agriculture, forestry, fishing	31.0	32.0	35.7	24.5	21.8
Industry	27.2	24.9	21.2	33.4	35.6
Manufacturing	12.0	12.6	8.2	7.6	7.3
Services	41.7	43.0	43.1	42.1	42.7
World					
Agriculture, forestry, fishing	9.5	6.9	4.0	4.1	4.5
Industry	37.3	37.4	30.2	29.3	29.5
Manufacturing	25.7	22.5	18.9	16.7	16.5
Services	53.3	55.6	65.8	66.6	66.0
World share of manufacturing					
Africa	2.27	2.35	2.07	2.70	2.77
South and Central America	5.18	6.49	5.76	6.02	6.15
Eastern and South-Eastern Asia	4.23	4.97	9.42	16.53	19.00
United States	27.77	26.15	27.24	25.86	25.34
Europe	43.42	41.61	36.14	31.92	30.02

Source: UNCTADstat

Figure 7 depicts the share of manufacturing value added in African countries in 2014. No economy in Africa has reached the threshold of 20 percent, and the only economies with a manufacturing share above 15 percent are Mauritius, the Democratic Republic of the Congo, and Côte d'Ivoire as well as the three North African economies Egypt, Tunisia, and Morocco. The world share of African manufacturing thus remains negligible. In contrast, Eastern and South-Eastern Asia gained a large share and became a new manufacturing hub of the world.

Figure 7: Share of manufacturing of total value added in African countries in 2014

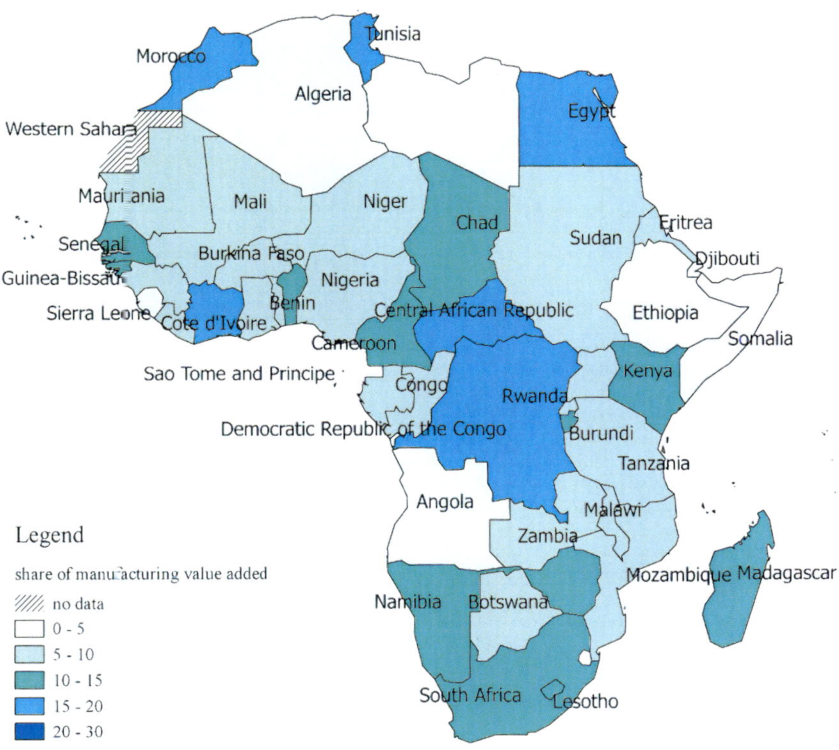

Source: Own depiction using QGIS, data from UNCTADstat

The rise of China and the East Asian economies paved the way for a Southern Consensus including the developmental state model as well as Latin American Neostructuralism. Until now, there is no African Development paradigm visible. However, in 1989 the ECA distanced itself from the Washington Consensus and the SAPs by providing an alternative framework. Among other things, it emphasized the need for structural transformation from primary products to consumer goods and services as well as the diversification of the economy towards more processed commodities and manufactured goods (ECA 1989: 34). Gore (2000: 802) argues that an African version of the Southern Consensus could emerge based on Mkandawire & Soludo (2003) and UNCTAD (1998: part 2). There is evidence that African economies (esp. Ethiopia and Kenya) have been increasingly following the Chinese model of development or the East Asian developmental state model in general (Fourie 2013: 379).

Even though African economies are trying to follow route of the NIC and China, it is not clear whether the developmental state model is replicable in Africa. On the one hand, the global economic environment has changed, the global share of manufacturing is steadily shrinking, and there is not much room next to the manufacturing center of the world China (this issue is discussed further in chapter 3). On the other hand, it is argued that African economies do not fit the special conditions, which had been in place in the East Asian economies, since they are mostly characterized as neo-patrimonial.

In addition to these negative prospects, there is an ongoing debate on the need for a democratic and socially inclusive developmental state in Africa. Despite only reaching a consensus in very few instances, 54 African economies have joined the African Union and have signed the 207 paragraphs of its latest development program called "New Partnership for Africa's Development" (NEPAD). Paragraph 79 of the policy paper reads as follows: *»It is generally acknowledged that development is impossible in the absence of true democracy, respect for human rights, peace and good governance".*

The most prominent representative in favor of an democratic developmental state is Thandika Mkandawire, who argues that there are examples of African countries which have clearly been developmentalist (Mkandawire 2001: 310). It is questioned whether it is possible to shift the focus purely to economic development in a democratic state (Öniş 1991: 121). Interestingly, the most widely cited examples for African developmental states, Mauritius and Botswana, are both democratic.51 Addition-

51 It is questioned whether Botswana is a flawless democracy. It scores high (+8 on a scale from -10 to +10) in the polity index, which is mainly based on legislation. Nonetheless, it is categorized as dictatorship in the ACLP dataset (ACLP is an acronym of the scholars: Michael *A*lvarez, José Antonio *C*heibub, Fernando *L*imongi und Adam *P*rzeworski), since it never had a change in government. The Botswana Democratic Party, founded in 1965, was never voted out of office.

ally, there has recently been a debate on the construction of a democratic developmental state in South Africa (Edigheji 2010). While the developmental state model is typically associated with industrial development and the promotion of the manufacturing sector, a democratic developmental state may focus on a service-led growth model. This view finds support by Eichengreen & Gupta (2009: 10), who identified a second-wave of services only observed in more outward-oriented (trade openness) and democratic countries.

3 Benchmarking structural change in Africa

Since the first industrial revolution in England, economic development has been linked to a rise in the share of the industrial sector and the capacity for production of manufacturing goods. Early development economics thus offered a variety of concepts for the process of industrialization. Probably the most famous concept of industrialization is the "Stages of Economic Growth" by Walt Whitman Rostow ([1960] 1997). He assumes that countries go through five stages characterized by a number of conditions. Industrialization is seen as a key driver of development, especially for low-income economies. Until today, several authors advocating a structural perspective on economic development argue that each developed country has gone through a process of industrialization (UNIDO 2011: 104, 2009: 4; United Nations Department of Economic and Social Affairs 2007: 7; Szirmai 2009: 35; Syrquin 2007: 208; Chenery et al. 1979: 70).52

In line with the theoretical concept of industrialization by Rostow and the industrialization experience of the most developed economies, a group of economist aimed to empirically substantiate these theories. According to the work of Kuznets and Chenery (Kuznets 1967; Chenery 1960; Chenery & Syrquin 1975; Chenery 1982; Syrquin & Chenery 1989), industrialization is regarded as one of the stylized facts of economic development. Their main findings can be summarized as follows: The share of agriculture in GDP and employment falls as economies grow richer; the share of industry in GDP and employment rises but the relationship between per capita incomes and the share of industry in employment is nonlinear; the share of services in GDP and employment rises unambiguously as economies grow rich. The idea of general patterns between sectoral

52 This hypothesis needs to be refined: There are several economies which are classified as high income countries according to the World Bank and/or are classified as very high developed by the United Nations but never exceeded a significantly share of twenty percent of manufacturing value added. However, these economies are either extraordinary small (Cayman Islands, Bermuda, Andorra, Aruba, Antigua and Barbuda, Bahamas, Turks and Caicos Islands, Greenland, Monaco, Seychelles, St. Kitts and Nevis, French Polynesia, Barbados) or resource rich (Oman, United Arab Emirates, Saudi Arabia, Kuwait, Bahrain) or both (Equatorial Guinea).

change and GDP per capita came to be known as the Chenery hypothesis. The framework was used to assess the progress of transformation of Eastern Germany (Ludwig 2010) as well as the Newly Liberalizing Economies in Central and Eastern Europe (Döhrn & Heilemann 1993; Raiser et al. 2004; Thießen & Gregory 2005). However, several newer studies (Dabla-Norris et al. 2013; Rodrik 2015) argue that the regularities of structural change have changed over time. According to them, the inverted-u-shape relationship between income and manufacturing output or employment has shifted downwards and peaks earlier in the development process.

A conceptual contribution of Chenery & Syrquin (1975: 5) is the differentiation of effects concerning a country's structural change: a) the effect of income, including the effects which relate to demand as well as to the supply side; b) the effects of other general factors, including all other factors on which the government has no or only little control, such as market size (population) or the endowment with natural resources; and c) the effect of the country's individual circumstances, including the country's individual history, its political and social circumstances as well as its economic and respectively industrial policy.

The chapter follows this differentiation: In the first part (section 3.3), the effects of income on employment and value added shares are analyzed. I use this relationship to represent the normal development path in the sense that economic development follows regularities that do not change between countries. This is in contrast to the idea that each country (or other economic entity) has its own economic style with its own characteristics. It should be emphasized that the "normal" development path cannot be regarded as a normative role model. As I will demonstrate, the normal development path changed substantially since 1960. Furthermore, I found substantial differences between the patterns in employment and value added shares. For this reason, the relationship between GDP per capita and relative productivity is analyzed in 3.3.2. In a last step, African economies are benchmarked within this general pattern of development.

In the second part of this chapter (section 3.4), the effects of other general control factors are considered in the analysis. For this, I include several control variables, such as population, resource rents, and time dummies. However, the equation does not comprise any policy-related, institutional and historical factors.53 As a result, the deviations from the estimated values can be regarded as industrial policy index.

3.1 Data set and benchmark countries

The primary dataset in this chapter is the GGDC 10-Sector Database, which provides an internationally comparable dataset on sectoral value added and employment for ten economic sectors and eleven sub-Saharan African economies, two North African economies, eleven Asian economies, nine Latin American economies, seven European economies, and the United States. The countries are listed in table 6. The data generally ranges from 1950 to 2011 for the European and Latin American economies. Most of the African and Asian economies are covered from 1960 onwards.

Table 6: Country sample of the GGDC 10-Sector Database

Africa	**Asia**	**Latin America**	**Europe and USA**
Botswana	China	Argentina	Denmark
Ethiopia	Hong Kong	Bolivia	Spain
Ghana	India	Brazil	France
Kenya	Indonesia	Chile	Italy
Malawi	Japan	Colombia	United Kingdom
Mauritius	Korea	Costa Rica	Netherlands
Nigeria	Malaysia	Mexico	Sweden
Senegal	Philippines	Peru	United States
South Africa	Singapore	Venezuela	
Tanzania	Taiwan		
Zambia	Thailand		
Egypt			
Morocco			

Source: Own depiction according to Timmer et al. (2016)

In order to estimate the normal development path, I exclude the African economies from the sample. None of the remaining 28 economies included in the dataset are extraordinarily small , but some of them exhibit ex-

53 A clear differentiation between general and political factors is impossible—especially in a single equation framework—since political factors are predestined to influence at least resource flow factors. Even population is conceivable as being open to influence, e.g., via family policy.

tremely high resource rents. The criterion of resource richness is commonly met if natural resource rents exceed 20 percent of the GDP. According to the data from the World Development Indicators this was or still is the case for the following countries in the sample: Bolivia, Chile, Mexico, Venezuela, Indonesia, and Malaysia. In Chile, Mexico, and Malaysia, the threshold is only exceeded in one or two years. Indonesia exceeded the threshold only in the 70s until 1981 and shows moderate resource rents since. Bolivia and Venezuela may be classified as resource-rich economies and are excluded from the benchmark sample. Our benchmark sample thus includes 26 economies. The sectors included in the dataset, their corresponding International Standard Industrial Classification (ISIC) as well as its abbreviation used later are listed in table 7.

Table 7: Sector classification in the GGDC 10-Sector Database

Sector	Abbr.	ISIC rev. 2	ISIC rev. 3
Agriculture, Hunting, Forestry and Fishing	AGR	1	A+B
Mining and Quarrying	MIN	2	C
Manufacturing	MAN	3	D
Public Utilities (Electricity, Gas, and Water)	PU	4	E
Construction	CON	5	F
Trade, Hotels, and Restaurants	WRT	6	G+H
Transport, Storage, and Communications	TSC	7	I
Finance, Real Estate, and Business Services	FIRE	8	J+K
Community, Personal, and Government Services	GCSPS	9	O+P+Q+L+M+N
Economy-wide	SUM		
Services	SER	6+7+8+9	G+H+I+J+K+ O+P+Q+L+M+N

Source: Own depiction according to Timmer et al. (2016)

3.2 The effects of income

In a first step, I estimate the relationship between GDP per capita and structural change. In line with the studies of Thießen & Gregory (2005) and Bah (2011), the dependent variable is the logarithm of the sector share either in value added or in employment. The regression equations54 thus take the form of:

54 For the sake of simplicity, the time and period indices in the equations are omitted for the whole chapter.

$$\ln \text{VAKS}_i = \beta_{i1} + \beta_{i2} \ln Y + \beta_{i3} (lnY)^2 + \varepsilon_i \qquad \text{Eq 1}$$

$$\ln \text{EMPS}_i = \beta_{i1} + \beta_{i2} \ln Y + \beta_{i3} (lnY)^2 + \varepsilon_i \qquad \text{Eq 2}$$

$VAKS_i$	constant value added share of industry i
EMPS_i	employment share of industry i
Y	GDP per capita
β_i	represents the corresponding coefficients
ε_i	residuum for the corresponding equation

Using the benchmark sample of 26 economies, I estimate a panel regression for the whole time period of equation 1 and 2 in least squares for each sector. To account for individual country circumstances, I include country fixed effects in the regression. In section 3.4, I analyze the effects of other general factors as well as other country specific variations more detailed. To account for variations over time, I also include fixed period effects in the panel regression. The results of these time period effects are discussed in section 3.3.1. The results of the panel regression with two-way fixed effects of equations 1 and 2 and white diagonal standard errors are shown in table a1 and table a2 in the appendix.

Figure 8 depicts the simulated relationship between the share of employment in agriculture, manufacturing, and services using the regression results of equation 1. My results confirm the earlier findings of Chenery and others. The share of agriculture in GDP and employment falls as economies grow richer; the share of manufacturing in GDP and employment rises but falls again at higher levels of GDP per capita; the share of services in GDP and employment rises unambiguously as economies grow rich.

The regression curves between value added and employment show in general the same tendencies. However, the share of employment in agriculture declines much slower than that of value added. The results further suggest that the value added share of manufacturing peaks much later in the development process and at a higher level than the employment share. These results confirm the findings of Rodrik (2015: 7).

Figure 8: Simulated relationship of employment shares and GDP per capita for major economic sectors, sample: benchmark economies

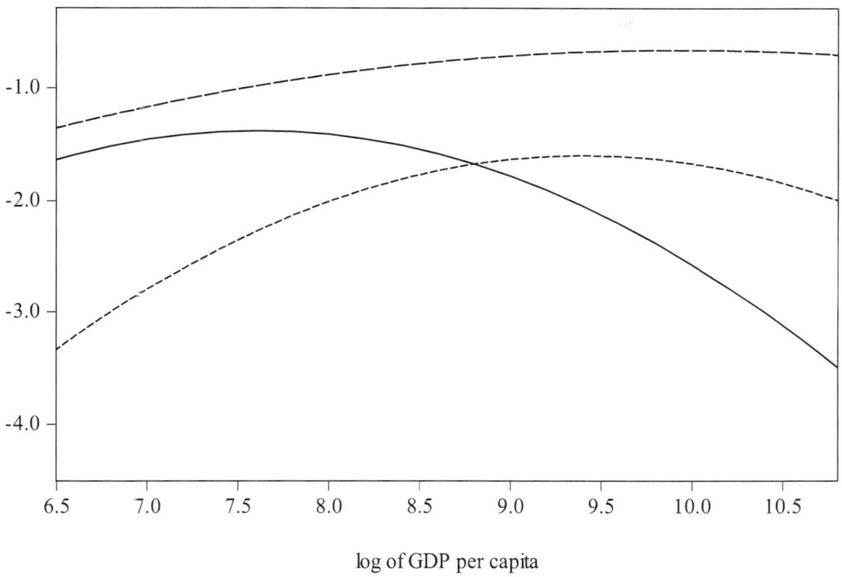

Source: own depiction base based on regression results of equation 2

3.2.1 Evolving patterns over time

The examination of fixed period effects in the panel regression allows an analysis of how these patterns were evolving over time. The period effect of regression 2 (see table a2) for manufacturing employment shares are continuously shrinking, whereas the period effects for the service sectors are continuously rising. Additionally, the period effects for the agricultural sector are also continuously decreasing.

Figure 9 presents the simulated relationship between employment shares of agriculture, manufacturing, and services and GDP per capita for the time periods 1960 and 2010. My results reveal that the manufacturing hub is substantially declining since 1960. According to the simulation, the manufacturing hub peaked at 25.5 percent in 1960. In 2010 the manufacturing hub peaked at only 14.5 percent. My results are thus in line with those of Rodrik (2015: 9–11) and Dabla-Norris et al. (2013: 16).

The share of agricultural employment shows a similar pattern, with a smaller employment share in recent years than it had been in 1960.55 In contrast, the employment share of the service sector for the corresponding GDP per capita ($12,226) rises from 41 percent in 1960 to 64.5 percent in 2010. This tendency is true for all service sectors but especially strong for market services, such as WRT and FIRE. In general, these findings strongly support the hypothesis that services will take the role of manufacturing in developing countries.

The decline in the manufacturing hub may have different causes. The most prominent argument is that with increasing world income the demand curve shifts to services. However, there are several other explanations for this phenomenon. One argument is that the decline of the manufacturing sector is a somewhat statistical phenomenon (Low 2013: 15). Due to increasing fragmentation of production and the segmentation into global value chains, formerly in-house production of services was outsourced and thus appears in statistics as services value added, formerly counted as manufacturing value added. This assumption formulates criticism on national accounting techniques, which the system of national accounts (SNA) is indeed well aware of and anxious to solve. Such hypothesis is supported by the results from input-output tables suggesting that the share of services as direct intermediate inputs in manufacturing increased substantially during this time (Falk & Jarocinska 2010: 4–5). The argument is closely related to the trend of servicification of manufacturing , which describes the increasing role of services in use, production and sales of manufacturing. The reasons are manifold: Firstly, increasing foreign trade requires more transportation services (Lodefalk 2014). Furthermore, services may help manufacturing firms to be more productive, not only through efficiency gains in logistics, management, and coordination but also by absorbing frontier technologies (Lodefalk 2015: 1). Lastly, due to international competition, manufacturing firms increasingly bundle their products by providing large volumes of installation, maintenance and technical support services to differentiate their offers (Kelle 2013: 1513). The differentiation between services and manufacturing thus becomes increasingly blurred.

55 These results cannot be confirmed once control variables are included (see table a10).

Figure 9: Simulated relationship between employment shares of agriculture, manufacturing, and services and GDP per capita over time, based on regression 2; sample: benchmark economies

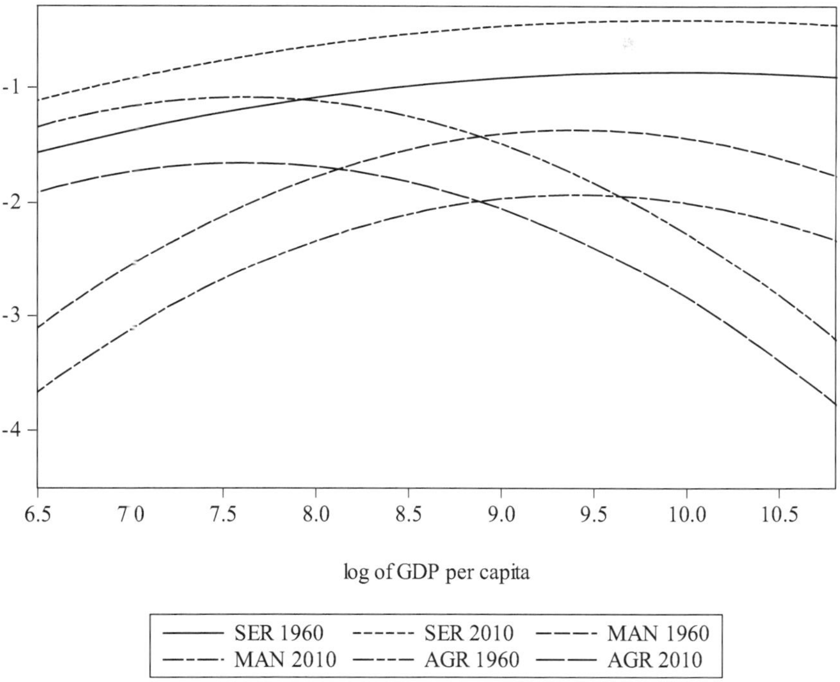

Source: Own depiction based on regression results of equation 2

Another explanation for the premature deindustrialization points to employment in the manufacturing sector that is reduced despite increasing output. Rowthorn & Wells (1987: 5), described the phenomenon as "positive de-industrialization". The reduction in employment may thus be explained by increased productivity in the manufacturing sector in contrast to other economic sectors. Indeed, the reduction in the value added share of employment is not as high as in employment. According to regression 1 (see table a1), the peak shifted from 28.8 percent in 1960 to 20.4 percent in 2010. Figure 10 depicts the simulated relationship between value added shares and GDP per capita, illustrating that the increase in the value added share of services between 1960 and 2010 is not as high as in employment shares. The value added shares of agriculture show an increase as opposed to the decrease of the employment share.

Figure 10: Simulated relationship between value added shares and GDP per capita over time, based on regression 1; sample: benchmark economies

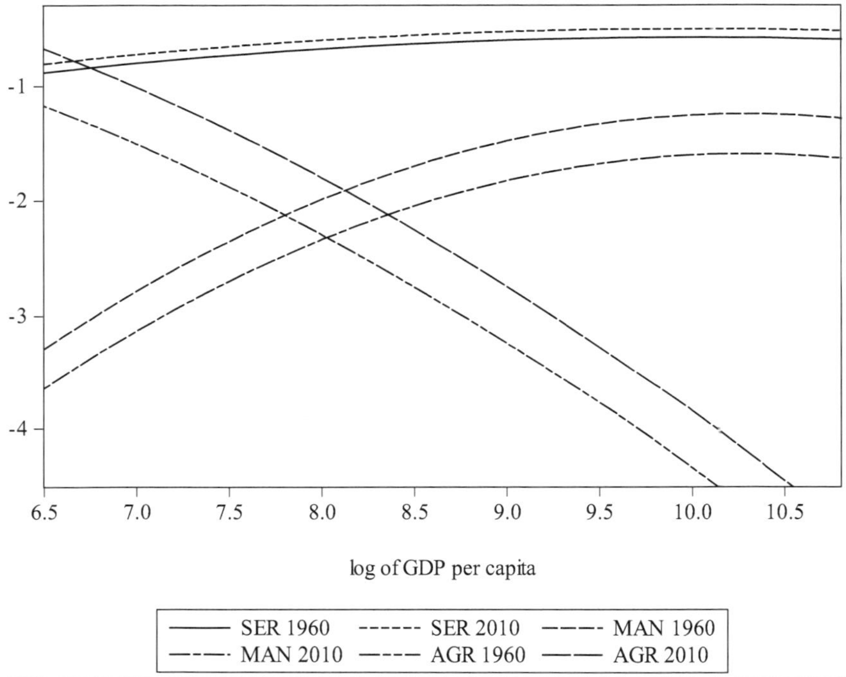

Source: Own depiction based on regression results of equation 3

3.2.2 Relative productivity

In the section above, it could be shown that the manufacturing hub of employment has experienced a dramatic reduction since 1960, whereas the same hub in value added shares has not. Subsequently, relative productivity of manufacturing increased with respect to other sectors. Relative productivity was calculated with the existing dataset by dividing the productivity of a sector through the total productivity in the country. To illustrate the changes of relative productivity during the development process, I used a similar approach as for employment and value added shares. Accordingly, I estimated relative productivity as a dependent variable of income. It turned out that the regression function is best explained by a third degree polynomial:

$$\ln RP_i = \beta_{i1} + \beta_{i2} \ln Y + \beta_{i3}(\ln Y)^2 + \beta_{i3}(\ln Y)^3 + \varepsilon_i \qquad \text{Eq 3}$$

RP_i	relative productivity of industry i
Y	GDP per capita
β_i	represents the corresponding coefficients
ε_i	residuum for the corresponding equation

Figure 11: Simulated relationship between relative productivity and GDP per capita over time, based on regression 3; sample: benchmark economies

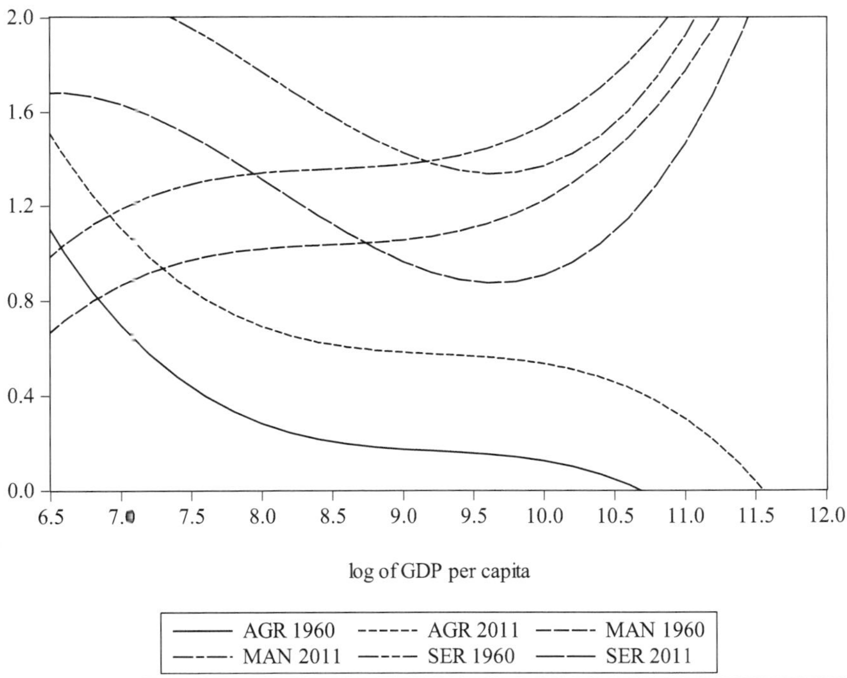

Source: Own depiction based on regression results of equation 3

Regression results are presented in table a3. The simulated relationship between GDP per capita and relative productivity for different time periods is shown in figure 11. The regression curve confirms the earlier results of Syrquin (1988: 239) in some aspects. At low levels of GDP per capita, the service sector has higher productivity than agriculture and manufacturing.

With rising GDP per capita, relative productivity of manufacturing increases while that of services and agriculture decreases. Syrquin (1988: 239) further suggests that at very high levels of GDP per capita, the relative productivity of manufacturing decreases and that of agriculture increases again. Those suggestions cannot be confirmed; on the contrary, an increase in relative productivity of services is found at high levels of GDP per capita.

Again, the more interesting results of regression equation 3 are the period effects. As depicted in figure 11, I found considerable changes in relative productivity of different sectors between 1960 and 2010. For the sectors manufacturing and agriculture, equation 3 shows increasing period effects since 1960, whereas the equation for service reveals decreasing time period effects. As a result, relative productivity of agriculture and manufacturing is much higher in 2010, though that of services is considerable lower. Especially in early periods of development, the difference between services on the one hand and manufacturing and agriculture on the other is dramatically reduced. The increased productivity of agriculture and manufacturing during earlier periods of development can be explained by increasing degrees of globalization. The result may be a faster technology transfer due to the integration into GVCs. This phenomenon is discussed more detailed in chapter 5.

3.2.3 Benchmarking African economies

With regard to the second chapter, I expect that African economies, especially the ones which had regimes of competitive exploitation, fit into the general pattern of development. According to this assumption these economies should fit the simulated relationship or have a positive deviation due to import substitution policies during the 1970s. Due to structural adjustment policies with a return to the ideology of comparative advantages, I suggest a negative deviation of the manufacturing share for the period after 1980 until today (see figure 12).

To examine the African specifities in comparison to other world regions, I split the sample of countries included in the GGDC 10-Sector Database into four world regions, as depicted in table 6. Regression results for the different samples are depicted in table a4, a5, a6, and a7. Figure 13 shows the corresponding simulated manufacturing employment shares for different world regions. According to those results, the employment share of manufacturing in Asia and Europe peaks at much higher levels than in Latin America.

Figure 12: Preliminary expectations on the structural transformation path in African economies

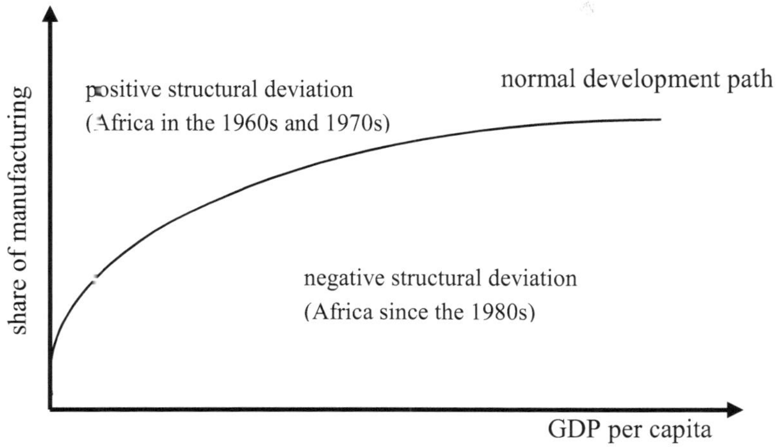

Source: Own depiction

Applying this to value added shares, the Asian sample's regression curve even outscores that of Europe and the United States. Figure 13 also illustrates that manufacturing peaks in Western economies at much higher levels of GDP per capita ($28,029) than in Asian economies ($12,223) or even in Latin America ($3,621).

In Africa, simulated employment shares are well below those of other regions, at least for low levels of GDP per capita. The quadratic term of the regression for the sample of African economies is close to zero. Accordingly, the simulated manufacturing share has no peak and increases steadily with GDP per capita. However, this does not indicate that the manufacturing share will rise steadily, but merely that most African economies did not reach their manufacturing peak yet.

The GGDC 10-Sector Database includes thirteen representative economies from all over Africa which in total account for about 55 percent of population and 65 percent of GDP on the continent (see table a8). To benchmark structural transformation in Africa, I compare the manufacturing share of African economies and its corresponding GDP per capita level with the "normal" path of economic development. Figure 14 reveals that the majority of African economies exhibit a manufacturing share below the regression line. However, the development paths differ substantially.

Figure 13: Simulated manufacturing employment shares for different world regions

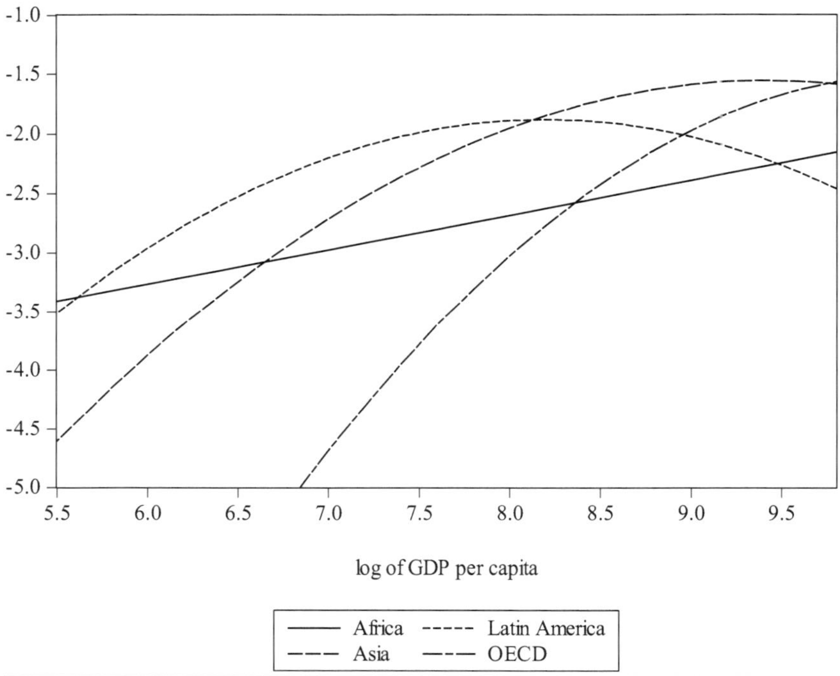

Source: Own depiction; regression curve based on regression results of equation 2

Botswana, one of the most successful developmental states in Africa, shows a tremendous growth between 1960 and 2010. It started at one of the lowest GDP per capita levels ($376) and has the highest GDP per capita level in the sample in 2010 ($14,992). Despite some slight increases in the 1980s and 1990s, the manufacturing employment share remains below seven percent. Nonetheless, while the "African miracle" Botswana displays a sectoral employment share lower than the "normal path", it increased its share steadily. This development is in line with the findings of Syrquin (2008: 57), arguing that resource-rich countries do industrialize, although with a delay. In Mauritius, another successful developmental state, the manufacturing employment share's peak can already be identified in 1990 when reaching 32 percent. Since then, it has shrunk to 18 percent, still being the highest African value in 2011.

Figure 14: Employment share of the manufacturing sector in logarithms in the African economies

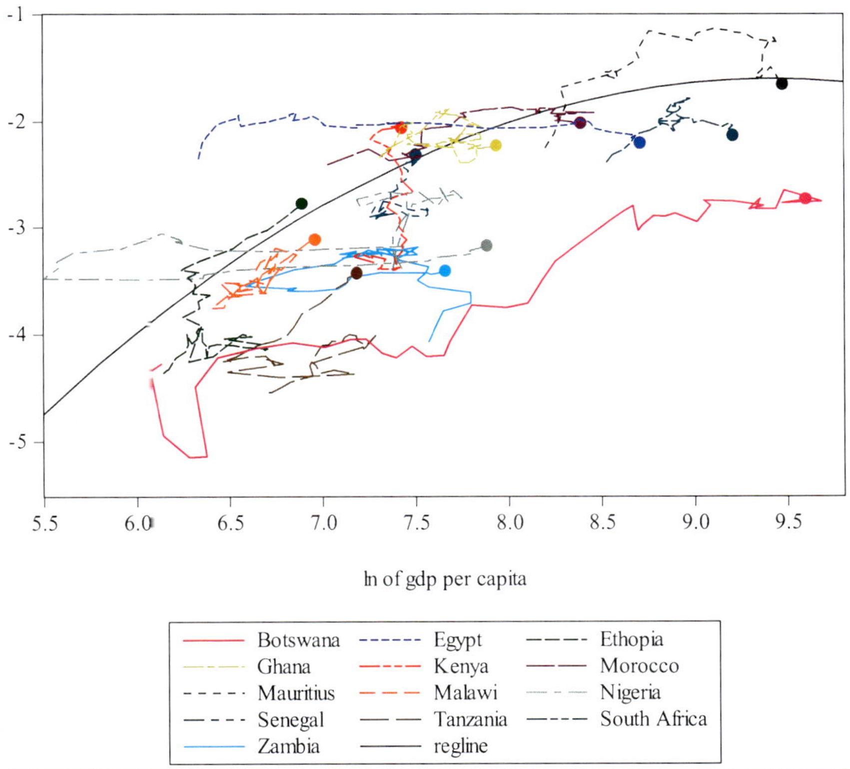

Source: Own depiction based on regression results of equation 2; filled circles indicate the values in 2010

South Africa, the largest African economy with a low growth record, shows a decreasing share of manufacturing employment, peaking in 1981 at only 17 percent and declining afterward to 11 percent in 2011. Egypt as the continent's second largest economy follows a development path with an astonishingly stable share of manufacturing employment of about 13 percent, which just recently declined to 10 percent. Morocco, also located in North Africa, generally shows lower growth rates. Despite a relatively stable manufacturing employment share, a manufacturing hub is visible.

Morocco started with a share of 9 percent in 1960, which peaked in 1985 at 15 percent and slowly declined afterward to 13 percent in 2011.For the three West African economies Ghana, Senegal, and Nigeria, no unambiguous development path can be identified. In Ghana, the manufacturing share rose up to 13 percent during the time of import substitution policies in 1978, declined afterward to about eleven percent and has remained stable since 1994. In contrast, GDP per capita declined almost steadily until 1983, thereafter increasing again. Senegal's economy shrank during the 1960s and experienced an explosive growth in the early 1980s. However, this growth ended in a severe crisis during the early 1990s. Since 1994 the country has experienced relatively steady growth rates. While its manufacturing share remained stable at about six percent until 1994, it increased up to ten percent in 2010. Another very interesting case is Nigeria: Despite its heavy reliance on oil, it increased its manufacturing share in the early 1960s from three to seven percent (still on a very low level) but only with moderate economic success. The economic collapse between the late 1970s and mid-1990s reduced the country's manufacturing share to three percent again. The economic success from the late 1990s until today is associated with only minor increases in the manufacturing share of employment up to four percent. Zambia increased its manufacturing share from an even lower level of 1.6 to 4 percent in the 1960s and early 1970s. However, GDP per capita declined from nearly $2,500 in 1967 to $724 in 1994. Since then, the country has experienced considerable growth rates, although with a stable and very low share of manufacturing of three percent. Kenya is the economy with the largest manufacturing sector in East Africa and the only economy besides Ethiopia showing a manufacturing employment share above the normal path. It experienced an almost steady growth of the manufacturing employment share from 4 percent to 13 percent in 2008. Despite this, its manufacturing share of value added has remained relatively stable since 1980. Kenya's GDP per capita growth was relatively high until 1978, after which its growth record became very unstable, and GDP shrank to $1,400 in 2003, recovering since. Tanzania, Malawi, and Ethiopia are the three poorest economies of the sample. These economies experienced at least moderate economic growth in the 1960s and early 1970s but also severe crises afterward until the mid-1990s or even early 2000s. However, these three East African economies have exhibited a considerable growth record in recent years which has been accompanied by a considerable increase in the manufacturing share, even though starting from a very low level. In Tanzania, the share of manufacturing started at 1.4 in 1995 and rose to 3.4 percent, in Malawi it went up from 2.4 in 2002 to 4.4 percent, and in Ethiopia from 1.4 in 1992 up to even 6.9 percent. Ethiopia, therefore, is becoming the new developmental state in Africa aiming to be the new manufacturing hub in Africa.

Besides the two flagship economies Mauritius and Ethiopia, the manufacturing record in Africa is disappointing. Several resource-rich economies such as Botswana, Zambia, Nigeria, Ghana as well as the two North African economies experienced economic growth without increasing their manufacturing share considerably. On the other hand, structural change took place without economic development. A shift towards manufacturing without economic development could be observed during the time of import substitution policies in the 1960s and 1970s in Ghana and Nigeria but also during the 1980s and 1990s in Kenya. Another phenomenon is the shift towards services without economic development. This was the case in Nigeria during the 1960s and 1970s, in South Africa during the 1970s until 2000 but also in Kenya and Malawi during the 1980s and 1990s. These findings confirm the results of Bah (2011: 17–18): Structural change takes also place during times of economic stagnation or decline.

3.3 The effects of other general factors

Reconsidering the conceptual contribution of Chenery & Syrquin (1975: 5), only effects of income have been regarded so far. To differentiate between the effects of other general factors that are not (or only to minor degree) influenceable and the effects of individual country experiences such as industrial policies, I measure the relationship including other control variables. In line with other publication of Chenery & Syrquin (1975: 16) but also the newer publication of Rodrik (2015: 6–7) and Dabla-Norris et al. (2013: 29), I control for the size of the economy, the share of mining value added, arable land per hectare as well as its geographical position56 (see table a9). The regression equations take the following form:

---

56 An island dummy is included which takes the value of one in the economies Indonesia, Philippines, Taiwan, and Singapore. It is further controlled for landlocked economies, however, the sample includes only one landlocked economy outside of Africa (Bolivia). Including the dummy suggests positive effects for the manufacturing employment share for landlocked economies. Extending the sample with African economies shows that the coefficient for the landlocked dummy becomes significantly negative, suggesting a negative effect on the

$$\text{lnVAKS}_\text{i} = \beta_{i1} + \beta_{i2}\ln Y + \beta_{i3}(lnY)^2 + \beta_{i4}\ln(pop) + \beta_{i5}\ln(alp) + +\beta_{i6}\ln(vaks_{min}) + \beta_{i7}\, island + \varepsilon_i \qquad \text{Eq 4}$$

$$\text{lnEMPS}_\text{i} = \beta_{i1} + \beta_{i2}\ln Y + \beta_{i3}(lnY)^2 + \beta_{i4}\ln(pop) + \beta_{i5}\ln(alp) + +\beta_{i6}\ln(vaks_{min}) + \beta_{i7}\, island + \varepsilon_i \qquad \text{Eq 5}$$

$VAKS_i$	constant value added share of industry i
EMPS_i	employment share of industry i
Y	GDP per capita
$vaks_{min}$	share of mining value added
alp	arable land in hectares per person
$island$	dummy variable for island economies
β_i	represents the corresponding coefficients
ε_i	residuum for the corresponding equation

In contrast to section 3.2, this section distinguishes between other general factors and the policy influenceable structural deviation. Therefore, all 28 non-African economies are included in the sample. The panel is estimated without country-fixed effects and includes only time-period effects in the panel regressions. The results of panel regressions with fixed period effects and white diagonal standard errors for different economic sectors are shown in table a10 and a11.

3.3.1 Interpretations

The size of a country has a significant positive effect on the share of agriculture, mining, and manufacturing but a negative effect on all other especially service sectors. The positive effect on manufacturing is in line with the findings of Dabla-Norris et al. (2013: 29) and Rodrik (2015: 40). The results suggest that the transition from agriculture is faster in smaller countries and that those countries move directly into services rather than manufacturing. The large negative coefficient in GCSPS also indicates that small countries principally have a higher share of the government sector than large economies. In general, smaller economies have larger shares

employment share of manufacturing. Thus, the dummy is not included in the regression.

of foreign trade and are thus able to deviate in larger scale from the normal development path. The economic structure of small countries conclusively has a larger variation (Perkins & Syrquin 1989: 1726).

The coefficient for arable land in hectare per person has a significantly positive effect on the share of agriculture. As expected, a negative coefficient for the employment share of manufacturing is found, however, the coefficient for most service sectors is positive.

The value added share of mining indicates whether a country is resource-rich or resource-scarce. The indicator misleads to some respect because it measures the share of mining value added in percent of GDP. If an economy is poor, its resource dependency increases considerably, whereas other countries which manage to develop a productive manufacturing sector (maybe with the help of resource rents) can reduce their resource rents share due to rising incomes (Brunnschweiler & Bulte 2008: 249). The indicator thus measures the dependency on mining but is not necessarily high if a country is resource-rich. As anticipated, the coefficient is significant negative for the manufacturing and the other industrial sectors. Regarding the value added shares, the regressions display negative coefficients for the most service sectors (with exception for FIRE). The coefficients for the employment shares in services are in general positive.

The island dummy has a negative coefficient for the employment share of manufacturing but a strong positive coefficient for value added. Manufacturing thus seems to have a higher productivity in island economies. The coefficient for the employment share in services is strongly positive but becomes insignificant for value added.

The period fixed effects for equation 5 (employment) generally confirm the results from section 3.3 for the manufacturing and the service sector. The time effects of manufacturing constantly decrease while those of services increase. In contrast to the results in section 3.3, time effects in the agricultural sector do not decrease but have shown a moderate increase since 1990.

The period effects for equation 4 (value added) in agriculture confirm the baseline results and show increasing value added shares, pointing to a strong increase in relative productivity in this sector. In contrast to the results of Rodrik (2015: 10), no decline in the manufacturing hub for value added is found when control variables are included. Indeed, the time dummies even indicate an increase in the hub between 1960 and 1990. The time dummies for the service sector as a whole decrease as well. However, some important differences within the service sector could be observed again: While the market services (especially TSC and FIRE) show substantial increases in value added, the GCSPS sector shows a substantial decrease which outweigh the effects.

My results suggest that premature deindustrialization, which is found in employment, is a "positive" deindustrialization driven by increased productivity in early periods of development. Employment shifts from the manufacturing sector to the service sectors. In the service sectors, I found generally losses in relative productivity but not across all sectors.

3.3.2 Structural deviations of African economies when accounting for control variables

In order to measure how the African economies have adjusted to the normal development path in terms of structural transformation, I calculate the deviation of the estimated employment and value added share to the actual shares. The estimated shares account for all control variables using the corresponding coefficients from table a10 and a11, no matter whether they are insignificant or not. They further account for the time period effects, which are included in the estimations. While Thießen & Gregory (2005, p. 5) consider all sectors simultaneously, I calculate the deviation for each single sector. The deviations are the same as the distance between actual shares and the normal development path in figure 14 while accounting for other general factors and the period effects. Table a12 and a13 show the deviations in employment and value added shares for the African economies in 1970, 1980, 1995, and 2010.

Assuming that structural change in absent of government intervention follows a general pattern as proposed by Chenery, the structural deviation index can be interpreted as industrial policy index. However, it is not accounted for other changeable variables, such as infrastructure, education, or institutional capacity, which could have a strong influence on the share of manufacturing.

To give a general overview of the structural deviation in Africa, I calculate the deviation for the average African economy which has average characteristics of all African economies included in the dataset. Figure 15 and figure 16 show the structural deviation in employment and value added shares over time for agriculture, manufacturing and, services. In general, the average African economy shows a strong positive deviation in the agricultural sector. The deviation in employment is even stronger than in value added which points to the low labor productivity in this sector. This finding is in line with Bah (2011: 17) and the literature addressing the low productivity in African agriculture (Collier & Dercon 2014; Oya 2010). While the strong positive deviation was substantially reduced from 1970 to 1980, it remained stable and even increased until 2010.

As expected, the deviation in manufacturing is negative in employment and value added shares. The comparison of time periods reveals some interesting insights. While the deviation in employment has continually declined since 1970, the deviation in value added has risen over time. The results imply that relative manufacturing productivity57 has decreased since 1970, at least in international comparison.

Figure 15: Structural deviation of employment shares in Africa over time

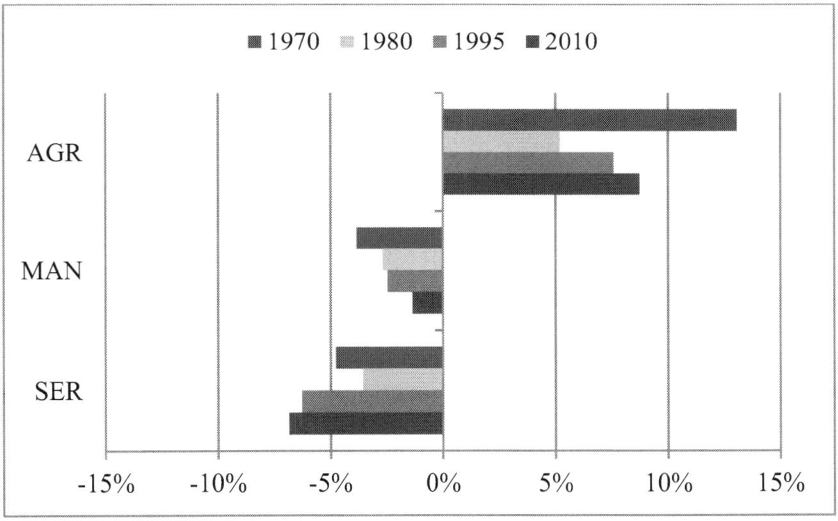

Source: Own depiction

57 As shares of total employment or production are regarded, the results point to relative productivity in comparison to total productivity in the economy. Even if total productivity decreases or remains stable, there could be changes in relative productivity between economic sectors.

Figure 16: Structural deviation of value added shares in Africa over time

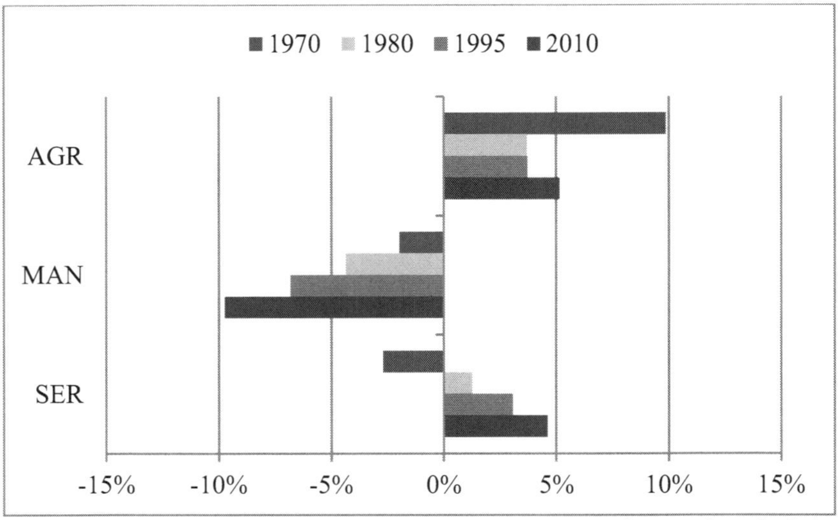

Source: Own depiction

Indeed, the declining deviation in the manufacturing employment share is solely a result of the time dummies that shift the manufacturing employment hub downwards. In contrast, the time period dummies for the value added hub had even increased until 2000 and have only recently decreased moderately. These findings suggest that in international comparison, relative manufacturing productivity increased heavily during this time, but the trend did not take place in Africa.

To give a more detailed record of the structural deviations in Africa's manufacturing sector, figure 17 compares the employment and value added shares for the African economies in the sample for the year 2010. While several African economies show a positive deviation in employment shares, all African economies display negative deviations in value added shares.

Figure 17: Structural deviation of manufacturing employment and value added shares in single African economies 2010

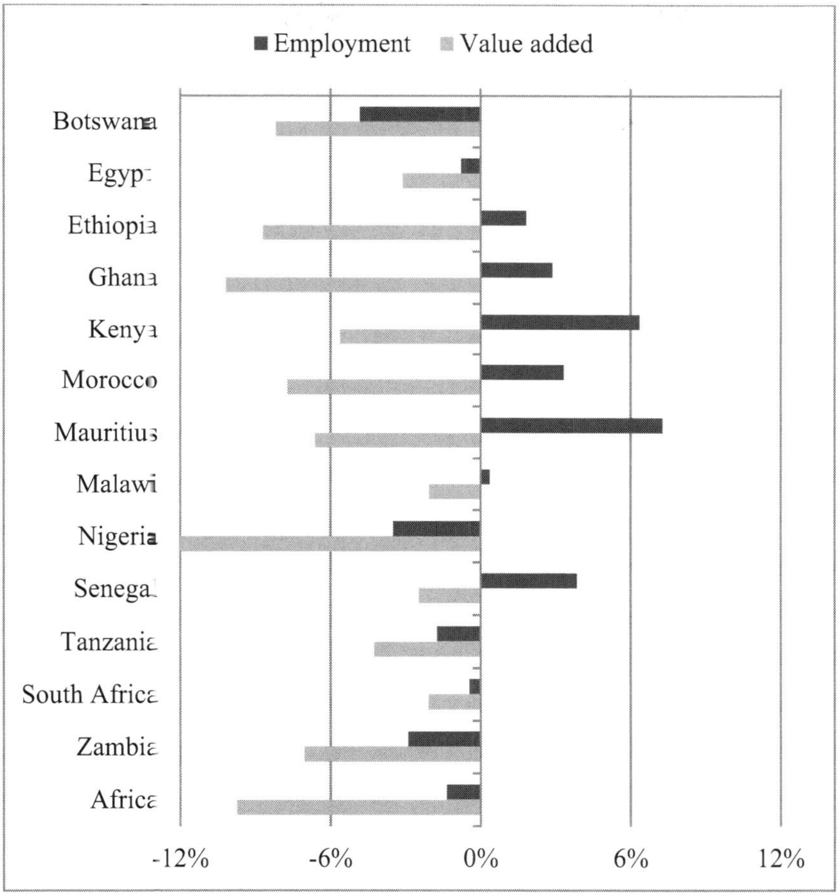

Source: Own depiction

The picture is dramatically different in services: The average African economy shows a negative employment deviation in the service sector. The deviation declined between 1970 and 1980 and increased afterward. It should be mentioned that the African employment share during this period increased substantially from 22 percent in 1980 to 39 percent in 2010. Again, the deviation is driven by the development of the benchmark economies which exhibit an increasing service share over time. In direct contrast to the increasing negative deviation of manufacturing value added, an increasing positive deviation is found in services value added. Indeed, such a positive deviation, especially in recent years (since 1995), can be identified in each African economy of the sample, except of Nigeria. The positive deviation confirms the results of Bah (2011: 13) who found surprisingly high service output shares at early stages of GDP per capita in Africa. The employment figures show that these high output shares are only partly a result of shifts in labor. In particular, they are a result of higher relative productivity in services. The relationship between employment and productivity is tackled in chapter 4.2 in more detail.

3.4 Interim conclusion

In this chapter the framework of Chenery and Kuznets is used to analyze the structural transformation path of non-African economies which serve as a benchmark for African economies. In contrast to earlier works in this line, the paper uses the GGDC 10-Sector Database, which makes it possible to distinguish between employment and value added shares. The result confirms the stylized facts of structural change: The share of agriculture decreases with GDP per capita, manufacturing shows a hub, and services increase with GDP per capita. However, these patterns have changed over time. The manufacturing hub in employment has been much smaller in recent years than it was in 1960, an effect which Rodrik (2015) calls "premature deindustrialization". Instead, services show higher shares of employment at early levels of development. These findings strongly support the hypothesis that services will take the role of manufacturing in developing countries.

However, these developments can only be found in the shares of employment. Considering value added share in constant prices, no reduction in the manufacturing hub occurred when control variables were included. Similarly, no increase in the value added shares of services is found. The phenomenon, which Rodrik calls "premature deindustrialization", is thus a "positive de-industrialization" (Rowthorn & Wells 1987: 5) that can be explained by the increase in relative productivity of the manufacturing sector.

Benchmarking African economies in this pattern indicates that African economies show comparable high shares of agriculture in value added and employment and corresponding low shares of manufacturing. The negative structural deviation in manufacturing employment has been reduced since 1970, whereas the negative manufacturing deviation in value added increased substantially. These results can be explained with the relative productivity of manufacturing that increased heavily during this period within the benchmark economies. However, this trend did not take place in the African economies. In the service sector, the opposite is the case. Relative productivity of services decreased in the benchmark economies but not in African economies. As a result, a strong and increasing negative structural deviation is found in service employment but an increasing positive deviation in service value added.

Future research should be directed to the analysis of sectoral patterns for single African economies in more detail and with the background of single country characteristics. Furthermore, research should focus on extending the data source. Firstly, data should be collected for more African economies. Secondly, analyzing a rather detailed sectoral aggregation provides the opportunity to determine whether changes in relative productivity can be explained by differing sectoral structures, such as the differentiation in high and low technology manufacturing. Furthermore, the provision of the capital stock and other variables opens the opportunities to analyze the patterns of structural change on a broader scale.

4 What is special with the manufacturing sector?

While the historical evidence for industrialization is overwhelming, the role of structural change in economic theory is not as straightforward as one would expect. In much of today's economic growth theory, structural change has been replaced with assumption. These sector-neutral theories (e.g., the Solow-Swan model) abstract from the differences in economic sectors and depict the production and consumption of the economy in a one-good-model. If structural change58 is not ignored, three strands of theories can be distinguished. Probably the most famous theory addressing structural change is Engel's law, which in newer economics is adapted by the assumption of an income elasticity smaller than one for primary products. The neoclassical framework assumes an open economy in which

58 The meaning of "structure" is often vague and sometimes misleading. The term does not only differ considerably depending on the context such as the structure of an econometric model or the price structure (in contrast to the price level), but is also used in a conceptual sense, such as "structural changes" referring to changes which are permanent or do not change too quickly. Finally, the term "structure" is also used in "Crypto-Apologetic Meanings" (Machlup 1958: 292), especially in the term "structural imbalances", which is used as a plea for foreign exchange restrictions or import barriers. It seems useful to refer to the great article of Machlup (1958) rather than enumerating the different meanings of structure and structural. In this thesis the term "structure" is used to refer to the separation of output or distribution of productive factors among various economic sectors. The sector can either be divided by its kind of output or, for example, by the arrangement of productive factors, such as capital-, labor- or technology-intensity. The meaning of structural change or structural transformation is the shift of agricultural production to industry respectively manufacturing as well as services. According to several authors such as Kuznets (1973: 249), structural transformation is one aspect of a variety of changes, which result in the process of "Modern Economic Growth". A broader measure for structural transformation thus considers institutional and technological change including educational systems, the governmental sector, business firms, and the functioning of markets (Kuznets 1973: 248). For further reading, see also Nelson & Winter (1982) and Douglass North who interprets structural change focusing only on institutional aspects but ignores the shift in the structure of production. These themes are only subsidiary aspects in this thesis.

structural change is driven by factor endowments. The third strand is the structuralist perspective.

The first one—addressing the demand-side of the economy—can be summarized with Engel's law which was named after the statistician Ernst Engel. He observed that the poorer a household, the higher its proportion of income spent on food (Engel 1895: 26). In newer economic literature this law is expressed as an income elasticity of demand smaller than one for food, which is tantamount to the assertion above. The income elasticity of demand expresses the responsiveness of demand for a good due to an increase in income.59 It is calculated as the percentage change of the quantity demanded divided through the percentage change in income.

Assuming a closed one-product economy, the income elasticity of the one good is exactly one. Fisher (1939) divides the economy into three sectors according to their hierarchy of needs and henceforth their income elasticity of demand: the primary sector satisfying the basic needs, the secondary sector with standardized products mainly manufacturing goods, and the tertiary sector with its new luxury goods. If the income grows, the economy automatically shifts production from the primary to the secondary and later to the tertiary sector. This explanation of structural change is acknowledged by various economist such as Kuznets (1967: 113–118), Syrquin (2007: 231), Chenery (1960: 624), or Pasinetti (1988). The theory is also incorporated into newer models of economic growth (Laitner 2000; Kongsamut et al. 1997; Foellmi & Zweimüller 2008).

Even though Engel's law is a widely accepted theory for explaining structural change, it loses relevance regarding small and open developing economies facing the challenges of globalization. Once the economy opens, the production structure can differentiate from the consumption structure. Thus, changes in demand do not necessarily induce changes in the production structure. In the neoclassical framework, the specialization of production according to the existing supply of production factors determines the production structure of an economy. Economic sectors are

59 The interpretation of this measure is based on the neoclassical microeconomics and can be looked up in every microeconomic textbook (e.g., Varian & Buchegger 2011: 315). It is assumed that income elasticities for goods are constant over time. Goods that exhibit a positive income elasticity are categorized as normal or superior goods, whereas inferior goods have a negative one. Furthermore, superior goods can be distinguished from luxury goods, showing an income elasticity above one, and essentials, having a positive income elasticity smaller than one (e.g., Kortmann 2006: 68).

distinguished either between capital and labor intensive sectors (e.g., Uzawa 1961; Teubal 1971) or between low and high technology sectors (e.g., Hatzichronoglou 1997; Lall 2000).

The essential causes for economic development in neoclassical theory are the endowment factors, including mainly capital (including physical and human capital) and labor (Lin 2011: 200). In accordance with these endowments, countries at different levels of development have the corresponding economic production structure. Developing countries facing scarce human and physical capital, hence exhibit their comparative advantage in labor- and resource-intensive but low technology production activities. In contrast, highly developed countries exhibit an endowment structure with abundant capital. Their comparative advantage is thus in knowledge and capital intensive industries (Lin 2011: 200). The developing countries can improve their endowment structure by accumulating capital, educating workers, and acquiring knowledge and thus change their comparative advantage. However, developing countries must first upgrade their endowment structure, which in turn may shift its comparative advantage (Ju et al. 2009). The advantages and disadvantages of external trade are discussed in chapter 5.

While in both above mentioned theories, Engel's law and the neoclassical framework, structural change is seen as a consequence of economic growth either driven by the demand or the supply-side, the third strand views structural change as a crucial part of economic growth, which spurs economic development. Policy recommendations of structural economists often propose industrial policy.

The term "old structuralist view" refers to the early development thinkers such as Rostow ([1960] 1997), Gerschenkron (1966), Hirschman (1958), but also Prebisch (1950) and Singer (1950) emphasizing the role of structural change in which government should play a crucial role. Import substitution was the recommended trade policy to initiate industrialization, since the manufacturing sector was/is considered being an "engine for economic growth". The early development economists, however, were not the first emphasizing the role of the manufacturing sector. Even long before the industrial revolution in Great Britain, the early mercantilist writers60 pointed to the inherent differences between economic activities and the advantages of the manufacturing sector compared to agriculture and the production of raw materials. The hypothesis that manufacturing is

60 The best example is Antonio Serra [1613] (2011).

the engine of economic growth is mainly attributed to Nicolas Kaldor and his inaugural lecture (Cantore et al. 2014; Su & Yao 2016).61 Emphasizing the role of the manufacturing sector, literature draws on three arguments: the structural bonus hypothesis, increasing returns to scale, and the relevance of backward and forward linkages.62 All three arguments are treated in detail in the next sections. A fourth argument may be that technology and knowledge transfer is faster in manufacturing than in other sectors. This argument is discussed in chapter 5.

---

61 Kaldor (1966: 5) found a highly significant relationship between the growth of manufacturing production and the growth of the whole economy. Thus, he attributed the slow growth rates in the UK but also in other regions of the world to the low share of the manufacturing sector. Kaldor's (1977: 193) explanation for the increasing differences in per-capita income between economies is the establishment of large scale enterprises in the manufacturing sector. He argued that neither important technological innovations nor Protestant Ethic but the establishment of the factory system was the decisive factor for transforming the productive powers of society. The long-term consequences of this factory system have been the acceleration of technological change and the opportunities for large scale capital investments, by e.g., installing bigger and better machines which allowed the production of goods on an ever-increasing scale (Kaldor 1977: 196). The former profit-maximizing enterprises, which had been prevalent only in the trade sector, thus entered the production sector. This started a dynamic and continuous phase of innovation and capital accumulation. Kaldor established three laws, whereby the first two laws were elaborated in Kaldors inaugural lecture (1966) and then supplemented by a third law (1975: 894–895). Kaldor's first law relates the growth of GDP to the growth of the manufacturing sector; the second law is also known as Verdoorn's law and is treated in chapter 4.2; the third law relates the productivity of the non-manufacturing sector to the growth of the manufacturing sector.

62 Szirmai (2011, 2009) lists eight arguments, including those three arguments. Other arguments are the empirical correlation between manufacturing and GDP, the structural change burden, the role of technological change, the role of capital accumulation as well as Engel's law. The empirical correlation between GDP and the manufacturing share is discussed in detail in chapter 3. The argument that manufacturing provides special opportunities for capital accumulation can be seen as rejected since in developed countries other sectors are more capital intensive than manufacturing (Szirmai 2011: 12). The rest of the arguments may be subsumed under one of the other.

4.1 Structural bonus hypothesis

Arthur Lewis (1954) provided one of the most influential models in development economics.63 He analyzed underdeveloped countries by dividing the economy into two sectors. He distinguished the low-productivity subsistence sector, including agriculture with diminishing returns to scale due to limited amount of land, from the capital-accumulating capitalist (industrial) sector. The model is build up on the assumption that marginal productivity in the subsistence sector is negligible (Lewis 1954: 141). As the price of labor is determined by the wage in the subsistence sector, there is unlimited supply of unskilled labor that Lewis called surplus labor.64 Industries can thus be established without the limit of an existing wage rate. Creating new and expanding old industries, the capitalist sector draws labor from the substistence sector (Lewis 1954: 142). The entrepreneurs are assumed to reinvest the profit made because of the fixed wage level. Output of agricultural sector and the wage level will remain unchanged until all surplus labor of the subsistence sector is absorbed.65 Especially the assumptions for capital accumulation, the existence of surplus labor, and the resulting constant urban wage rate have been subject to critique (Todaro & Smith 2006: 111–115). Nonetheless, the Lewis model was a major milestone in development economics and has provided some valuable insights on the sectoral interaction during the development process.

In recent empirical literature, the concept has become prominent again under the notion of the structural change bonus. The structural change bonus hypothesis suggests that labor productivity in the agricultural sector is much lower than in industry. A shift of production from agriculture to industry would thus automatically enhance labor productivity. Higher productivity in the manufacturing (or industry) sector is mostly associated with higher capital intensity or advanced technology. Especially empirical

---

63 Arthur Lewis draws on Boeke (1942) who originally created the concept of the dual economy. However, the Lewis model is probably the most famous one which provided the underlining framework and induced a whole series of dual sector models. Examples can be found in: Fei & Ranis (1963), Jorgenson (1961), Zarembka (1970), Harris & Todaro (1970), and Dixit (1973).

64 The concept surplus labor by Lewis (1954), in which the marginal product of labor is zero, should not be confused with the classical value concept of Karl Marx. I use the concept surplus labor only in reference to Lewis.

65 For further applications of the dual sector model, see Bhaduri (2006: 222–223).

literature, analyzing the East-Asian industrialization experience, emphasizes the role of the structural bonus hypothesis (Timmer & Szirmai 2000; Fagerberg 2000; Ark & Timmer 2003; McMillan et al. 2014; Timmer et al. 2014).

4.1.1 Productivity differences between sectors

Using the GGDC 10-Sector Database productivity[66] and employment shares for the average African, economy is calculated and depicted in figure 18.

Figure 18: Productivity (vertical axis) and employment share (horizontal axis) for nine industrial sectors, average of 12 African economies

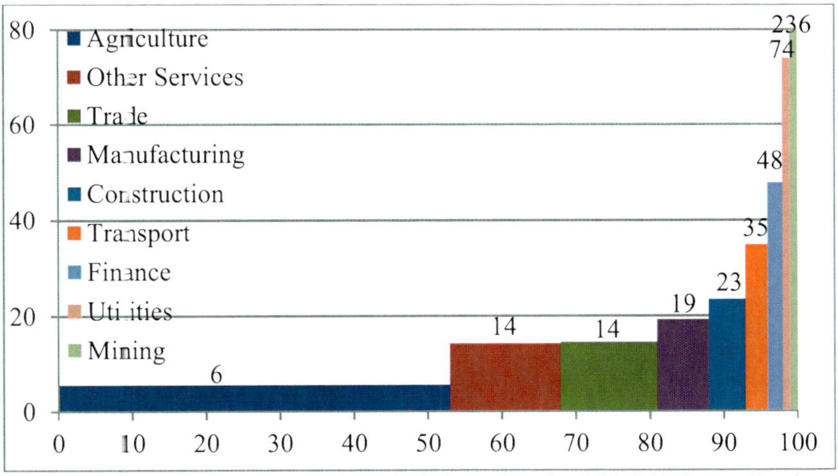

Source: Own depiction using the GGDC 10-Sector Database

The graph illustrates the huge productivity gaps between economic sectors in Africa. Mining shows the highest productivity followed by public utili-

66 To obtain an international comparable data, productivity is calculated using the constant value added shares of the GGDC 10-Sector Database multiplied with output-side real GDP at chained PPPs (in million 2005 USD) from the PENN World Tables, divided by employment (in thousands) from the GGDC 10-Sector Database. Productivity is thus measured in thousand USD (PPPs of 2005 USD) per person employed in the corresponding sector.

ties and financial and business services. Agriculture has the by far lowest productivity while maintaining the by far largest sector in employment shares. Manufacturing, accounting for only 7.5 percent of total employment, shows a productivity slightly above the average of 14 percent. The average African economy thus seems to provide a good example of a Lewis economy at early stages of development.67 Following the Lewis model, low productivity in agriculture could be explained by limited supply of land and can be reduced by shifting labor to other high productivity sectors. Table 8 compares productivity levels of ten economic sectors between different world regions. As expected, agriculture has the lowest productivity in all regions. In contrast, mining followed by public utilities has the highest productivity across all sectors. Furthermore, it shows that productivity in services sectors differ substantially. Productivity of financial and business services outscores by far that of wholesale and retail trade or government and social services.

Table 8: Labor productivity for economic sectors in world regions in 2010

	Africa	Asia	Latin America	Europe & US
AGR	6	13	13	58
MIN	318	351	185	766
MAN	19	61	36	96
PU	74	213	118	331
CON	23	24	21	71
WRT	14	37	15	64
TSC	35	53	36	103
FIRE	48	64	30	65
GCSP	14	38	17	63
SER	18	42	20	67
SUM	14	43	23	73

Source: GGDC 10-Sector Database; own calculation; Africa, Asia Latin America, and Europe & United States are the average values of the economies included in the data.

The most striking result concerns the differences in productivity between economic sectors that are less pronounced in other regions than in Africa. The data generally show that productivity differences in developed econ-

67 Single African economies differ substantially in their economic structure. While Ethiopia with 75 percent shows the highest agricultural employment share in the sample, only 7 percent of the labor force work in this sector in Mauritius.

omies are considerable smaller than in developing economies (Bhaduri 2006: 220; Caselli 2005: 721). While in Africa labor productivity in manufacturing and services is more than three times higher than in agriculture, this is not the case for other regions. The same ratio for the Western economies is 1.6 for manufacturing and 1.1 for services; in Latin America the ratio is 2.7 for manufacturing and only 1.5 for services. Only in Asia, the ratio with 4.8 for manufacturing and 3.3 for services outscores that of Africa. It shows that despite higher levels of GDP per capita, productivity differences between sectors are much higher in Asia than in Latin America.68 Indeed, there is no linear relationship between economy wide productivity and the ratio of agricultural labor productivity to non-agricultural productivity. McMillan et al. (2014: 17) suggest that productivity differences first increase and then decrease so that the relationship takes the form of an u-curve. The data further shows that Africa, in fact, has the by far lowest labor productivity in agriculture but also in manufacturing. While in other regions productivity of manufacturing outscores that of services, this is not the case in Africa. Of course, this pattern is not applicable for all African economies: In South Africa, Egypt, Tanzania, and Malawi, labor productivity of manufacturing considerably exceeds that of services.

4.1.2 Methodological issues

Reconsidering the results of chapter 3, developing economies shift resources from the agricultural sector to the industry and the service sector during the development process. As there are huge productivity gaps between economic sectors and assumingly constant returns to scale (see chapter 4.2), productivity of the whole economy increases when labor is shifted from a low to a high productivity sector.

To assess the impact of structural change on economic growth, an empirical method known as shift-share analysis is used quite frequently (e.g., Fabricant 1975; Maddison 1952). The method decomposes productivity growth into an intra-sectoral effect and the effect of sectoral re-allocation of labor (the inter-sectoral effect). The decomposition can be derived as follows:

68 These patterns may be explained by different development models, see section 2.7.

$$\Delta P = P^1 - P^0 \; mit: \qquad \text{Eq 1}$$

$$P^t = \frac{Y^t}{L^t} = \sum_{t=1}^{n} \frac{Y_i^t L_i^t}{L_i^t L^t} = \sum_{t=1}^{n} P_i^t S_i^t \qquad \text{Eq 2}$$

$$\sum_{t=1}^{n} P_i^1 S_i^1 - \sum_{t=1}^{n} P_i^0 S_i^0 =$$

$$\sum_{t=1}^{n} (P_i^1 S_i^1 - P_i^0 S_i^0) + \left(P_i^0 S_i^1 - P_i^0 S_i^1\right) + \left(P_i^0 S_i^0 - P_i^0 S_i^0\right) + (P_i^1 S_i^0 - P_i^1 S_i^0) \qquad \text{Eq 3}$$

$$\Delta P = \sum_{t=1}^{n} (P_i^1 - P_i^0) S_i^0 + \sum_{t=1}^{n} (S_i^1 - S_i^0) P_i^0 + \sum_{t=1}^{n} (S_i^1 - S_i^0)(P_i^1 - P_i^0) \qquad \text{Eq 4}$$

1 2

P_i^t	productivity in industry i at period t
S_i^t	share of branch i in total output at period t
Y_i^t	output of branch i at period t
L_i^t	labor of branch i at period t

Equation 4 decomposes overall productivity growth into three effects:

1. *The within effect*: the contribution from productivity growth within individual industries, weighted by the share of these industries
2. *The static shift effect*: productivity growth from shifts in the allocation of labor towards industries with higher productivity
3. *The dynamic shift effects*: productivity growth from shift in the allocation of labor towards industries which exhibit productivity growth

However, a number of criticisms and several applications concerning this purely descriptive technique have been raised (Timmer & Szirmai 2000: 282 ff.). Even a formulation of shift-share regressions to differentiate random effects and provide statistical test was proposed (Patterson 1991). Nonetheless, the method is applied to uncover the effects of structural change in several newer publication using the GGDC 10-Sector Database (Vries et al. 2015; Timmer et al. 2014; McMillan et al. 2014). Since the results are discussed in detail in the named publication already, only the major results are recapitulated in this thesis. However, the results presented differ slightly to that of the other publication because the periodization of chapter 2 is used. It is thus distinguished between the period of import substitution industrialization from 1960 to 1980, the period of the Washington Consensus from 1980 to 1995, and the time thereafter: 1995-2010.

4.1.3 Results

The most striking result of the decomposition points to Africa which productivity growth between 1960 and 1980 was predominantly driven by structural change (see figure 19). Except of Latin America, which exhibit a similar pattern during this period, such a development remains irreproducible during all period and regions. In the other periods, the within effect remains the most dominant driver for productivity growth. In general, the static shift effect is positive since workers move from lower to higher productivity sectors. An exception is the region Europe & United States for the most recent period from 1995 to 2010 showing a slightly negative static shift effects (figure 22). The negative static shift effects may be attributed to the problem of deindustrialization. Indeed, the main shifts were from the manufacturing sector towards financial and other business services a sector which, in average, had substantially lowered labor productivity in 1990. The dynamic shift effect is most often negative. Vries et al. (2015: 18) attribute this general tendency to problems of adjustment frictions or problems in organizational restructuring. Such negative effect means that labor productivity generally decreases in the sector that experiences labor inflows. In turn, a reduction in labor productivity implies that output did not increase in the same rate as labor did, which indicates the presence of decreasing returns to scale. The relationship between output and productivity growth is discussed in detail in chapter 4.2.

The dynamic shift effect captured for Africa revealed only small negative values besides considerable negative values in the years 1960 until 1980 so that structural change remained the main driving force of productivity growth. Between 1980 and 1995, the negative dynamic shift effect even exceeded the positive static shift effect so that structural change had an overall negative effect on productivity growth. Since 1995, the dynamic shift effect has remained high and negative but has been exceeded by the positive static shift effect so that structural change has a positive effect on productivity growth.

Figure 19: Decomposition results for Africa

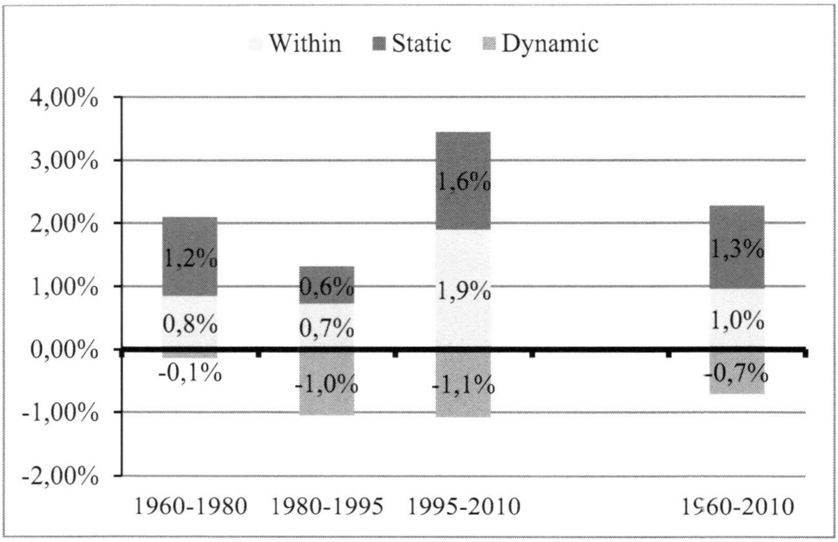

Source: Own depiction based on own calculations following Timmer et al. (2016)

Figure 20: Decomposition results for Latin America

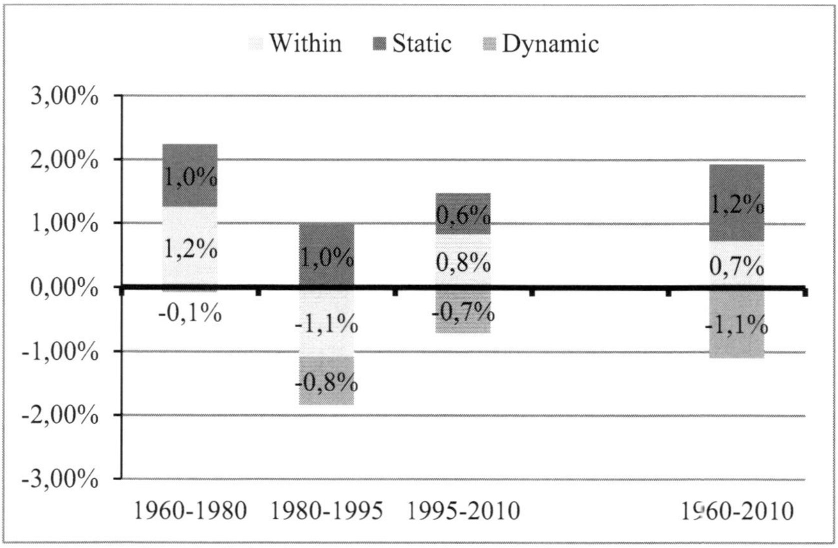

Source: Own depiction based on own calculations following Timmer et al. (2016)

Figure 21: Decomposition results for Asia

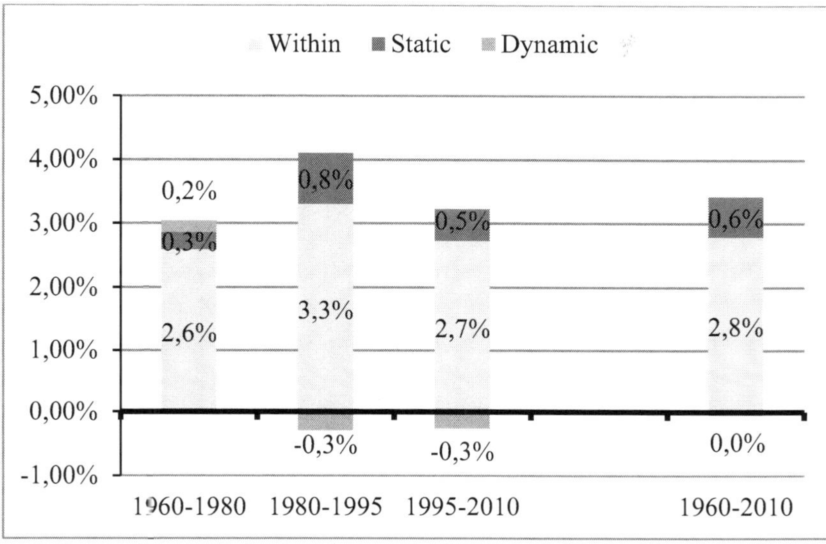

Source: Own depiction based on own calculations following Timmer et al. (2016)

Figure 22: Decomposition results for Europe & United States

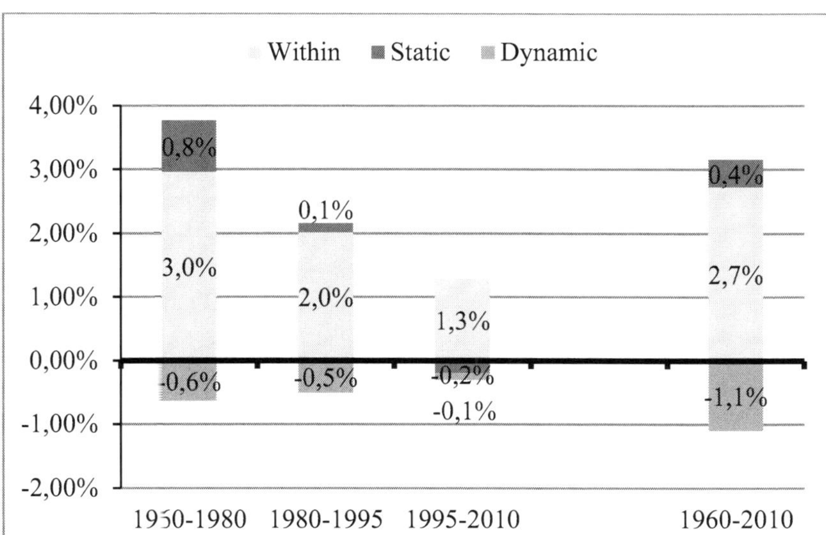

Source: Own depiction based on own calculations following Timmer et al. (2016)

The decomposition results of Latin America (figure 20) show similar patterns as in Africa. The results concerning Asia demonstrate positive static effects and only very small negative dynamic shift effects (figure 21). In Europe & United States, the negative dynamic shift effect outscores the static shift effect which continually decreased from 1960 until 2010 (figure 22). However, the effects of structural change in Asia as well as in Europe & United States plays only a minor role, whereas the within effect remains as the main economic driver of productivity growth.

Results for single Africa economies are shown in table a17. Indeed, individual country experiences in Africa unveil a lot of heterogeneity. In the latest period, Egypt and Botswana suffer from considerable negative static and dynamic structural change effects. The same with South Africa and Senegal: The negative dynamic effect outscores the small positive static shift effect. As to all the other African economies, the positive static shift effect exceeds the negative dynamic effect insofar that structural change in general show a positive effect on productivity growth. However, the dynamic shift effect was not always negative. Especially in the period 1960 to 1980, several economies such as Botswana, Egypt, Nigeria, and South Africa exhibit positive static and dynamic shift effects. Positive dynamic effects indicate that the output increases at higher rates than labor. The relationship between output and labor is subject of the next chapter.

4.2 Testing Verdoorn's law in Africa

As explained, African economies face huge productivity gaps between economic sectors. The structural bonus hypothesis suggests that shifting labor or output from the agricultural to the manufacturing sector would raise productivity immediately. Still not enough: In contrast to the agricultural sector (as well as the service sector), the manufacturing industry is supposed to exhibit increasing returns to scale. That is, if labor is shifted from the agricultural to the manufacturing sector, productivity in manufacturing is growing even more. The hypothesis that an increase in the volume of production is associated with an increase in productivity is known as Verdoorn's law.

This law has been subject of several long-lasting controversies and its interpretation is not always straightforward. The following section thus briefly outlines the historical background before discussing several theoretical and methodological issues. In section 4.2.4, the GGDC 10-Sector Database is used to provide cross-section estimates of the returns to scale in different economic sectors. To give a more detailed record on African economies, section 4.2.5 provides time series estimates of Verdoorn's law for three African economies.

4.2.1 Historical background

Verdoorn's law is named after the Dutch economist Petrus Johannes Verdoorn, who postulated an empirical relationship between growth of output and productivity in the manufacturing sector. The empirical relationship is supposed to indicate the existence of increasing returns to scale. Although the Italian article by Verdoorn (1956) did not attract much attention, it was taken up by Kaldor in his inaugural lecture in 1966, coining the term Verdoorn's law (Kaldor 1966: 35). According to Kaldor, the slow economic growth rates in the UK between 1953 and 1963 can be attributed to the low share of the manufacturing sector. Kaldor (1966: 5) found a highly significant relationship between the growth of the manufacturing production and that of the whole economy. As Kaldor (1966: 8–11) pointed out, the only plausible explanation for this is the existence of increasing returns to scale. Kaldor (1966: 11 and 16) emphasized that this relationship is especially prevalent in the manufacturing sector and that the application beyond this sector is very limited. The Kaldorian interpretation is the most prominent version whenever Verdoorn's law is discussed. Nevertheless, the theoretical contributions by Verdoorn himself are very limited. He relied on the explanations given by Young (1928) and Smith (2008 [1776]), both pointing to the role of the market size for the advantages of the division of labor. Indeed, increasing returns are often ascribed to the classical economist Adam Smith. Smith may be the most prominent economist but definitely not the first one. Several authors (Schefold 1994; Reinert & Reinert 2003; Schumpeter & Schumpeter 2009: 332) traced the idea of increasing returns back to Antonio Serra and his pioneering work *Breve Trattato* (1916)[69]. He addresses the hypothesis of increasing returns to scale in his statement by suggesting that multiplication in manufacturing is possible "at a proportionately lower cost" (Serra et al. 2011: 121). Nonetheless, he did not give any explanation of his reasoning. According to Adam Smith, the wealth of nations is a product of the division of labor

69 The first English translation is provided by Sophus Reinert (Serra et al. (2011))

which itself relies on the extent of the market (Smith 2008 [1776]: 20 ff.). Alfred Marshall also emphasizes in his "Principle of Economics" the existence of increasing returns in the sectors in which the production factor land does not play any role (Marshall 1920 [1890]: 185). Likewise, Young (1928) revived Smith's ideas about increasing returns to scale in manufacturing industry due to the division of labor. The primary explanation of increasing returns is "that with the division of labor a group of complex processes is transformed into a succession of simpler processes, some of which, at least, lend themselves to the use of machinery."

In 1922, the economic historian Clapham questioned the forerunner of neoclassical economics, Marshall and Pigou, for a classification of industries according to the "empty boxes" of decreasing, constant, and increasing returns to scale. In default thereof and with the purpose of deriving economic recommendations, he tried to categorize the hat industry. He thereby met the problems of time and regional dependent differences in factor supply, the elusive quest of distinguishing internal and external effects, and the presence of joint products. Conclusively, he questioned the utility of such a categorization insofar as they might be inapplicable to real economic problems. Clapham's article became the starting point of a long-lasting debate on increasing returns in the economic journal between 1922 and 1930, in which especially Sraffa (1991: 191) criticized the upcoming/prevailing, perfect competition-based Marshallian analysis due to its incompatibility with decreasing and increasing returns. These theoretical shortcomings were only partly solved by the endogenous growth theory of Romer (1990).

4.2.2 Theoretical and methodological issues

Despite the fact that increasing returns to scale seem to play such an important role for economic development, relatively little attention is payed to them in economic textbooks. Increasing returns are always related to a production function. I assume the production of a commodity y to be characterized by a function f of the required inputs x_i, i.e.:

$$y = f(x_1, x_2, \dots, x_n) \qquad \text{Eq 1}$$

If all inputs x_i are multiplied by an arbitrary constant c > 0, the production function exhibits:

- constants returns to scale if:

$$cy = f(cx_1, cx_2, \dots, cx_n) \qquad \text{Eq 2}$$

- increasing returns to scale if:

$$cy < f(cx_1, cx_2, \ldots, cx_n) \qquad \text{Eq 3}$$

- decreasing returns to scale if:

$$cy > f(cx_1, cx_2, \ldots, cx_n) \qquad \text{Eq 4}$$

It should be noted that the production function is regarded as a technical relationship and does not claim to reflect a causal production function. I do not assume that the output automatically rises when more inputs are provided. On the contrary, the causal relationship may be the other way around: When demand increases, more inputs are used for the production process. Additionally, other factors may influence inputs and outputs of the production function simultaneously. In this section, I leave it open to debate in which cases causality runs in which direction.

The typical inputs considered in economic textbooks are land, labor, and capital, which can be traced back to Jean-Baptiste Say who departs from the classical labor theory of value in this point (e.g., Krelle 1989). In most cases, the traditional production factor land is subsumed under the factor capital; in some cases, however, the list of inputs is extended by natural resources, human capital, knowledge etc.

The identification of inputs is important to distinguish *the law of decreasing returns to scale*, which assumes a change in the volume of production factors, from the *law of diminishing marginal returns*, which assumes a change in the factor proportion.70 However, the distinction between those two laws is not straightforward since production factors, i.e., their quality, differ in reality. When production is increased, the returns decrease because some production factors are not available in the same quality.71 Following these arguments, it is plausible to argue that "dimin-

---

70 The law of decreasing returns goes back to Steuart (1767) who explained what later was called the extensive margin: With increasing population but equal claimable lands, the population must deal with poorer soils so that equal amount of labor will lead to lower harvest (Schumpeter & Schumpeter 2009: 333). Turgot discovered the other case of decreasing returns which was later called the intensive margin: Assuming that equal amounts of labor were applied to a given piece of land, the resulting additional quantities will first increase with labor up to a certain amount as soon as the ratio between the increment of labor and product will reach a maximum; beyond that point, additional labor will lead to lower increments of output (Schumpeter & Schumpeter 2009: 333).

71 For such a case some classical economist (e.g., Ricardo) argue that there is more fertile and less fertile land, and whenever production is increased, one in-

ishing returns to all factors together are not conceivable" (Kaldor 1934: 66).72 Given that not only the quantity but also the quality of production factors needs to be considered, it is a nearly impossible task for empirical researchers to measure the extend of increasing returns to scale. In the following, capital and labor are thus assumed to be the only production inputs with equal quality. These assumptions are of special relevance for the primary sectors agriculture and mining in which land and natural resources are disregarded as production factors. I account for those circumstances in the interpretation of results, especially in those sectors.

The most common operationalization of Verdoorn's law was suggested by Kaldor (1966)73:

$$p = \beta_1 + \beta_2 q \qquad \text{Eq 5}$$

$$e = \beta_3 + \beta_4 q \qquad \text{Eq 6}$$

p	annual growth rate of labor productivity
q	annual growth rate of output
e	annual growth rate of employment

The constant terms β_1 and β_3 can be interpreted as exogenous or autonomous technological and employment growth. The Verdoorn coefficient β_2 measures the extent to which productivity grows if the growth of output rises. Productivity is measured as the output divided by employment, the definition of equation 7 holds:

$$p \equiv q - e \quad \text{since} \quad P = Q/E \qquad \text{Eq 7}$$

P	denotes labor productivity
Q	denotes the level of output
E	denotes the level of employment

The definition implies that the constants β_1 and β_3 add up to zero while β_2 and β_4 sum up to unity. This can be seen by adding equation 5 and 6. In the case of constant returns to scale, no correlations should be expected, thus: $\beta_2 = 0$ and $\beta_4 = 1$.

---

evitably need to use less fertile land. However, the argument is also attributed to the factor of labor: "The best lands and the best men are limited" (Robbins 1928: 401). In several cases, the entrepreneur is assumed to be a constant factor (e.g., Coase 1937: 405).

72 See also Sraffa (1991: 143) for a detailed discussion of this argument.

73 Kaldor explicitly referred to output, employment, and productivity of the manufacturing sector. However, the theory is applied to the overall economy.

4.2.2.1 Labor elasticity and Verdoorn's law

Equation 6 is not only a common operationalization of Verdoorn's law but also the core of the labor demand equation, which is often used in literature (Bhorat & Oosthuizen 2008: 53; Hanson & Leautier 2013). The renewed interest in manufacturing is not only associated with the shift from low to higher productivity activities and the existence of increasing returns but also with a higher potential for employment creation. This argument comes up especially in the light of India's jobless growth experience (Singh 2012: 318; Kannan & Raveendran 2009). In some cases, it is argued that opportunities for employment creation is due to its increasing returns (UNIDO 2011: 6).

By definition, an increase in manufacturing output needs to be traced back either to employment or to productivity growth. Substituting equation 7 for equation 5 yields:

$$e = -\beta_1 + (1 - \beta_2)\, q \qquad \text{Eq 8}$$

Equation 8 shows that there is a clear contradiction between job creation and increasing returns to scale at least in a closed economy framework.74 The greater β_2 is, the higher are the returns to scale, but the lower is the employment elasticity to output β_4.

4.2.2.2 Capital

Kaldor's operationalization of Verdoorn's law does not include capital as a regressor which builds upon the assumption that the growth of the capital stock (c) equals the growth of output (q). Kaldor (1966: 16) claims that increasing returns are, by far, a more important cause for productivity growth than investment bevavior. He thus argues that the rate of growth of capital itself is a function of the growth of output and later confirms that capital and thus investment is an important prerequisite for economic development Kaldor (1977: 193–194). However, since capital is necessarily a result of human economic activities, he raises concerns over the possibility to separate cause and effect. For him, it is simply more plausible that capital accumulation results from the industrial development rather than

74 The challenge to compete in a global world and the role of global value chains is discussed in chapter 5 of this thesis.

being the cause of it. However, most of the studies prefer to include the growth of capital (net-investments) (c) as a regressor into equation 4:

$$p = \beta_1 + \beta_2 q + \beta_5 c \qquad \text{Eq 9}$$

4.2.2.3 Demand vs. supply-side models

Rowthorn (1975a), referring to the argument that labor shortage is the cause of the slow rates of economic growth in the UK75, reformulates the Kaldor equation in such that productivity growth is explicitly linked to employment growth76:

$$p = \beta_6 + \beta_7 e \qquad \text{Eq 10}$$

Rowthorn (1975b) regards equations 5 and 6 as an implicit and unusual method and prefers the direct method proposed by himself. Applying this formulation to the post-war period in industrialized countries, Rowthorn (1975b) did not find any significant relationship between productivity and employment growth in the manufacturing sector.

Indeed, Kaldor's equation may be directly derived from a production function approach.77 Assuming a production function of the form:

$$Q = \mathrm{A}\, E^{\beta_8} C^{\beta_9} \qquad \text{Eq 11}$$

Q	level of output
E	level of employment
C	capital stock
A	technical progress

Taking the logarithm on both sides of equation 11 gives:

$$lnQ = \mathrm{lnA} + \beta_8\, \mathrm{lnE} + \beta_9\, \mathrm{lnC} \qquad \text{Eq 12}$$

which in terms of growth rates reads:

75 The argument of Kaldor (1966: 25–31) was later rejected by himself (Kaldor 1975: 895).

76 Using the definition e ≡ q – p, it can be shown that: $\beta_6 = \beta_1/(1 - \beta_2)$ and $\beta_7 = \beta_2/(1 - \beta_2)$.

77 It should be noted that this derivation of the production is only based on analytically treatable relationships and should not be interpreted as a causal relationship. According to Kaldor, output is not a function of supply factors but is determined exogenously or by the economy's competitiveness.

$$q = \beta_{10} + \beta_8 \, \mathrm{e} + \beta_9 \, \mathrm{c} \qquad \text{Eq 13}$$

q	growth rate of output
e	growth rate of employment
c	growth rate of the capital stock

Using the definition from equation 7, the Verdoorn's law can thus be derived as:

$$p = \left(\frac{\beta_{10}}{\beta_8}\right) + \left(\frac{\beta_8 - 1}{\beta_8}\right) \mathrm{q} + \left(\frac{\beta_9}{\beta_8}\right) \mathrm{c} \qquad \text{Eq 14}$$

Following Kaldor and assuming that capital grows at the same rate as the output (c = q), equation 14 simplifies to78:

$$p = \left(\frac{\beta_{10}}{\beta_8}\right) + \left(\frac{\beta_8 + \beta_9 - 1}{\beta_8}\right) \mathrm{q} \qquad \text{Eq 15}$$

Kaldor's (1975) response to Rowthorn stresses his initial concern not to measure the coefficient between employment and output. Instead, he abandons the interpretation of his inaugural lecture that the slow rate was due to labor shortages. Instead, he emphasizes the validity of Verdoorn's law given in equation 5. Kaldor prefers equation 6 because in any situation in which employment growth is zero or constant, there must be a perfect correlation between productivity and output growth. Since Kaldor (1975: 892) generally regards output as an exogenous variable determined by demand, he concludes that "a sufficient condition for the presence of static or dynamic economies of scale is the existence of a statistically significant relationship between e and q, with a regression coefficient which is significantly less than 1" (Kaldor 1975: 893). Equation 10 is rejected for testing the Verdoorn's law by Kaldor (Kaldor 1975: 892). Acknowledging the assumption that output is exogenously determined by demand, one should use the Kaldor equations 5 and 6 to identify the presence of increasing returns to scale.

Parikh (1978: 83) argues that the results of Kaldors specification 5 and 6 as well as Rowthorn's equation 10 suffer from a simultaneous equation bias which led to incorrect estimates. He, therefore, proposes a simultane-

78 Whereby $((\beta_8+\beta_9-1)/\beta_8)$ reflects the Verdoorn coefficient which is measured by Kaldor. Accordingly, a Verdoorn coefficient of $0.5 = ((\beta_8+\beta_9-1)/\beta_8)$ and assuming that $\beta_8 = \beta_9$ (e.g., McCombie & Roberts 2007) yields $\beta_8 = \beta_9 = 0.67$ which implies a return of scale in the value of 1.33.

ous equation model. Due to the possibility of simultaneous causation, there have been several attempts to identify the causal structure of the relationship between output and productivity using methods from time series analysis. The results are partly inconclusive, for example see: Fase & Van Den Heuvel (1988), Mohammadi & Ram (1990), Castiglione (2011). Recent empirical work deal with the problem of simultaneous equation in different ways: Angeriz et al. (2008) estimate not only the demand-side version of Verdoorn's law but also a supply-side version. They find considerably different estimates for the two versions in the order of magnitude of returns to scale. Millemaci & Ofria (2014: 144) use the method of instrumental variables to solve the simultaneity problem. Another approach was conducted by Harris & Lau (1998) as well as Harris & Liu (1999) using the Johansen methodology to deal with the simultaneity. In this section, the usual demand-side version is estimated first. Later, the demand and supply-side version are estimated using time series data for three African economies. Additionally, an error-correction model is used to estimate the long-run cointegration relationship.

4.2.2.4 Capacity utilization

Another problem in estimating the relationship between output and productivity growth is posed by the possible occurrences of business cycle fluctuations, which affect both the utilization of capital and labor. The relationship between unemployment and the gap of output to potential GDP is also known as Okun's law (Okun 1962).79 According to Okun, an increase of one percent in the unemployment rate is associated with a three percentage decrease in output. The unemployment rate is used as indicator for all kinds of idle resources. The problem for the measurement of increasing returns to scale emerges because the intensity of the use of resources changes during the business cycle (e.g., underutilized machinery or underemployed workers during downswing). If output increases in the short term and underemployed workers are available, productivity increas-

79 It should be noted that the concept of Okun refers to an imaginary potential GDP as a "supply concept" which is achieved when all production factors are fully used. Such a concept would be neglected by Kaldor, assuming that output is predominantly dependent on the demand of an economy.

es as well. This positive relation between output and productivity has sparsely to do with increasing returns to scale.

One possibility to solve the problem involves constructing and controlling for indices of capacity utilization (e.g., unemployment rate, stocks or deviations of the capital-output ratio from the trend), however, amplitude differences of business cycles would pose problems to such a method. McCombie (2002: 98) thus proposes to use average cross-sectional growth rates calculated with peaks of the business cycle as initial and terminal point. This procedure is realized by León-Ledesma (2002) and Fingleton & McCombie (1998). Another possibility to distinguish the long-term influence of demand from influences of the short term business cycle is to include a time lag (Millemaci & Ofria 2014: 143). I tackle the problem by using ten years averages of growth rates in the cross-section estimates. In the time series analysis, I include several time lags and estimate an error-correction version which models the adjustment to the long-run equilibrium.

4.2.2.5 The issue of convergence

In advanced economies, the main factor of productivity growth is the technological change, mainly driven by research and development. Developing economies in contrast have the advantages of backwardness (Gerschenkron 1966) and can profit from technology transfer. Another control variable, which should be taken into account especially for developing economies, is speed of convergence. The literature suggests that productivity convergence is not similar across economic sectors.

Bernard & Jones (1996) show that the manufacturing sector does not display any pattern of convergence. As convergence is present in aggregate productivity, it is claimed to be driven by non-manufacturing activities, mainly services. Bernard & Jones (1996) explanation is based on the distinction between tradable and non-tradable goods sectors. While the non-tradable sectors will converge in productivity levels, the tradable goods sectors will specialize across countries due to comparative advantages. To the extent that different countries produce different goods, there is no reason for productivity convergence between economies.

In contrast to those results, Rodrik (2013) finds strong unconditional convergence of manufacturing industries, whereas aggregate and non-manufacturing activities reveal absence of unconditional convergence. Rodrik (2013) further hints at the sectoral convergence which gets stronger, the more disaggregated sectors are considered. Rodrik (2013: 201) also refers to the distinction of tradable and non-tradable goods, but his explanation is exactly the opposite of the arguments from Bernard & Jones (1996). He argues that these manufacturing sectors produce tradable goods which can be rapidly integrated into global production chains and networks, facilitating technology transfer and absorption. Further tradable goods sector are constantly under competitive threat from foreign companies which is, according to him, not the case for traditional agriculture, non-tradable services, and especially informal economic activities.

Using the GGDC 10-Sector Database, Castellacci et al. (2014) also find that the results of Bernard & Jones (1996) are not robust against the inclusion of developing economies. Services sectors do not converge when non-OECD countries are included into the sample. They further figure that the convergence hypothesis is only true for some country-sectors (e.g., services and manufacturing) above a certain threshold of initial productivity. Convergence in contrast is absent for agriculture. They call those sectors "convergence island in oceans of non-convergence" (Castellacci et al. 2014: 1001).

To control for convergence and technology transfer, I include the productivity gap in the cross section estimations.

4.2.2.6 The static-dynamic paradox of Verdoorn's law

Assuming that increasing returns to scale hold, how can one explain that Switzerland with a much smaller manufacturing sector exhibits the same productivity as the United States manufacturing sector? Since Verdoorn's law in the operationalization of Kaldor is expressed in terms of growth rates, it does not account for differences in the total output:

$$p = \beta_1 + \beta_2 \, q + \beta_5 \, k \qquad \text{Eq 9}$$

However, following the production function approach and using equation 7, one can rearrange equation 12 in such that:

$$lnP = \text{lnA} + (\beta_8 - 1)\,\text{lnE} + \beta_9 \,\text{lnK} \qquad \text{Eq 16}$$

Equation 16 is also known as the static version of the Verdoorn's law since it accounts for the total value of output. McCombie (1982) astonishingly finds that in nearly all cases results from measuring static returns to scale do not reject the prevalence of constant returns to scale (McCombie 2002: 102)[80]. Estimating the dynamic version of Verdoorn's law should yield the same results.

McCombie & Roberts (2007) argue that the static-dynamic paradox of Verdoorn's law may be attributed to the spatial aggregation bias, also known as ecological inference fallacy (King et al. 2008), describing, in general, statistical phenomena when conclusions are drawn from statistical aggregates. The phenomena emerge when data is aggregated to e.g., nation states and when the relationship between the average values is different from the relationship between the individual values. Assuming a country exists out of several functional economic areas from which each is showing increasing returns to scale, McCombie & Roberts (2007: 192ff) argue that the static version of Verdoorn's law at the aggregated level will show constant returns to scale. In contrast, by measuring cross-section data, expressed in growth rates, the asymptotic bias will become negligible. That is why the dynamic version of Verdoorn's law coefficient will yield the same results at all levels of aggregation (McCombie & Roberts 2007: 196). Time series data of the static and the dynamic version of Verdoorn's law will lead to unbiased results (McCombie & Roberts 2007: 200).

4.2.3 Recent empirical research

In analyzing historical datasets of industry, Verdoorn finds a constant relation between growth of labor productivity and the volume of industrial production. According to his statistics, a 10 percent increase of volume of production is associated with a 4.5 percent increase of labor productivity. This elasticity seems to be fairly constant for the countries Switzerland, United Kingdom, United States, and Germany (in contrast it differs between industrial sectors) (Verdoorn 2002: 30).

Kaldor (1966: 36–38) confirms the results of Verdoorn and estimates a coefficient of about 0.5 for manufacturing as well as public utilities and construction. He did not find any correlation between output and productivity in the transport sector and a Verdoorn coefficient near to unity for commerce and the agricultural sector. A coefficient of unity implies no correlation between employment and output, suggesting that the inflow of labor will not increase output in those sectors.

---

80 For an exception see Leon-Ledesma (2000).

McCombie et al. (2002) compile a list of studies from Kaldor's works until 2002 and conclude that a robust Verdoorn coefficient between 0.3 and 0.6 was found in the literature in most cases for the manufacturing sector. In the recent literature, Verdoorn's law has been tested for European regions for different economic sectors but mostly had a focus on the manufacturing sector (Harris & Lau 1998; Leon-Ledesma 2000; Millemaci & Ofria 2014; Pons-Novell & Viladecans-Marsal 1999; Angeriz et al. 2008; Fingleton & McCombie 1998; Alexiadis & Tsagdis 2010).

Other economies are investigated by Timmer & Szirmai (2000) who examine four East Asian economies or by León-Ledesma (2002) testing the Verdoorn's law for 17 OECD economies. Harris & Liu (1999) use the Penn World Tables to test the Verdoorn's law for more than 60 countries including 12 African economies, however, the Penn World Tables do not provide sectoral data. Pieper (2003) considers 30 developing and thereof 8 African economies and 9 economic sectors. Wells & Thirlwall (2003) draw on data from the African Development Bank as well as the World Bank to test Verdoorn's law for 44 African economies. They reveal a Verdoorn coefficient of nearly 0.9 for the manufacturing sector and a coefficient near to unity in the other sectors. The Verdoorn's law is not yet tested for the GGDC 10-Sector Database which is the best source on sectoral data for African economies.

4.2.4 Cross section estimates

In a first step, I use the GGDC 10-Sector Database to test Verdoorn's law for cross section estimates of the 41 economies included. The dataset provides employment and value added data (from which productivity data can be calculated) for nine sectors. To distinguish the long-term effects from short term business cycle effects (Okun's law), I calculate the average growth rates of 10 years from 1970 to 2010 in 10-years intervals. I further use a modified version of the original specification (equation 5) and include the growth of the capital stock. I unfortunately do not have any data on capital accumulation or investment on a sectoral level. Instead, the growth rate of the aggregate capital stock in constant national prices is used to control for changes in the capital stock. Due to missing data, it is thus assumed that the growth rate of sectoral capital stocks equals the aggregate stocks. This is a daring assumption I come back to later.

Since productivity is the dependent variable in the model, the specification allows to test for the convergence hypothesis. Accordingly, I use the initial productivity gap to the United States to control whether the distance to the technological frontier has an influence on productivity growth. Positive or negative coefficients of the productivity gap thereby correspond to productivity convergence or divergence to the United States, respectively. Since the GGDC 10-Sector Database measures value added in national prices, only sectoral value added shares and the output-side real GDP in PPP from the World Penn Database is used to construct comparable sectoral productivity data in constant 2005 US Dollar.

The modified version of the Kaldor specification is given in equation 17[81]:

$$p_i = \alpha_{1i} + \alpha_{2i}q_i + \alpha_{3i}pg_i + \alpha_{4i}c + \varepsilon_{1i} \qquad \text{Eq 17}$$

p_i	average growth rate of labor productivity in industry i
q_i	average growth rate of output in industry i
pg_i	productivity gap to the United States of industry i
c	average growth rate of the aggregate capital stock
α_{vi}	coefficient for the corresponding variable v and industry i
ε_{1i}	residuum for the regression equation of industry i

Table a18, a19, a20, a21 contain coefficients and p-values of the cross section results for four periods, table a22 presents the results of the panel regression when the sample includes all four periods.

4.2.4.1 Verdoorn coefficient

The empirical literature suggests values between 0.3 and 0.7 for the Verdoorn coefficient. In the cross section estimates, I find very small values in some cases, which are not significantly different from zero, but also considerable high values that are not significantly different from unity. However, regarding the panel regression in which all four periods are included, I detect values between 0.3 and 0.8, which is within the spectrum of the expected values. The Verdoorn coefficient for the total economy shows the highest value with 0.85. The lowest values over all four periods are found in the manufacturing sector, followed by construction and public utilities. Agriculture shows the highest Verdoorn coefficient, followed by the service sectors: FIRE, WRT as well as GCSPS. Especially for the

81 The cross-section indices as well as period indices (for the panel regression) are omitted in the equation for the sake of simplicity.

manufacturing sector, the results differ substantially between decades. The coefficient is relatively high for the period 1970–1980 (0.47) and 1990–2000 (0.62). It is very low and even insignificant for the period 1980–1990 as well as 2000–2010. The results question the stability of the coefficients over time.

Reconsidering equation 15, which is derived from the production function approach, as well as the assumption, that the output elasticities of capital and labor are equivalent ($\beta_8 = \beta_9$), a Verdoorn coefficient of 0.5 implies that $\beta_8 = \beta_9 = 0.67$, which in turn suggests a return of scale of about 1.33. Accordingly, the coefficient in manufacturing of 0.31 implies returns to scale of 1.18, and the coefficient of 0.85 for the total economy implies returns of scale of 1.74. In general, a high Verdoorn coefficient indicates high returns to scale. However, what entails the Verdoorn coefficient going up to unity? In this case, output growth is independent of employment growth, meaning that an increase in employment would not change output or the other way around.

Indeed, a coefficient near to unity is often measured in the literature. Kaldor (1966: 36–38) himself finds those coefficients for the agricultural and service sector. He interprets the results as the existence of surplus labor in those sectors. Wells & Thirlwall (2003) also reveal a Verdoorn coefficient of roughly 0.9 for the manufacturing sector and a coefficient close to unity in the other sectors. They grasp the results as evidence for substantial returns to scale in the manufacturing sector and conclude for the other sectors: “No economic meaning can be attached to this result except that employment growth in these two sectors seems to be independent of output growth” (Wells & Thirlwall 2003: 97). No matter whether one assumes the demand-side or supply-side interpretation of the Verdoorn’s law, the economic meaning of such a coefficient is everything but negligible. In the demand-side interpretation, this would mean that if demand grows, output can be enhanced without increasing labor. Such a growth would be in accord with the jobless growth experiences in several developing and emerging economies.82 As the result, labor productivity increases with the same rate as output grows. In the supply-side interpretation, an increase in labor input would have no effect on output growth and would result in a reduction of labor productivity. Implications, especially for the structural bonus hypothesis (see chapter 4.1), are enormous.

82 See as an example Bhorat & Oosthuizen (2008) for South Africa and Kannan & Raveendran (2009) for India.

4.2.4.2 Productivity gap

The distance to the technological frontier has a negative effect on productivity growth for the total economy. Nonetheless, this result is only true for the aggregate economy. Agriculture is the only sector in which the coefficient is always significantly negative. In all other sectors, the coefficient is mostly not significant. Thus, I conclude that the data does not confirm the hypothesis of unconditional convergence neither in manufacturing nor in service industries. However, I find evidence of productivity divergence in the agricultural sector. Nonetheless, divergence was mostly present in former decades; the coefficient has been constantly decreasing from 1970 on and was barely significant in the latest period 2000-2010. In contrast, the coefficients are significantly negative for manufacturing in the latest period's 1990-2000 and 2000-2010, suggesting an increasing divergence rather than convergence in the manufacturing sector. These results are in contrast to the unconditional convergence hypothesis of Rodrik (2013).

4.2.4.3 Capital

The coefficients in the sectoral regressions should be regarded carefully since no sectoral capital shares are available, and the aggregated growth rate is assumed to be the sectoral growth rate. However, only in rare occasions, the coefficients for capital in the regressions are significantly different from zero. According to Kaldor and other authors (e.g., Fingleton & McCombie 1998: 91), regressing capital (c) on output (q) will yield an β_5 of zero and a β_6 which is not significantly different from unity83:

$$\mathrm{c} = \alpha_5 + \alpha_6 q + \varepsilon_2 \qquad \text{Eq 18}$$

Since capital data is not available on the sectoral level, the regression is only estimated for the total economy. The regression results are presented in table a. In this case, the confidence interval for p = 0.05 is between 0.78 and 1.02 which shows that the coefficient is, as expected, not significantly different from unity.

---

83 Again, the cross-section indices as well as period indices are omitted in the equation for the sake of simplicity.

4.2.5 Times series analysis

To provide estimates which sectors in the economies of Africa show increasing or decreasing results, I encounter several problems. Firstly, I do not have enough cross sections to provide estimates for the economies of Africa. I thus rely on time series data rather than cross section differences. Secondly, I face problems how to compile sectoral data for the capital stock. Thirdly, the previous chapter has already revealed that the interpretation of Verdoorn coefficient is not straightforward. A high Verdoorn coefficient does not only indicate the existence of substantial increasing returns but is an indicator for low employment elasticity to output. In the following, I try to solve those problems.

4.2.5.1 Model discussion

According to the literature, four models can be distinguished. Model 1 and 2 are the Kaldorian demand-side models. Model 2 "represents the 'cleanest' form of the law for the investigation of the existence of increasing returns" (Pieper 2003: 836). However, model 1 is the most frequently used model since control variables such as technology transfer as well as capital or investment can directly be interpreted. Model 3 and 4 are supply-side models, meaning that the supposed causality leads from input factors to output and not the other way around. The more frequently used model 3 was suggested by Rowthorn (1975b). Model 4 is directly derived from the production function; its coefficient can be easily interpreted.

Model 1 $$p_{it} = a_{7i} + a_{8i}q_{it} + \alpha_{9i}c_{it} + \varepsilon_{3i} \quad \text{Eq 19}$$

Model 2 $$e_{it} = \alpha_{10i} + \alpha_{11i}q_{it} + \alpha_{12i}c_{it} + \varepsilon_{4i} \quad \text{Eq 20}$$

Model 3 $$p_{it} = \alpha_{13i} + \alpha_{14i}e_{it} + \alpha_{15i}c_{it} + \varepsilon_{5i} \quad \text{Eq 21}$$

Model 4 $$q_{it} = \alpha_{16i} + \alpha_{17i}e_{it} + \alpha_{18i}c_{it} + \varepsilon_{6i} \quad \text{Eq 22}$$

p_{it} average growth rate of labor productivity in industry i, at time t
q_{it} average growth rate of output in industry i, at time t
e_{it} average growth rate of employment in industry i, at time t
c_{it} average growth rate of the capital stock in industry i, at time t
α_{vi} coefficient for the corresponding variable v and industry i

All four models are estimated for the total economy ($i = sum$) using the dataset from 0, including all four periods. Table a24 depicts the results of the panel regression for all four models. It shows that the results of the demand-side model 1 are in line to those of model 2. In the same way, the supply-side models 3 and 4 correspond to each other. However, the results of the demand- and supply-side models differ. The Verdoorn coefficient in the demand-side models shows a value of 0.76. This value suggests substantial increasing returns to scale of about 1.6. In contrast, the coefficient for labor in model 3 reveals a significant and high negative value. In the Rowthorn interpretation, such a coefficient indicates substantial decreasing returns to scale. The coefficient is in accord to the coefficient in equation 4 which is clearly below unity. Accordingly, an increase in labor supply would enhance output by much less than the initial increase in labor, hence, labor productivity would decrease immediately. The returns to scale indicated by model 4 are constant if not decreasing (0.95). In the following section, I present results for model 1 and model 4.

To distinguish the short-run effect of possibly underutilization of resources (see Okun's law) from a long-run effect, I follow Millemaci & Ofria (2014: 11) and include time lags in model 1[84]:

Model 1B $$p_{it} = a_{19i} + a_{20i} q_{it} + \alpha_{21i} c_{it} + \alpha_{22i} q_{it-1} + \alpha_{23i} p_{it-1} + \varepsilon_{7i}$$ Eq 23

The Verdoorn long-run elasticity (v) for equation 2 is then calculated as:

$$v_i = \frac{(a_{19i} + a_{20i})}{(1 - a_{23i})}$$ Eq 24

Furthermore, it is plausible that even if there is no relationship between employment and output in growth rates, there may be a cointegration relationship in the sense of a long-run equilibrium between the absolute levels. Therefore, I estimate the production function in logarithms. To control for technological progress, a time trend is included in the regression:

Model 4B $$logQ_{it} = \alpha_{24i} + \alpha_{25i} trend + \alpha_{26i} logE_{it} + \alpha_{27i} logC_{it} + \varepsilon_{8i}$$ Eq 25

84 The optimal lag length is tested. The results are unambiguous according to all criteria and indicate an optimal lag length of one for all sectors.

$logQ_{it}$	logarithm of output in industry i, at time t
$logE_{it}$	logarithm of employment in industry i, at time t
$logC_{it}$	logarithm of the capital stock in industry i, at time t
$trend$	trend dummy
α_{vi}	coefficient for the corresponding variable v

I use the ADF (augmented dickey fuller) statistic to test whether the residuals are stationary of order one (I(1)), which is a condition for a long-run cointegration relationship between the three variables. I further estimate the error correction model:

Model 4C $$q_{it} = \alpha_{286i} + +\alpha_{29i}q_{it-1} + \alpha_{30i}e_{it} + \alpha_{31i}c_{it} + \alpha_{32i}e_{it-1} + \alpha_{33i}c_{it-1} + \alpha_{34i}\varepsilon_{8i} + \varepsilon_{9i}$$ Eq 22

With regard to model 4B, ε_{8i} is the residual indicating the deviation from the predicted long-term equilibrium. Estimating model 4C, the coefficient α_{34i} is of special interest because it indicates the influence of the deviation from the long-term equilibrium. If the coefficient is significantly negative, a stable long-run relationship is assumed, as suggested by model 4B.

4.2.5.2 Data

The GGDC 10-Sector Database provides a promising dataset of employment and value added on the sectoral level for eleven economies in sub-Saharan Africa. Nonetheless, testing the Verdoorn's law requires independent measurement of employment and value added data. Data examination shows that sectoral employment in the GGDC 10-Sector Database is inter- or extrapolated in various cases using average productivity growth rates (Vries et al. 2013: 21). This is especially the case for the African economies. Time series information from estimating the effect of employment growth or output growth on productivity growth will thus give pointless results in those cases. For countries in which the sectoral employment data is smoothed, I use the assumption of constant productivity growth for: Botswana, Ethiopia, Ghana, Malawi, Nigeria, Senegal, Tanzania, Zambia. Time series in which this assumption is not used concern: Kenya, Mauritius, and South Africa (after 1970) (nonetheless sometimes interpolation has been done). Thus, I focus on these three countries to give an exemplary indication of sectoral returns to scale for African economies. The sectoral capital stock for South Africa is derived from historical macroeconomic time series of the Quarterly Bulletin from the South African

Reserve Bank.[85] No official data for the sectoral capital stocks in Mauritius and Kenya are available. To construct the data, I firstly compile data on gross capital formation. For Kenya, I was able to compile sectoral data on gross capital formation from the Economic Survey Publications[86] for the period 1964 to 2003. For Mauritius, sectoral data on gross capital formation for the period 1976 to 2011 is compiled from historical national accounts series from Statistics Mauritius.[87] In both cases, data sets in constant prices with varying base years are available. Thus, I use the growth rates to compile consistent time series in prices of the latest base year in national prices. Calculating the capital stock, data on the depreciation rate as well as on the initial capital stock is needed. Since no data for industry specific depreciation rates are available, I use the depreciation rate of the total economy from the PENN World Tables. The initial capital stock is then estimated according to the method used by Tobin (1973)[88] who used this approach to estimate the initial capital stock for different sectors in Kenya. Using the initial capital stock as well as the depreciation rate and gross capital formation, a time series for the capital stock is constructed.

The final dataset consists of the three variables: employment as well as value added and capital stock each in constant national prices. The sample includes the corresponding sectors in the GGDC 10-Sector Database and more than 30 years in each country: South Africa (1960-2010), Kenya (1970-2004), and Mauritius (1977-2010). In Mauritius, data on capital formation was only available for the years 2007 onwards. The mining sector in Mauritius is thus excluded from the sample.

4.2.5.3 Results

Table a25, a26, and a27 present the coefficients and p-values of the models 1, 1B as well as 4 and 4B for all nine sectors and the total economy in

---

85 South African Reserve Bank: https://www.resbank.co.za/Publications/QuarterlyBulletins/adhoc/Pages/default.aspx (last access: May 5, 2016)

86 Economic Survey Publications are available for download from the Kenya National Bureau of Statistics (last access: May 5, 2016)

87 Statistics Mauritius is under the aegis of the Ministry of Finance & Economic Development: http://statsmauritius.govmu.org/English/StatsbySubj/Pages/NationalAccounts.aspx (last access: May 5, 2016)

88 Other approaches such as the steady state approach has been tried but led to highly implausible results. See Berlemann & Wesselhöft (2014) for a compilation of different methods estimating the initial capital stock.

South Africa, Kenya, and Mauritius. The complete estimates (output sheets) are available on demand. The regression results are discussed in the following.

South Africa

As expected, in the demand-side model 1 and 1B, the coefficients for capital growth are in general not significantly different from zero. An exception is the negative coefficient in manufacturing and mining. The coefficient in manufacturing is only significant in the model 1A and becomes insignificant when lags are included. The results for mining are altogether very inconclusive.

The Verdoorn coefficient differs substantially between sectors. For the total economy as well as the sectors AGR, WRT, TSC, and FIRE, the Verdoorn coefficient is not significantly different from unity, indicating that output is independent from employment. Indeed, the findings are confirmed by the results of model 4A. In the same sectors, the coefficient for employment growth is not significantly different from unity. I can also refute a positive long-term cointegration relationship between output and employment in the absolute levels for those sectors. The Engle-Granger two-step procedure rejects the existence of such a relationship. The adjustment coefficient in the error-correction model shows significant negative values for WRT as well as FIRE, but the coefficient for employment in the long-term regression is not significantly different from unity in those sectors.

In the sectors MAN, CON as well as GCSPS, the Verdoorn coefficient is between 0.4 and 0.7. The results indicate the existence of increasing returns in the Kaldorian sense.

Accordingly, I find positive coefficients between employment and output growth in the supply-side model. The coefficient for the manufacturing sector has the highest value. The sum of the coefficients of capital and labor in the supply-side model indicate the extend of returns to scale. According to this procedure, the only sector which shows increasing returns is FIRE (yet only because of the extraordinarily high coefficient of 2.4 for capital). In construction (0.72) and GCSPS (0.35), I detect substantial decreasing returns. At least manufacturing shows constant returns to scale (1.04). In absolute levels, I find evidence for moderate increasing returns in manufacturing and construction. The tests whether there is indeed a long-run cointegration relationship remain ambiguous. The simple two-step procedure of Engle-Granger indicates no cointegration relationship. The adjustment coefficient of the error-correction, in contrast, is significantly negative suggesting the existence of such a long-term relationship.

In the sector PU, the Verdoorn coefficient is not significantly different from zero. In Kaldor's interpretation, this is the case when constant returns to scale prevail because output and employment grow with the same rate, which is why output growth has no correlation with the growth of labor productivity.

The most likely explanation for the difference between supply- and demand-side results is the misspecification of the production function. As I have argued in section 4.2.2, the measurement of increasing returns in the supply-side version requires a full list of input factors. Otherwise, the law of diminishing marginal returns is measured.

The results suggest that there is labor surplus in agriculture and in the most service sectors. Only in manufacturing, construction, and the sector GCSPS I found a positive labor elasticity below unity indicating the existence of increasing returns to scale.

Mauritius[89]

Similar to regression results of South-Africa, the coefficient for capital is insignificant in the demand-side models.

The Verdoorn coefficient is close to unity in agriculture but also in the service sectors FIRE and GCSPS. In the other sectors, the results of model 1A and 1B differ, thus, I focus on the long-run elasticity as the coefficients in model 1A may be biased due to short-term business cycle fluctuations. The long-run elasticity of output on productivity is very small in manufacturing (0.10), construction (0.32), PU (0.33) as well as WRT (0.14). It reaches expected values in TSC (0.48) and in the total economy (0.68).

As expected, the supply-side models illustrate that output is independent of labor in the sector in which the Verdoorn coefficient shows very high values: AGR, FIRE, and GCSPS. This is also the case in the sector PU (despite the long-run Verdoorn coefficient of zero). I further find no indication for a cointegration relationship between labor and output in the sectors PU, FIRE as well as GCSPS. In agriculture, both the Engle-Granger test and the adjustment coefficient indicate the existence of a

89 Due to missing capital data, the mining sector is excluded in Mauritius.

long-run cointegration relationship. However, the coefficients for employment are not significantly different from zero.90

In the sectors manufacturing, construction as well as the service sectors TSC and WRT, the coefficient shows a relatively low but significantly positive correlation between employment and output. Unexpectedly, the coefficients for capital are also insignificant for the most cases in the supply-side models except for the sector GCSPS. In the sector FIRE, a strong, counter-intuitive negative coefficient for capital is found. Considering the sum of coefficients for labor and capital in the supply-side model, I do not find any indication for increasing returns to scale.

The results suggest that there is surplus labor in agriculture, public utilities as well as the service sectors FIRE and GCSPS. In manufacturing, construction, and the service sector TSC, I found a positive labor elasticity. The labor elasticity is relatively high, suggesting that there are only small productivity gains when output is expanded.

Kenya

In model 1A, the coefficient for capital shows some unexpected positive values in agriculture, manufacturing, and WRT and even a negative coefficient in PU. However, the coefficients become insignificant in model 1B except for the positive coefficient in WRT.

The Verdoorn coefficient differs from unity in only three sectors: MIN (0.19), WRT (0.47) as well as FIRE (0.45). In all other sectors the coefficient is not significantly different from unity and sometimes even higher (TSC and PU). Those results are in general confirmed by model 1B with the exception of the long-run Verdoorn coefficient for FIRE, which takes a value near to zero.

The supply-side models confirm that employment growth is independent of output growth in all sectors except for the two service sectors with significant but relatively low positive coefficients: WRT (0.29) and FIRE (0.46). As I do not find positive coefficients for employment in the absolute levels (model 4B), I can also refute a cointegration relationship for the

90 Testing for cointegration between either two of those variables indicates a negative long-run relationship between capital and output. I further find a positive short-run relationship between capital and labor.

other sectors.91 Again, the coefficients for capital are insignificant for most sectors except GCSPS as well as FIRE.

The results for Kenya suggest the independence of labor and output, and thus the existence of labor surplus in all sector except of WRT. The results for WRT suggest the existence of increasing returns to scale.

4.2.6 Interim conclusion

The returns to scale differ substantially between sectors. However, these characteristics are not robust with respect to time and between countries. Testing the Verdoorn's law for a cross section of countries using the GGDC 10-Sector Database, the Verdoorn coefficient appears especially high in agriculture and FIRE. The lowest value is found in manufacturing and construction. The higher the Verdoorn coefficient, the higher are the returns to scale. The data thus clearly rejects the hypothesis that the manufacturing sector is important because it shows the highest returns to scale. However, a high Verdoorn coefficient is a double-edged sword. A high Verdoorn coefficient near to unity reveals independence between employment and output growth. The phenomenon is interpreted as surplus labor. Hence, manufacturing and construction can be regarded as sectors with the highest output elasticity on employment, thereby providing the most opportunities for job creation. However, the tests for different periods show that the results are not very robust over time.

Testing Verdoorn's law in time series data for the African economies Kenya, Mauritius, and South Africa, I find very high Verdoorn coefficients indicating independence of output and employment for the majority of sectors. Table 9 summarizes in which sectors a positive relationship between output and labor (positive) are found and in which both variables are independent from each other. I interpret those results as the existence of surplus labor. In some sectors the results are inconclusive. In the Kaldorian interpretation, those sectors with a Verdoorn coefficient between zero and unity exhibit increasing returns to scale, meaning that labor productivity increases when demand for output rises. The analysis of

91 The Engle-Granger test also indicates that there is no cointegration. The error correction model suggests adjustment to the long-run equation in construction and public utilities, but the coefficients in the long-run equation are very small and insignificant.

South Africa and Mauritius confirms the cross section results and indicates a positive output-elasticity on employment in manufacturing and construction while several other sectors point to the existence of surplus labor. In Kenya, the only sector with a positive relation between output and labor is WRT.

The supply-side version confirms a positive relationship between employment and output in most cases in which a Verdoorn coefficient is between zero and unity. However, I could not identify any indication for increasing returns to scale in the supply side version.

Table 9: Relation between output and labor

	South Africa	Mauritius	Kenya
AGR	surplus labor	surplus labor	surplus labor
MIN	-	-	-
MAN	positive	positive	surplus labor
CON	positive	positive	surplus labor
PU	-	surplus labor	surplus labor
WRT	surplus labor	-	positive
TRS	surplus labor	positive	surplus labor
FIRE	surplus labor	surplus labor	surplus labor
GSCP	-	surplus labor	-
SUM	surplus labor	-	surplus labor

Source: Own depiction; "surplus labor" indicates independence between output and labor, "positive" suggests a positive relationship, and a dash indicates that the results are unclear.

Future research should be directed to solving the puzzle of the supply-side and demand-side version of Verdoorns' law. I assume that the misspecification of the production function is the underlying reason for unclear results. Better results should be expected when more reliable data on the capital stock is used and other input factors such as human capital and knowledge are included in the production function. By this, it should be possible to identify whether or not the phenomenon of surplus labor exists only for unskilled workers.

4.3 The role of linkages: results of input-output tables

The third major argument in favor of the manufacturing sector is that linkage effects are stronger than in agriculture and services (Szirmai 2011: 14; Cornwall 1979: 130 ff.). The concept of linkages has originally been introduced by Albert Hirschman. It has especially attracted attention to identify economic key sectors. Indeed, Albert Hirschman (1958) proposed the idea of unbalanced growth in contrast to a strategy of balanced growth.92 In contrast to the neoclassical view of steady state growth and continuous equilibrium, Hirschman recommended a development policy which presumptively produces disproportions, tensions, and disequilibria as these are the main driving powers for economic development (Hirschman 1958: 66–67).

The major characteristic of Hirschman's theory are complementarities, meaning that in any state, given a certain price, a rise in the production of one good affects the demand of another good. According to the concept of complementarities, the increased supply of one good will thus stimulate the production of another good even if there is no direct relationship between these two goods. The arguments are based on the assumption that investment decisions are rather driven by demand than by the availability of monetary funds. The effect can be understood as a multiplier in a sense that every investment causes a sequence of subsequent investments (Hirschman 1958: 69–71). Trying to maximize induced investments, Hirschman introduced the concept of forward and backward linkages, describing them as follows:

- Backward linkages – are the effects which are induced by an economic activity to produce the inputs which are required for this economic activity (Hirschman 1958: 100).
- Forward linkages – are the effects which are induced by an economic activity to utilize this output as an input for the production of other goods (Hirschman 1958: 100).

According to this definition, economic sectors that produce primary products do not show any backward linkages, and economic sectors which

92 Rosenstein-Rodan (1943) and Nurkse (1953) proposed a development strategy in which investments should be in accordance with the increase in demand measured by the income elasticity of demand. This strategy, called "balanced growth", was questioned by the concept of "unbalanced growth" as postulated by Albert Hirschman (1958).

produce output that is used directly for final demand do not show forward linkages.

Hirschman argued that, due to these linkages, particular industries can spur economic growth in the whole economy. Conclusively, the promotion of a lead sector would cause disequilibria which in turn would induce private investment (due to the profit motive). Hirschman (1958: 105–110) based his conclusion on the analysis of Chenery & Watanabe (1958) who analyzed input-output tables of four countries93 and observed that the pattern of interdependence among sectors are similar enough to apply the results to other countries.

Indeed, Imbs & Wacziarg (2003) demonstrate that economic development is associated with industrial diversification rather than specialization. They found an empirical relationship between sectoral concentration and per capita income, expressed in a graph forming a U-curve. Accordingly, countries first diversify in the sense that economic activity is spread among various sectors. Only relatively late in the development process ($9,000 – $11,000), countries tend to specialize again.

The results are also in line with the findings of Syrquin (2008), who claims the increased use of intermediates as a relatively robust trend in the process of development. The density of an input-output matrix can be regarded as a measure for the use of intermediates, reflecting the change to a more complex system of production with a higher degree of fabrication (Syrquin 2008: 54). The findings underpin modernization theories which emphasize the role of industrialization in the development process.

The purpose of this chapter is to test whether the manufacturing sector shows stronger production linkages than other economic sectors. I use input-output tables from the GTAP Africa Database to analyze the backward and forward linkages across sectors in African economies.

4.3.1 Methodological problems

Hirschman, despite using the input-output framework, has challenged the use of input-output tables for the measurement of linkages since "input-output analysis is by nature synchronic, whereas linkage effects need time to unfold" (Hirschman 2013: 159). He thus argues that historically oriented studies are more illuminating in testing the linkage hypothesis.

---

93 These four countries are Norway, Italy, Japan, and United States.

Hirschman proposes further extensions and generalizations on several lines to the concept of linkages. He affirms that the fiscal linkage is much more straightforward than the production linkage since the linkages of an industry depend heavily on the degree of technological differences of the new sector in relation to the established sectors (Hirschman 2013: 166). This conception is very much in line with the discussion of "absorptive capacity"94.

For the analysis of the fiscal and the consumption linkage, more in-depth research is needed since both cannot be identified with the help of input-output analysis. As the results of case studies have revealed, the extend of forward as well as backward linkages in the domestic economy not only depends on sector characteristics but also on several other factors, such as ownership, infrastructure provision, the policy environment as well as capabilities especially in the system of innovation (Morris et al. 2012: 38–43). The results of the analysis of input-output tables abstract from these differences but can only count for differences resulting from sector characteristics.

4.3.1.1 The input-output framework

Assuming a closed economy with no imports and exports but n-sectors, table 10 shows a simplified input-output framework:

Table 10: Input-output table – general example

		Purchasing Sector 1	…	n	Final Demand	Total Output
Producing Sector	1	z_{11}	$\cdots$	z_{1n}	y_1	x_1
	$\vdots$	$\vdots$	$\ddots$	$\vdots$	$\vdots$	$\vdots$
	n	z_{nn}	$\cdots$	z_{nn}	y_n	x_n
Value Added		v_1	$\cdots$	v_n		
Total Input		x_1	$\cdots$	x_n		

Source: Own depiction

The top left part of the table shows the transaction-matrix (**Z**) which is the

94 See the publication of Cohen & Levinthal (1990), which is considered as the origin of the concept, or the World Bank (2011) for a recent application of the concept in Southern Africa.

heart of the input-output table including the coefficients (z_{ij}) representing the intermediary goods sold from industry i to industry j. Conclusively, z_{ij} shows intra-sectoral trade if i = j and inter-sectoral trade if i ≠ j.

$$\boldsymbol{Z} = \begin{pmatrix} z_{11} & \cdots & z_{1n} \\ \vdots & \ddots & \vdots \\ z_{n1} & \cdots & z_{nn} \end{pmatrix} \qquad \text{Eq 1}$$

4.3.1.2 Industry vs. commodities

In the input-output framework, the rows and columns of the transaction matrix either represent industries (sectors) or commodities (products). In general, the both are classified in the same way; commodities are defined by the characteristics of the corresponding industries.95 Since some producing units produce more than one good, the assumption of a homogeneous branch is made, according to which an industry produces only one product. If a production unit produces more than one unit, it is assigned to the commodity which accounts for the greatest part of its output. In reality, of course, an industry produces more than one type of good; an approach to more complex, and thus realistic commodity-by-industry frameworks, in which by-products and secondary products are accounted for, has been already introduced (Miller & Blair 2009: 184–209). There are various types of industry-by-industry and commodity-by-commodity models, each with its own advantages and disadvantages.

The level of secondary products as well as the production of products in secondary industries seems to be relatively low. The manual of Eurostat & EC (2008: 306) thus concludes that "*the difference between product-by-product input-output tables and industry-by-industry input-output tables is relatively small. Both transformations can be regarded as valid options for impact analysis.*"

The data I will use (global input-output tables) is a compilation of national input-output tables with different types.96 It should be noted that

95 For the construction of an input-output table, the national accounts as well as the external trade statistics need to be harmonized. While the former is usually based on an industry classification (e.g., SIC and NACE), the latter is based on a goods classification (e.g., SITC or ISIC).

96 In the GTAP Africa Database used in this chapter, the original input-output table of e.g., Uganda is an industry-by-commodity table, Namibia is of a commodity-by-industry format and the one of Kenya is constructed of a commodi-

for my purpose—the measurement of linkages—I follow Hirschman by interpreting the coefficient in the input-output framework as sales and purchases, respectively. I thus use the notation of "sectors" for rows and columns.

$$\boldsymbol{y} = \begin{pmatrix} y_1 \\ \vdots \\ y_n \end{pmatrix} \qquad \text{Eq 2}$$

Finally, the vector of total demand ($\boldsymbol{x}$) represents the gross output of each sector (x_i) which is determined by the sum of intermediary consumption and final demand for each sector:

$$\boldsymbol{x} = \begin{pmatrix} x_1 \\ \vdots \\ x_n \end{pmatrix} \qquad \text{Eq 3}$$

whereby:

$$x_i = \sum_{j=1}^{n} z_{ij} + y_i \qquad \text{Eq 4}$$

Since total demand needs to equal total inputs or total production, the transposed vector $\boldsymbol{x}'$ is below the transaction matrix $\boldsymbol{Z}$:

$$\boldsymbol{x}' = (x_1 \quad \cdots \quad x_n) \qquad \text{Eq 5}$$

The vector $\boldsymbol{v}$ is a row vector including the value added of a specific sector (v_j). It is simply calculated as follows:

$$v_j = x_j - \sum_{i=1}^{n} z_{ij} \qquad \text{Eq 6}$$

Hirschman's backward linkage (BLH) is calculated as the ratio of inter-industry purchases to total production (Hirschman 1958: 106–107):

$$BLH_j = \frac{\sum_{i=1}^{n} z_{ij}}{x_j} \qquad \text{Eq 7}$$

The Hirschmanian forward linkage (FLH) is calculated as the ratio of inter-industry sales to total demand:

$$FLH_i = \frac{\sum_{j=1}^{n} z_{ij}}{x_i} \qquad \text{Eq 8}$$

---

ty-by-commodity table. The description of individual input-output tables can be found in the GTAP documentation (Aguiar et al. 2016). The preference of the GTAP is on commodity-by-commodity tables (Huff et al. 2000: 2).

Combining both linkages with emphasis on the backward linkage, Hirschman provides a ranking of industry that economist-planners of underdeveloped economies should take into account in their industrial policy. At the top of the list appear the intermediate manufactures (especially iron and steel followed by nonferrous metals and paper products).

In the next step I define the technological matrix $\boldsymbol{A}$ with the dimension n x n, which consist of technological coefficients a_{ij} that represent the share of value of intermediary goods i used to produce one unit of good j:

$$\boldsymbol{A} = \begin{pmatrix} a_{11} & \cdots & a_{1n} \\ \vdots & \ddots & \vdots \\ a_{n1} & \cdots & a_{nn} \end{pmatrix} \qquad \text{Eq 9}$$

whereby:

$$a_{ij} = \frac{z_{ij}}{x_j} \qquad \text{Eq 10}$$

The sum of rows and columns needs to be smaller than one since there has to be at least some final demand and value added. The matrix $\boldsymbol{A}$ is called the technological matrix as it can be interpreted as the technology of production in the sense of a production function. Given the technology A, one need a_{ij} (in terms of value) of sector i to produce one unit of output x_j. Certainly, it is implausible to assume that one industry applies only one technology. The use of different applied technologies may, however, lead to a similar utilization of production inputs which are typical for the respective kind of industry. Despite the misleading interpretation of the notion "technological matrix", I retain the notion because of its standard use in the literature. It should be noted that most applications of input-output tables assume that these technological coefficients are at least stable over time.97

Given the technological matrix $\boldsymbol{A}$, the relationship between input and output can be described by the following formula:

$$\boldsymbol{x} = \boldsymbol{A}\boldsymbol{x} + \boldsymbol{y} \qquad \text{Eq 11}$$

Rearranging leads to:

$$\boldsymbol{x} = (\boldsymbol{I} - \boldsymbol{A})^{-1}\, \boldsymbol{y} \qquad \text{Eq 12}$$

or:

$$\boldsymbol{x} = \boldsymbol{B}\boldsymbol{y} \qquad \text{Eq 13}$$

97 This is consistent with the assumption of constant returns as well as fixed factor proportions, meaning that the factors of production cannot be substituted. Such a production is also called a Leontief production function.

whereby $$\boldsymbol{B} = (\boldsymbol{I} - \boldsymbol{A})^{-1} \qquad \text{Eq 14}$$

The Leontief inverse matrix ***B*** is the central element of the standard model of input-output analysis, it is also called the total requirement matrix. The coefficients (b_{ij}) indicate how many direct and indirect purchases are required to produce one unit of output.

4.3.1.3 Accounting for indirect effects

Since the backward and forward linkages, which were introduced by Hirschman (1958: 100), only account for direct effects, the column sum of the Leontief inverse matrix is proposed to be a better measure for backward linkages (Yotopoulos & Nugent 1973):

$$BLJ_j = \sum_{i=1}^{n} b_{ij} \qquad \text{Eq 15}$$

The Danish economist Poul Nørregaard Rasmussen (1956) had already used the column sum of the Leontief inverse matrix in his PhD thesis "Studies in Intersectoral Relations", but called it "index of dispersion" (Rasmussen 1956: 133).98 Assuming that the "government wants to increase final demand in such a way that the economic activity is increased in all industries", the industries in which an expansion in final demand would "lead to a general increase in economic activity embracing all or at least most industries" might be called "key industries" (Rasmussen 1956: 141).

For the index of dispersion, Rasmussen (1956) averaged the column sum with the number of industries (n). In order to compare them with other industries, he further normalized them with the overall average:

$$BLR_j = \frac{\frac{1}{n}\sum_{i=1}^{n} b_{ij}}{\frac{1}{n^2}\sum_{j=1}^{n}\sum_{i=1}^{n} b_{ij}} \qquad \text{Eq 16}$$

98 The Leontief inverse matrix (***B***) is interpreted as representing the structure of the economy. Changes in the elements of ***B*** are thus interpreted as structural change. "The problem is to find convenient and relevant indices describing ***B***" (Rasmussen 1956: 133).

Hirschman (1958: 108) cited the earlier study of Rasmussen (1956) and acknowledged the index as a more "refined measure of backward linkage". Despite his acknowledgment, Hirschman did not use the "refined" measure but based his analysis on his the much simpler definition. Although Rasmussen was first to present a more refined measure, which is widely accepted in the literature, the notion of backward and forward linkages as introduced by Hirschman has become part of the economic language and is indivisibly connected to his name.

4.3.1.4 Forward linkages and the output inverse (Ghosh model)

Arguing with the "pressure of demand", Hirschman (1958: 117) postulated the importance of the backward linkage over the forward linkage. He did not consider the forward linkage as an independent inducement mechanism. Thus, the question had been raised, which economic meaning could be attributed to the forward linkage.99 The input-output table represents primarily utilization structure rather than sales and purchase interrelations. Nevertheless, the forward linkage is widely used in economic analysis. Ghosh (1958: 58) argued that it would be meaningful at least for monopolistic markets or wherever a general shortage of resources occurs. Indeed, several case studies support his view: A classic example is the diamond sector which helped to develop the cutting and polishing industry in the early 1980s in Botswana (Mbayi 2011). Another example is the processing industry which is induced by the tropical timber industry in Gabon (Terheggen 2011).

These case studies demonstrate that even if the backward linkage turns out to be the more important factor in almost all cases, the forward linkages may have relevance. In addition, as a considerable amount of literature uses this concept, I will include the forward linkage in the analysis but remain tentative in interpreting the results.

One should further bear in mind that sales from industry 1 to 2 in the input-output framework are counted as backward linkage of industry 2 and simultaneously as forward linkage for industry 1. Due to this double counting, only half of the linkages, which are measured in the total, can be

99 The question was especially put forward to me by Georg Quaas in "Forschungsseminar Politik und Wirtschaft" (www.forschungsseminar.de) on May 7, 2015.

effective in a causal sense. Recalling our experiment, for one industry it might still be possible that all its linkages are causal. The measured backward and forward linkages are thus interpreted as purely descriptive and no causal relationship should be read into it.

However, the measurement of the forward linkage is also subject of controversial debate. Hirschman (1958: 105) considers the ratio of inter-industry purchases (column sum) to output as backward and the ratio of inter-industry sales (row sum) to total output as forward linkages. While the use of the column sum of the Leontief inverse matrix as an element of the backward linkage is straightforward, the use of the row sum for the forward linkage is controversial (e.g., Cai & Leung 2004: 68).

Since the Hirschman linkage (share of inter-industry use to total demand) does not account for indirect effects, I am looking for a forward linkage which is equivalent to the column sum of the Leontief inverse matrix.

According to Jones (1976: 325–329), the row sum of the output inverse matrix, instead of the Leontief inverse matrix, should be the appropriate measure for the forward linkage. The output inverse matrix is calculated similarly to the Leontief inverse matrix, though with the output coefficients (z_{ij}/x_i) instead of the input coefficients (z_{ij}/x_j). It was first introduced by Ghosh (1958) who assumed that the output coefficients could be more stable than the input coefficients, at least in monopolistic markets or wherever a general shortage of resources is present (Ghosh 1958: 58).

Introducing the output-coefficient matrix ***C***:

$$\boldsymbol{C} = \begin{pmatrix} c_{11} & \cdots & c_{1n} \\ \vdots & \ddots & \vdots \\ c_{n1} & \cdots & c_{nn} \end{pmatrix} \qquad \text{Eq 17}$$

whereby:

$$c_{ij} = \frac{z_{ij}}{x_i} \qquad \text{Eq 18}$$

Then the output inverse matrix ***D*** with the coefficients d_{ij} total is calculated by:

$$\boldsymbol{D} = (\boldsymbol{I} - \boldsymbol{C})^{-1} \qquad \text{Eq 19}$$

The forward linkage according to Jones (1976: 328) (FLJ) then is measured as the row sum of the output inverse matrix ***D***:

$$FLJ_i = \sum_{j=1}^{n} d_{ij} \qquad \text{Eq 20}$$

Several authors have endorsed the use of the output inverse matrix for the measurement of forward linkages (Beyers 1976; Miller & Blair 2009: 558; Drejer 2002) just as Hirschman (2013: 188, note 6) appreciates it himself. Nonetheless, the use of such matrix for the measurement of the forward linkage is opposed by other authors due to implausibility of the supply-driven Ghosh model (e.g., Oosterhaven 1988).100 According to Lenzen (2003: 6), the Ghosh model can be used in order to identify key sectors as well as for international comparative studies but should not be used for impact studies. Therefore, the Ghosh model is suitable to serve the purpose of this study. However, I refute the old interpretation of Hirschman with an allusion to causal relationsships and use the following definition of forward and backward linkages:

- Backward linkages are the interrelations of an economic sector along the whole upstream supply chain.
- Forward linkages are the interrelations of an economic sector along the whole downstream supply chain.

4.3.1.5 Discussion on weighting and elasticities

Cuello et al. (1992) sums up the diverse criticism on Hirschman's and Rasmussen's linkages approach. The main argument addresses their use of ratio of averages, which is supposed to be misleading as multiplier effects do not necessarily need to have a high number of linkages but could have a few strong ones. Cuello et al. (1992: 289) try to resolve some problems by weighting the coefficients in the Leontief inverse matrix with final demand or total output of the corresponding sector.

In line with the arguments of i.e., Cuello et al. (1992) is the study by Mattas & Shrestha (1991: 247), who argue that "neither multipliers nor linkages contain information on the relative size of a sector in an economy". They thus propose the use of input-output elasticities instead of multipliers101 (see also Ciobanu et al. 2004; Miller & Blair 2009: 283).

---

100 Cella (1984: 77–78) argues that the Gosh model based forward linkages cannot be combined with the Leontief based backward linkages towards one total linkage index since both are built upon assumptions which are inconsistent with each other (fixed input vs. fixed output coefficients).

101 Elasticities measure the percentage change in output induced by a change in input of one percent, whereas multipliers measure the unit change of output which is induced by a change of input of one unit.

Although weighting could be useful for policy analysis when key sectors (in the sense of comparative advantages, technological forerunners) should be identified, neither weighting of the Leontief inverse coefficients nor the use of elasticities are plausible and useful for my purpose since I am interested in the "nature" or specificities of economic sectors. Instead, it is the multiplier effect—in the sense of: how much does the output increase if the final demand is increased by unit one?—that is searched for. Thus, I use the unweighted sum of coefficients to measure forward and backward linkages.

4.3.1.6 The open economy

In the above sections, a closed economy with no trade relations to other economies assumed. However, I need to cope with imports and exports in the input-output framework somehow. Referring to the literature, there are several ways of dealing with imports, but one can generally distinguish between two types:102

Table 11: Input-output table with separate import matrix (variant D)

		purchasing sector			final demand		output
		1	⋯	n			
producing sector	1	z_{11}	⋯	z_{1n}	e_1	y_1	x_1
	⋮	⋮	⋱	⋮	⋮	⋮	⋮
	n	z_{nn}	⋯	z_{nn}	e_n	y_n	x_n
imports	1	i_{11}	⋯	i_{1n}	e_1^i	y_1^i	x_1^i
	⋮	⋮	⋱	⋮	⋮	⋮	⋮
	n	i_{nn}	⋯	i_{nn}	e_n^i	y_n^i	x_n^i
value added		v_1	⋯	v_n			
total input		x_1	⋯	x_n			

Source: Own depiction

In the first version (variant D), all imports are classified by commodities and are represented in a separate import matrix. Similarly, the exports are

102 The literature often refers to four variants (A; B; C; D) which are defined in UN (1973: 53–63). While Kronenberg (2012: 183) introduced an additional variant E (for Eurostat), these descriptions are not used any more in the newer "Handbook of Input-Output Compilation and Analysis" (UN 1999).

shown as a column vector which adds up with the domestic final demand to total final demand. Since imports are represented in an extra row but may be consumed or re-exported directly, I need to introduce the vectors for directly consumed imports (y_i^i), directly exported imports (e_i^i), and the total demand for imports (x_1^i). The interpretation of the matrix $\boldsymbol{A}$ as the technological matrix, however, seems problematic as not all inputs are entered in the matrix $\boldsymbol{Z}$ (Holub & Schnabl 1985: 54).[103] Nevertheless, this is the version that is published by most statistical offices in the system of national accounts (e.g., Eurostat) since all other versions can be calculated from this version (Holub & Schnabl 1985: 54).

It makes sense, therefore, that another version (variant A) should be used for input-output analysis, in which the imports are classified by commodities and added up to the domestic sectors. As in this version the row sums would be higher than the total inputs, a negative import-column is typically inserted before the total demand vector (Holub & Schnabl 1985: 56–57).[104]

Table 12: Input-output table including imports in the transaction matrix (variant A)

		purchasing sector			final demand		imports	output
		1	…	n	exports	dom.		
producing sector	1	$z_{11} + i_{11}$	…	$z_{1n} + i_{1n}$	e_1	y_1	$-i_1$	x_1
	⋮	⋮	⋱	⋮	⋮	⋮	⋮	⋮
	n	$z_{nn} + i_{nn}$	…	$z_{nn} + i_{nn}$	e_n	y_n	$-i_n$	x_n
value added		v_1	…	v_n				
total input		x_1	…	x_n				

Source: Own depiction

103 There is a similar version (variant B) in which the imports are only separated according to their use and not to their origin; they are thus shown in a row-vector instead of a matrix.

104 The third possibility (variant C) is to differentiate from competitive imports, which are also produced within the country, and non-competitive imports, which are either not producible or not yet produced in the country (UN 1999: 155). While the competitive imports are treated in the same fashion as domestic products and thus the value is added to the corresponding row as inputs to a certain industry, non-competitive imports are shown in a separate row in the use table (UN 2008: 156–158).

New types of datasets are multi-region or even world input-output tables, which have only emerged in the last years. In these types of tables, several national input-output tables are merged into one table. To visualize an input-output framework with n sectors and g countries, I add a superscript to the variables z, y, x, and v which denotes the country (1 to g) while the subscript (1 to n) still represents the sector in such manner that z_{ij}^{kl} represents the sales from industry i in country k to industry j in country l.

In the case that k = l (the gray shaded area in table 13), intra-country linkages are shown and in the case that k ≠ l, import-export relationships are represented. Final demand is, in contrast to a national input-output framework, represented by a matrix rather than a vector with the dimension of n*g rows and g columns. The coefficient y_i^{kl} thus represents final demand which is produced in sector i of country k and consumed in country l. The case of a world input-output table (when all countries are included) has the advantage that, again, a closed system can be regarded in such a way that I do not need to account for further imports and exports than those represented in the transaction matrix ***Z***.

Table 13: World input-output table

		countries									final demand			output
		1			...			g						
		sectors			sectors			sectors			countries			
		1	...	n	1	...	n	1	...	n	1	...	g	
country 1	sector 1	z_{11}^{11}	...	z_{1n}^{11}		...		z_{11}^{1g}	...	z_{1n}^{1g}	y_1^{11}	...	y_1^{1g}	x_1^1
	⋮	⋮	⋱	⋮				⋮	⋱	⋮	⋮	⋱	⋮	⋮
	n	z_{n1}^{11}	...	z_{nn}^{11}				z_{n1}^{1g}	...	z_{nn}^{1g}	y_n^{11}	...	y_n^{1g}	x_n^1
⋮	sector 1													
	⋮		⋮			⋱			⋮		⋮	⋱	⋮	⋮
	n													
g	sector 1	z_{11}^{g1}	...	z_{1n}^{g1}				z_{11}^{gg}	...	z_{1n}^{gg}	y_1^{g1}	...	y_1^{gg}	x_1^g
	⋮	⋮	⋱	⋮		...		⋮	⋱	⋮	⋮	⋱	⋮	⋮
	n	z_{n1}^{g1}	...	z_{nn}^{g1}				z_{n1}^{gg}	...	z_{nn}^{gg}	y_n^{g1}	...	y_n^{gg}	x_n^g
value added		v_1^1	...	v_n^1		...		v_1^g	...	v_n^g				
total input		x_1^1	...	x_n^1		...		x_1^g	...	x_n^g				

Source: Own depiction

Similarly to the variant D of the national input-output framework, there is a problem with the interpretation of the matrix ***A***. Calculating the matrix ***A*** of the compounded transaction matrix ***Z*** could not be interpreted as a technological matrix as long as domestically produced products of type 1 can be substituted by products of the same type that are produced in another country. The framework in contrast treats the sectors from one country as different to the "same" sectors of another industry. Interpreting the matrix ***A*** as a technological matrix would thus only be plausible if all sectors would be non-competitive, which is very questionable in economic terms.105

A world input-output table allows to measure world linkages as well as domestic linkages. After calculating the Leontief inverse matrix (***B***), the domestic backward linkage (DBL) for industry j of country l would be calculated as follows:

For all k = l:
$$DBL_j^l = \sum_{i=1}^{n} b_{ij}^{kl} \qquad \text{Eq 21}$$

Accordingly, the world backward linkage (WBL) for industry j of country i is:

$$WBL_j^l = \sum_{i=1}^{n} \sum_{k=1}^{g} b_{ij}^{kl} \qquad \text{Eq 22}$$

After calculating the output inverse matrix (***D***) the domestic forward linkage (DFL) for industry i of country k is calculated:

For all l = l:
$$DFL_i^k = \sum_{j=1}^{n} d_{ij}^{kl} \qquad \text{Eq 23}$$

Accordingly, the world forward linkage (WFL) for industry i of country k is:

$$WFL_i^k = \sum_{j=1}^{n} \sum_{l=1}^{g} d_{ij}^{kl} \qquad \text{Eq 24}$$

4.3.1.7 Domestic vs. world linkages

Chenery & Watanabe (1958) use the latter version (variant A) for their analysis in their pioneering work, which is straightforward since they focus on the nature of interdependence of production between economic sec-

105 The interpretation of ***A*** as a technological matrix is not necessary since I am not interested in impact analysis but solely in the sum linkages of industries. The use of the matrix ***A*** for the calculation of the Leontief inverse matrix is only necessary to include direct and indirect linkages.

tors. Assuming that technology is identical across countries, the measure of linkages should lead to the same results in each country if the technological matrix (domestic plus imported) is used. If variant D—and thus only domestic flows—are used, the linkages would differ depending on the level of imports in this economy. To identify special characteristics of the manufacturing sector, it is therefore reasonable to use world linkages.

In contrast, Jones (1976: 330) and Bulmer-Thomas (1978) criticize the use of variant A since no differentiation between domestic and foreign inputs is made. Similarly, no reference to export possibilities is provided. However, since the Hirschmanian idea of calculating linkages was to identify potential linkages, the potential import-substituting investments should also be included (McGilvray 1978: 55). Several authors thus use variant A with the reference to potential import substitution (e.g., Lenzen 2003: 6).

It is difficult to answer a priori to which extent domestic investments can substitute foreign linkages and, thus, can incorporate them into the domestic economy as a valid reply depends on several factors:

First of all, it is unsure whether the economy is able to produce the same products. Resource endowments or climatic preconditions may be one reason for the inability to produce the imported products within the economy, another is the technological ability. Linkages to foreign resource sectors, which are not available in the home country, are thus irrelevant for the identification of key sectors. Furthermore, as Jones (1976: 330) stresses, linkages may exist to foreign sectors since the domestic sectors do not exhibit the technological ability to produce the commodities. While resource endowments are difficult to change, technological knowledge, education, etc. is a factor which is changeable, and more importantly, desirable to develop.106 In the literature on global value chains (GVCs), upgrading the GVC and thus substituting foreign by domestic value added is seen as a key for economic development. Morris et al. (2012) discuss sev-

106 While most proponents of the neoclassical school argue that economies need to acquire the respective technological knowledge and accumulate enough physical and human capital before they can enter the more advanced industry, it may be argued that technological capabilities are acquired in concrete production experiences. The arguments are elaborated by Ha-Joon Chang in the discussion of whether industrial policy should conform or defy comparative advantages (Lin & Chang 2009: 490 ff.). In line with the experience of the East Asian NICs, industrial policy can be seen as a matter of managing technological change (e.g., Pack & Westphal 1986; Wade 1990; Aoki et al. 1997).

eral African case studies and show how and under which circumstances "one thing may lead to another".

Another important factor is the degree of policy space for import substitution and industrial policy in the light of the current global policy environment. Rodrik (2004: 32 ff.) gives a good overview of this discussion and criticizes "that the pendulum between policy autonomy and international rules may have swung too far in the direction of the latter in recent trade rounds" (Rodrik 2004: 35) but also concludes that "there is plenty of scope for industrial policies in the present international economic environment" (Rodrik 2004: 38).

The relationship between domestic and world linkages is discussed in detail in the next chapter. In this chapter the focus is on the specific characteristics of manufacturing in contrast to other economic sectors. Hence, I concentrate on world linkages.

4.3.2 The data

In recent years, there has been a renewed interest in the analysis of input-output tables which was also driven by environmental concern.[107] Besides, the increasing fragmentation of production has generated a new interest in the measurement of trade in value added, which also depends on the provision of reliable input-output tables. Conclusively, there are several attempts to provide multiregional input-output tables. While Tukker & Dietzenbacher (2013) give an overview of the existing MRIO database, Inomata & Owen (2014) provide a comparative evaluation of these databases.

The most extensive database is the Eora MRIO Database which includes 187 countries with up to 600 sectors on a yearly base from 1990 to 2011. The Eora MRIO Database comprises 74 input-output tables from different countries and also three African economies (Kenya, Mauritius, and South Africa) (Lenzen et al. 2013: 48–49). Countries for which no input-output tables are available, a proxy input-output table with a template

107 World input-output tables make it possible to trace emissions from the producer to the consumer. In the light of an emerging consensus that consumers should pay (be responsible) for the emissions during the production process, this is an important tool even for the international climate policy negotiations.

input-output structure based on an average of the Australia, Japan, and United States tables is used (Lenzen et al. 2012: 8375).

The GTAP 8 Database, in contrast, comprises input-output tables of 129 regions and 57 sectors and is thus (except for the Eora MRIO Database which predominantly uses proxies) the most extensive source for input-output tables especially for Africa economies. The GTAP further provides a freely available GTAP Africa Database, including 42 regions (32 African regions plus 10 other aggregated regions) and the 57 sectors of the GTAP 8 Database. In contrast to Eora MRIO, the GTAP 8 Database relies on only two years, 2004 and 2007.

Table 14: Datasets for international input-output tables

database	origin and access	coverage
World Input-Output Database (WIOD)	European Commission www.wiod.org	1995-2011 23 EU + 13 other 35 industries
Global Trade Analysis Project (GTAP) Database	Situated at the Center for Global Trade Analysis (Purdue University) www.gtap.agecon.purdue.edu/	2004 and 2007 129 regions 57 sectors
The Trade in Value Added (TiVA) Database	Joint OECD and WTO initiative stats.oecd.org/Index.aspx?DataSetCode=TIVA_OECD_WTO	1995, 2000, 2005, 2008, 2009 57 countries 18 industrial sectors
Eora MRIO Database	funded by the Australian Research Council http://worldmrio.com/	1990-2011 187 countries 25-600 sectors
IDE JETRO Asian Input-Output Tables	Institute of Developing Economies, Japan External Trade Organization (IDE-JETRO) http://www.ide.go.jp/English/Data/Io/index.html	1970, 1975, 1985, 1990, 1995, 2000, 2005 8 Asian countries 76 sectors

Source: Own depiction following Tukker & Dietzenbacher (2013)

Although the GTAP provides a computable general equilibrium model, which in its standard form assumes perfect competition and constant returns to scale, it does not provide a multi-regional input-output table (unless the data is at hand). Based on the work of Peters et al. (2011), it was thus necessary to convert the GTAP Africa Database into a multiregional input-output table. To allocate the transport margins to the transport users, I construct the version with endogenous international transportation pool.

4.3.3 Results

Using the constructed MRIO from the GTAP Africa Database, I calculate the domestic and world backward and forward linkages for 42 regions and 57 sectors. The results are presented in three steps. To give an overall impression and to place the Africa region in a global context, I first present aggregated data for only four sectors in the major regions in the world (chapter 4.3.3.1). In a second step, I provide detailed sectoral data for the African region and compare it with the average linkages in the world (chapter 4.3.3.2). Finally, I present data for four major economic sectors for the single African economies included in the dataset (chapter 4.3.3.3).

4.3.3.1 Comparing world regions

To get a first impression on some general features of linkages, I construct the MRIOT with only four sectors[108] and ten regions.[109] The results for all four types of linkages are shown in figure 23.

Overall, the structure of linkages is similar between regions. Manufacturing and utilities reveal considerable stronger backward linkages than primary industries and services. Manufacturing exhibits the strongest backward linkages in nearly all regions. Concerning the forward linkage, figure 23 shows that agriculture, followed by manufacturing, exhibits considerable stronger linkages than utilities and services. This is true for almost all regions and all four linkages.

The service sector in general has very weak forward and backward linkages. While the primary sectors show world forward linkages above three, the service sector only slightly exceeds the value of two in some world linkages.

108 These four sectors are "primary sectors" comprising the sectors 1-18 of the GTAP sector classification, "manufacturing" comprising the sectors 19-42, "utilities" with the sectors 43-46, and "services" comprising sectors 47-57. For concordances between the GTAP sector classification and other sector classifications such as CPC and ISIC see https://www.gtap.agecon.purdue.edu/databases/contribute/concord.asp (last access: June 16, 2015).

109 The regions are Oceania, East Asia, South-East Asia, South Asia, North America, Latin America, the European Union (EU), Middle East and North Africa (MENA), sub-Saharan Africa, and the rest of the world (ROW). A detailed list of which economies are included in these regions can be found in Narayanan et al. (2012).

Figure 23: World and domestic, forward and backward linkages in aggregate regions and four economic sectors

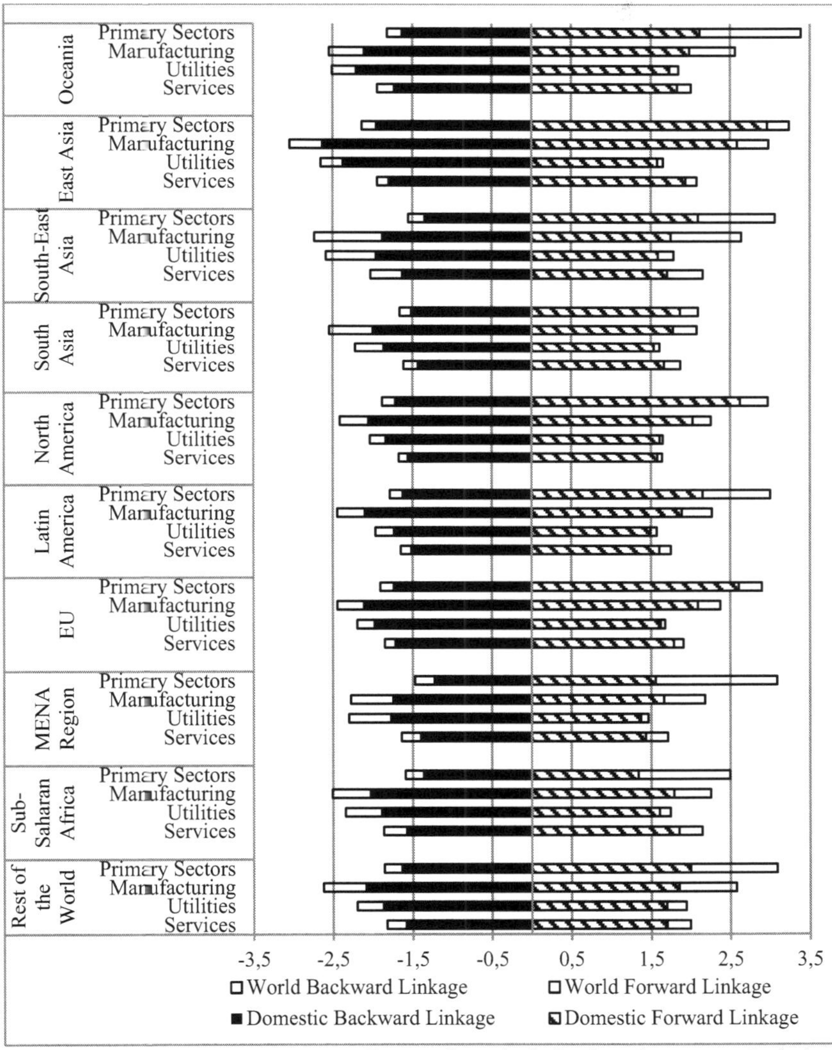

Source: Own depiction based on own calculations

Nonetheless, differences between regions are undeniable: Very strong linkages are evident in East Asia, concerning both the strongest backward linkages in the manufacturing sector and the forward linkage in services and manufacturing. The weakest linkages show up in the MENA region with the exception of strong world forward linkages in the primary sectors.[110] Another remarkable feature is the exceptional weak domestic forward linkage of the primary sectors in sub-Saharan Africa. African linkages are discussed in more detail later.

The differences between regions do not suggest any general relationship between the level of economic development (respectively industrialization or productivity) and the size of linkages as proposed by Deutsch & Syrquin (1989). On the contrary, the world linkage for, e.g., manufacturing (which is their object of investigation) is very similar between regions with substantial differences.

The world linkage is by construction always stronger than the domestic linkage. As explained in the methodological chapter, it is arguable to interpret the world linkage as the (technologically given) potential linkage. The comparison between domestic and world linkages reveals that some regions are able to integrate more of the potential linkages into their domestic economy. The relative difference between domestic and world linkage may be interpreted as the degree of integration into the global economy or the participation in GVCs. The issue is discussed in detail in section 5.3.

4.3.3.2 Detailed sectoral analysis

After the first impression on the altitudes of linkages and their differentials between the major world regions, I inspect the 57 sector classification which is provided by the GTAP Africa Database. The GTAP Africa Database includes 18 primary sectors and 24 manufacturing sectors. It further distinguishes between 11 service sectors and comprises the utility sectors: electricity, gas, water as well as construction.

Figure 24 depicts linkages of the average world[111] in comparison with Africa. Since the size of a region determines the size of the domestic linkage to a large extent, I only use the world linkage for this comparison. Figure 24 demonstrates that the average linkages in the world regions are not substantially different from those in Africa. Nonetheless, especially in

---

110 The strong world forward linkages in the MENA region result from the high share of the oil sector which shows considerable strong world forward linkages of about 4.3.

111 I use the average of nine world regions included in the Africa database: Oceania, East Asia, South Asia, North America, Latin America, EU27, Rest of Europe and the Middle East. I exclude Africa for reasons of comparison.

the primary sectors, some deviations occurred. The largest deviations in the backward linkages can be found in the mineral sectors: coal, gas, and oil, which are 25 to 30 percent stronger than in the world average. The deviations in the forward linkages are also present in the primary sector, including cereals, forestry, oil seed, and animals.

These forward linkages are 35 to 60 percent weaker than in the world average. It is noteworthy that the world backward linkages are very similar in all other sectors and generally do not exceed 10 percent.

The analysis reveals that the primary sectors are very different concerning the size of their linkages. While agricultural, fishing, or animals show low forward linkages, the mineral sectors (coal, oil, gas, and minerals not elsewhere classified (nec.)) exhibit extraordinary strong forward linkages. Indeed, minerals are the sectors with the strongest forward linkages. The backward linkages are comparably weak and only in some cases exceed the value of two.

In contrast, no manufacturing sector reveals a backward linkage below two. While the backward linkages are very similar between manufacturing sectors, there are considerable differences concerning the forward linkage. The first group shows only weak forward linkages which are below the value of two. The second group, which includes metals, chemical, rubber and plastic products, petroleum but also paper products, exhibits considerable strong forward linkages.

Interestingly, the second group is nearly exactly the group of intermediary manufactures with strong backward and forward linkages that Hirschman (1958: 106) had identified on the basis of the analysis of Chenery & Watanabe (1958).

The utilities are very diverse: Electricity and construction exceed the value of two in the backward linkage, but construction shows very weak forward linkages. In contrast, electricity and gas as well as manufacture distribution present considerably strong forward linkages.

The same is true for most service sectors, apart from recreation, dwellings, and the public sector, which generally show very weak linkages. However, only the transport sectors, especially sea and air transport, also show strong backward linkages. The typical business services—communication, financial services, and insurance—have all linkages below the value of two.

Figure 24: World backward and forward linkages, world average (left) and Africa average (right)

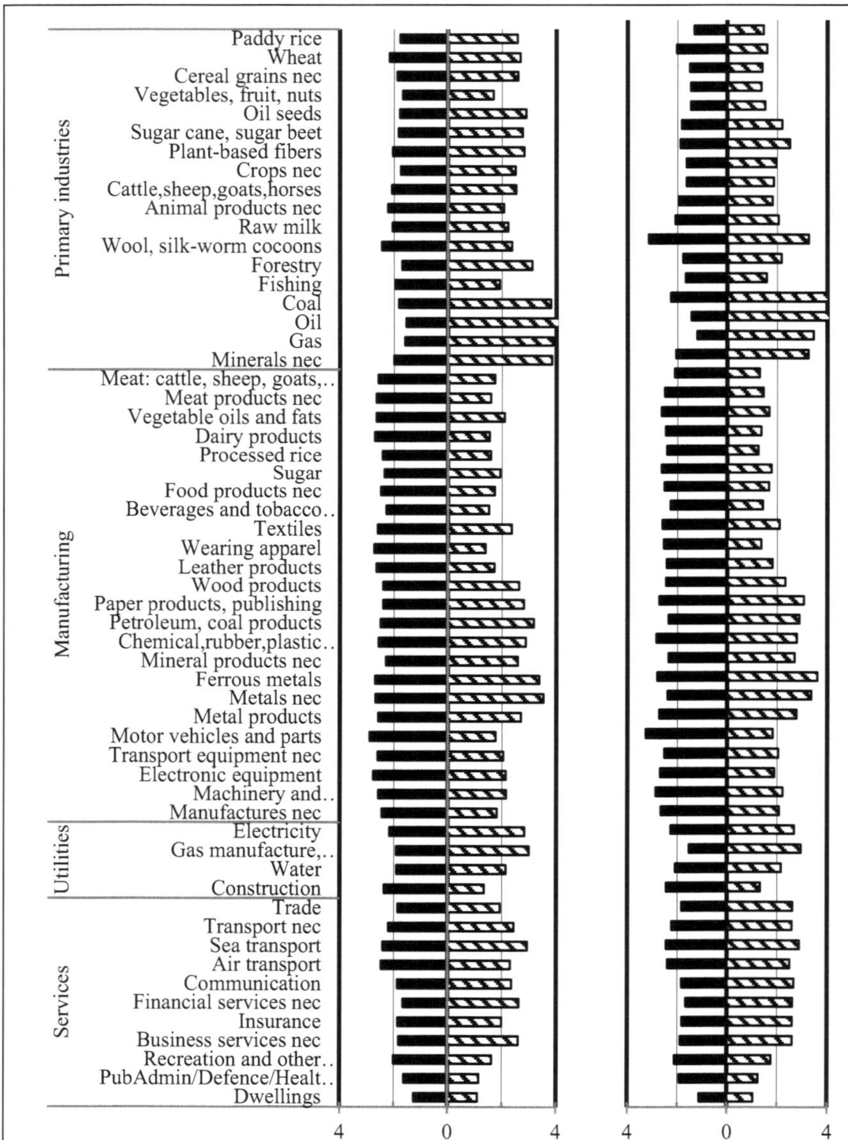

Source: Own figure, bars to the left show backward and bars to the right show forward linkages; world averages are calculated out of nine world regions except Africa; Africa is the average of 32 African economies

4.3.3.3 Linkages in single African economies

Up to this point, I have analyzed the African region as a whole and found that the linkages do not distinguish themselves substantially from other world regions. In the next step, I further investigate to which extend African economies differ from each other. Thus, I construct an aggregated multiregional input-output table for 33 regions, including 32 African regions, and the rest of the world comprising all other regions which are outside of Africa. For reasons of simplicity, the sectors are, again, aggregated into four sectors. Table 15 and table 16 show the backward and forward linkages in African regions that are calculated from this input-output table. I again distinguish domestic from world linkages. Since the only foreign countries of the "world" are the African economies, the domestic linkages of the rest of the world cannot be compared with the national economies, and I thus present only the world linkages for this region.

However, it is useful to compare the domestic and world linkages between the African economies. Indeed, there are some economies in which considerable differences between world and domestic linkages, especially in manufacturing, appear. Examples are Togo, Egypt, Tunisia, Senegal but also Mauritius, Benin, Zimbabwe, and Botswana. The interpretation of these results and more detailed data analysis are subject to chapter 5.3. In the following, I concentrate on the analysis of world linkages.

As to backward linkages, the same pattern emerges as in the world average. Either manufacturing or, in some cases, utilities reveal the strongest linkages. The weakest linkages are found either in agriculture or in services. Nonetheless, there are some significant deviations between these economies. Rather strong linkages are present in South Africa , Malawi , or Togo. In contrast, there are some countries which show considerable weak linkages in all four sectors. The most obvious case for weak linkages is Nigeria, followed by Burkina Faso and Botswana. While Nigeria and Burkina Faso exhibit rather weak linkages in nearly all sectors , Botswana's weak linkages mainly result from minerals nec., vegetable oils and fats, petroleum and coal products as well as ferrous metals and metals nec.

Other peculiarities emerging from the detailed sectoral analysis of African economies are the extraordinary weak linkages in several manufactures but also the strong linkages in several agricultural sectors in Mauritius. Even stronger linkages in the agricultural sector appear in Namibia and Zimbabwe, reaching the by far strongest linkage with a value of eight in the wool and silk worm cocoons sector, a sector that shows mostly strong backward linkages in nearly all African economies.

Table 15: World and domestic backward linkages for four aggregated sectors in African economies

		Domestic linkages				World linkages			
		PRI	MAN	UTI	SER	PRI	MAN	UTI	SER
	World					1.8	2.6	2.2	1.8
North Africa	Egypt	1.2	1.6	1.7	1.4	1.4	2.5	2.3	1.9
	Morocco	1.6	2.0	1.8	1.8	1.8	2.7	2.3	2.2
	Tunisia	1.5	1.7	1.6	1.3	1.8	2.7	2.4	1.7
Western Africa	Benin	1.2	1.5	1.7	1.2	1.4	2.2	2.8	1.8
	Burkina Faso	1.2	1.5	1.5	1.3	1.3	1.9	2.0	1.5
	Cameroon	1.5	2.1	2.0	1.6	1.7	2.4	2.3	1.8
	Cote d'Ivoire	1.6	1.9	1.9	1.4	1.8	2.4	2.4	1.6
	Ghana	1.4	1.6	1.2	1.5	1.6	2.2	1.7	1.8
	Guinea	1.2	1.7	1.2	1.2	1.8	2.0	1.7	1.4
	Nigeria	1.1	1.5	1.3	1.3	1.2	1.8	1.7	1.7
	Senegal	1.1	1.4	1.4	1.3	1.3	2.2	2.1	1.6
	Togo	1.3	1.5	1.4	1.2	1.8	2.8	2.9	2.2
East Africa	Ethiopia	1.2	2.0	1.8	1.4	1.3	2.5	2.4	1.8
	Kenya	1.5	1.8	1.5	1.6	2.0	2.4	2.2	2.1
	Madagascar	1.4	2.0	2.2	1.4	1.6	2.6	3.0	1.8
	Malawi	1.6	2.0	2.0	1.7	1.9	2.7	2.9	2.3
	Mauritius	1.2	1.4	1.4	1.3	1.7	2.2	2.2	1.7
	Mozambique	1.3	1.7	1.2	1.3	1.7	2.5	1.7	2.0
	Rwanda	1.2	1.9	1.6	1.3	1.4	2.2	1.9	1.6
	Tanzania	1.2	1.7	1.5	1.4	1.3	2.1	1.9	1.7
	Uganda	1.2	1.8	1.3	1.4	1.4	2.3	1.8	1.6
	Zambia	1.7	2.2	1.6	1.5	2.1	2.9	2.2	1.9
	Zimbabwe	1.5	1.7	1.5	1.4	2.5	2.6	2.1	2.1
Southern Africa	Botswana	1.1	1.4	1.6	1.3	1.3	1.9	2.3	1.6
	Namibia	1.4	1.9	1.5	1.5	1.9	2.6	2.4	1.9
	South Africa	2.0	2.2	2.3	1.7	2.3	2.8	2.8	2.0

Source: Own calculations; PRI: primary sectors, MAN: manufacturing sectors, UTI: utilities, SER: services, see also footnote 108; world comprises the simple average of all regions except Africa.

The most obvious result, however, is that several African economies show considerably strong backward linkages, especially in the coal sector but also in the other mineral sectors gas, oil, and minerals nec. The most obvious cases are Togo, Guinea, Ghana, Cameroon but also Madagascar, Zambia, Malawi, Ethiopia, and Kenya.

Regarding the forward linkage, the results show that even though most African economies show weaker linkages in the primary sector than the world average, this is still the sector with the strongest linkages for most of the African economies.

Table 16: World and domestic forward linkages for four aggregates sectors in African economies

		Domestic linkages				World linkages			
		PRI	MAN	UTI	SER	PRI	MAN	UTI	SER
	World					3.0	2.5	1.7	1.8
North Africa	Egypt	1.9	1.5	1.3	1.2	2.4	1.9	1.4	1.5
	Morocco	1.8	1.9	1.4	1.9	2.2	2.3	1.4	2.1
	Tunisia	1.9	1.4	1.4	1.5	2.6	2.1	1.5	1.9
Western Africa	Benin	1.7	1.4	1.2	1.3	2.0	1.6	1.2	1.4
	Burkina Faso	1.3	1.4	1.3	1.3	2.2	1.5	1.3	1.4
	Cameroon	1.6	1.8	1.5	1.8	2.3	2.1	1.6	2.2
	Cote d'Ivoire	1.5	1.5	1.6	1.9	2.1	2.1	1.8	2.3
	Ghana	1.3	1.3	1.2	1.8	1.6	1.9	1.3	2.1
	Guinea	1.1	1.1	1.2	1.9	2.2	1.6	1.4	2.4
	Nigeria	1.1	1.2	1.3	1.4	2.2	1.3	1.4	1.6
	Senegal	1.3	1.2	1.2	1.4	1.6	1.6	1.2	1.6
	Togo	1.3	1.2	1.2	1.5	2.0	1.7	1.2	1.9
East Africa	Ethiopia	1.3	1.4	1.3	1.8	1.5	1.5	1.3	2.1
	Kenya	1.2	2.0	1.6	1.5	1.5	2.3	1.7	1.7
	Madagascar	1.6	1.9	1.2	1.9	2.2	2.2	1.3	2.2
	Malawi	1.3	1.6	2.4	2.0	2.2	2.0	2.8	2.3
	Mauritius	1.5	1.3	1.3	1.3	2.9	2.0	1.4	1.9
	Mozambique	1.1	1.2	1.5	1.6	1.9	2.6	2.7	2.2
	Rwanda	1.2	1.3	1.3	1.7	1.9	1.5	1.4	1.9
	Tanzania	1.4	1.2	1.4	1.6	1.9	1.8	1.5	2.0
	Uganda	1.3	1.5	1.2	1.5	2.3	1.8	1.3	1.6
	Zambia	1.7	1.4	1.5	2.3	2.4	2.5	1.7	2.9
	Zimbabwe	1.8	1.4	1.8	1.6	3.1	2.6	2.3	2.1
Southern Africa	Botswana	1.2	1.3	1.4	1.4	3.2	2.2	1.5	1.6
	Namibia	1.7	1.3	1.4	1.8	3.0	2.1	1.5	2.1
	South Africa	1.8	1.9	1.8	2.1	2.8	2.5	2.0	2.4

Source: Own calculations; PRI: primary sectors, MAN: manufacturing sectors, UIT: utilities, SER: services, see also footnote 108; world comprises the simple average of all regions except Africa.

As it has been shown in the detailed sectoral analysis, the strongest forward linkages result from the mineral sectors and not from agricultural products, which is also true for nearly all African economies. However, the strong forward linkages are only the case for the world linkages since the large difference between domestic and world linkage in the primary sectors is apparent in most African economies. Explicit cases are Botswana, Guinea, Nigeria, and Mauritius, but nearly all other African economies show similar patterns. African economies are not able to use the strong forward linkages to increase domestic value added.

The results support the findings of the Making the Most of Commodities Programme. The program questions the conventional wisdom of the resource curse and identifies the size, nature, and development of the downstream and upstream linkages in the mineral sector with the help of case studies. My results confirm that in most African economies, the production linkage provides a huge potential for "climbing up the value chain"; they explain how "one thing might lead to another" (Morris et al. 2012).

The results look rather different when analyzing the services sector. Several African economies show by far stronger linkages in the services sector than the world average. Additionally, a much higher fraction of these linkages are pursued in the domestic economy. As mentioned above, the differences between domestic and world linkages are discussed in detail in chapter 5.3.

The economy with the strongest linkages in services is Zambia, followed by South Africa and Guinea. Aside from trade and transport, business services—communication, financial services, and insurance—show comparably strong forward linkages. The forward linkages of recreation, public services as well as dwelling, in contrast, are negligible.

4.3.4 Interim conclusion

The results of input-output tables indicate that the manufacturing sectors show the strongest backward linkages, followed by utilities, services, and the primary sector. According to the data used in this chapter, the manufacturing sector in sub-Saharan Africa exhibits backward linkages with a value of 2.5, whereas those of services take the value of 1.8 and of primary sectors only 1.6. Primary sectors, in contrast, show the strongest forward linkages with a value of 2.5, followed by manufacturing (2.3) and services (2.1). These linkages are similar to other regions in the world.

A detailed sectoral analysis reveals that in primary sectors, it is not agriculture but only the mineral sectors showing the strongest forward linkages. Sectors that can be qualified as lead sectors in the sense of having both strong backward and forward linkages are found in the intermediary manufactures, such as metals, chemical, paper, or coal industries, as already suggested by Chenery & Watanabe (1958: 493).

If one acknowledges the superior importance of demand rather than supply, therefore emphasizes the role of the backward linkage, I can confirm the hypothesis that the manufacturing sectors show stronger linkages than all the other sectors. Despite substantial differences in the values of these linkages between countries, this is true for nearly all African economies.

African linkages in general conform to the values found in other regions of the world. However, this is only true for the world linkages and not for the linkages which relate to domestic value added. African economies face huge gaps between the domestic and the world linkage, especially in the mineral sectors. The opposite is the case in service sectors. Whether or not a relatively high share of domestic value added in the value chain is a good sign, is discussed in the next chapter.

5 Africa – the limbo of the international system?

As described in chapter 2.5, the intellectual thinking during the first post-colonial era until 1980 was dominated by structuralism, dependency, and world system theory. While the primary object of most modern economic theories is the nation state and its economic policy, the world system theory rejects the idea of the sovereign state as entity of analysis (especially in the case of Africa) and explains changes as a consequence of evolution and interaction within the world system (Wallerstein 1974: 7). In this context, Africa is often deemed to be in isolation or thought of as an enclave and is thus supposed to be the limbo of the international system (Bayart & Ellis 2000). However, the prescribed economic policy originating from these trade theories is not to integrate the African economies into the global system but to isolate them from international trade by import substitution policies.

In consequence of the economic crisis at the end of the 1970s and the increasing influence of the Washington Consensus (see chapter 2.6), the succeeding generations of economists and policy makers have advocated import-liberalization and export-promotion as the preferred trade strategy. The strategy is based on three major arguments.

Firstly, the main argument for strengthening free trade is the concept of comparative advantages, which is supposed to be one of the crown jewels of the economic profession (Rodrik 1998: 3). While the theory has been heavily criticized for its oversimplifying assumptions, its proponents love it for its clarity; it reduces the complexity of real world problems and helps to explain the advantages of free trade even to non-economists. However, policy conclusions stemming from this theory should be valued cautiously. The concept suggests in most cases that it would be advantageous for latecomer economies to specialize on primary products. The presumed gains of national specialization (according to factor endowments) are not the only argument in favor of free trade.

The second major argument promoting free trade is put forward by Alexander Gerschenkron (1966). In his book "*Economic backwardness in historical perspective*", he emphasizes the role of technology and innovation for economic development in latecomer economies. His theory implies that developing economies can benefit from adopting technological innovation from more developed economies and are thus able—due to their "advantage of backwardness"—to grow faster and catch up to already developed countries (Gerschenkron 1966: 8). This process is dependent on the import of foreign machinery and know-how, and therefore the conditions vary from industry to industry (Gerschenkron 1966: 9). A customary method to account for this catch-up growth is applied in chapter 4.2.4. The gap between an industry's productivity and that of the technological frontier is used as a dependent variable to explain productivity growth. However, catch-up growth is not an automatic mechanism. The failure of early industrialization efforts in sub-Saharan Africa in contrast to the success in East Asia is often attributed to the neglect of technology and knowledge transfer via international trade.112 The exploitation of those advantages depends heavily on the capabilities of the latecomer economies to absorb the necessary technologies.113

Thirdly, as discussed in chapter 4.2, not all industries are characterized by constant returns to scale. It is apparent that opening the economy provides the opportunity to exploit the advantages of increasing returns to scale. In line with the new trade theory as mainly established by Paul Krugman (Helpman & Krugman 2002; Krugman 1985, 1979), increasing returns are a fundamental cause of international trade and serve as a major argument for the export-oriented growth model.114 While in principal all economic sectors can benefit from knowledge and technology transfer, the actual profit from increasing returns depends on the possibility to trade the specific products. Therefore, the basic distinction between tradable and non-tradable goods is an important element of international economics.

The export-oriented industrialization, fostering knowledge and technology transfer and allowing the exploitation of increasing returns to scale

112 The discussion is mostly held under the notion of import substitution versus export promotion; see Krueger (1985) for the neoclassical view.

113 This is a widely discussed issue in international economics but is not the focus of this thesis. A study focusing on Southern African enterprises is provided by Goldberg & Kuriakose (2011).

114 The Ricardian as well as the Heckscher-Ohlin model are based on the assumption of constant returns to scale. Ignoring this assumption, the concept of comparative advantages becomes very vague. Comparative advantages depend not only on factor endowments but also on the amounts produced. In sectors with increasing returns to scale, an economy could simply increase its output and would in this way get a comparative advantage in this sector. The starting point of the new trade theory was a model developed by Paul Krugman (1979). In this model, trade is not driven by comparative advantages but by increasing returns to scale which are internal to the firms.

while using the cost advantage of low wages, became virtually synonymous with economic development policy for a number of nations, especially Asia.

Simultaneously to the rise of the Post Washington Consensus Consensus, there is an acute awareness about the fact that the gains of globalization are not always evenly distributed between nations. Several authors point to the trend of increasing vertical disintegration in the global production structure which results in rising intra-industry trade rather than inter-industry trade (Sturgeon & Memedovic). Subsequently, a number of scientists argue that the involvement of low development countries in intra-industry trade provides the basis for economic peril (Kaplinsky 1998, p. 4).

According to the literature, an increasing amount of trade is not solely organized on market relations. In contrast, trade takes place within a framework of global buyers and is governed by a few companies. These so-called lead firms and in particular their headquarters are mostly located in developed nations and include either multinational manufactures or large retailer and brand-name firms (Gereffi et al. 2001: 1). The research concerning these issues circulates nowadays under the notion of global value chains (GVCs) and follows in a certain way the footsteps of dependency theorists. Applying the concept of economic rents, the distribution of margins between producers is found to be strongly influenced by power relationships. Gereffi (1994) showed that the markets for commodities produced in developing countries exhibit an increasing concentration of global retailers and he thus emphasized the role of governance in GVCs.

The view that the proliferation of GVCs is a defining feature of trade in the new century is also shared by large international organizations (OECD et al. 2013; OECD 2014). While the original literature is based on case-studies, international organizations endeavor to collect comparable data on integration into and participation in GVCs. The OECD and the WTO have recently published a new dataset on trade in value added (TiVA). Additionally, the Eora MRIO Database provides the necessary input-output tables for developing economies. The limitation of these data sources has already been discussed in chapter 4.3.2. This chapter also applies the multiregional input-output table calculated from the GTAP Africa Database to assess Africa's position in the international economic system.

The chapter is structured as follows: Section 5.1 introduces the concept of trade in value added to re-evaluate the conventional trade statistics and questions the differentiation of tradable and non-tradable goods. Section 5.2 uses the new TiVA data to calculate the revealed comparative advantage for African economies and gives an overview of economic sectors showing an export surplus or deficit. Section 5.3 provides a short overview of the theory of GVCs and measures African economies' participation in GVCs.

5.1 Measuring trade in value added

The basic distinction between tradable and non-tradable goods is an important element of international economics. The issue is of special relevance since increasing returns to scale (see chapter 4.2) can only unfold its strengths if the demand for the goods produced is large enough. Conclusively, the exploitation of increasing returns depends on the tradability of the respective goods or services.

In conventional sector classifications, primary products as well as manufacturing goods are characterized as tradable goods, whereas utilities and the service sectors are regarded as non-tradable (Goldstein & Officer 1979: 426).[115] Even though several service industries show up in the conventional trade statistics, the statistics still support the view of international trade dominated by manufacturing goods.

The increasing importance of GVCs as well as rises in intra-industry trade and in the fragmentation of production challenged the conventional use of trade statistics. In conventional trade statistics, intermediate goods are counted at their full value each time they cross a border. Employing the added value embedded in the traded good instead of the gross flows may change the observed patterns of trade. In the next paragraphs, this difference is explained by using a fictitious example. The applied approach is in line with the TiVA data published by the OECD and the corresponding literature (Koopman et al. 2010; Koopman et al. 2012, 2014; Maurer & Degain 2010; Hummels et al. 2001).

Given a country 1, the industry A produces intermediary goods for industry B worth 150€. Industry B of country 1 adds 50€ in value and exports the good to country 2. In country 2, the imported goods are further processed in industry B before exported to country 3. Industry C of country 3 adds a value of 50€ before the good is consumed in country 3. The described value chain is depicted in figure 25.

---

115 An overview of differing results in the definition of the tradable and non-tradable sector can be found in Knight & Johnson (1997).

Figure 25: Trade in value added – example

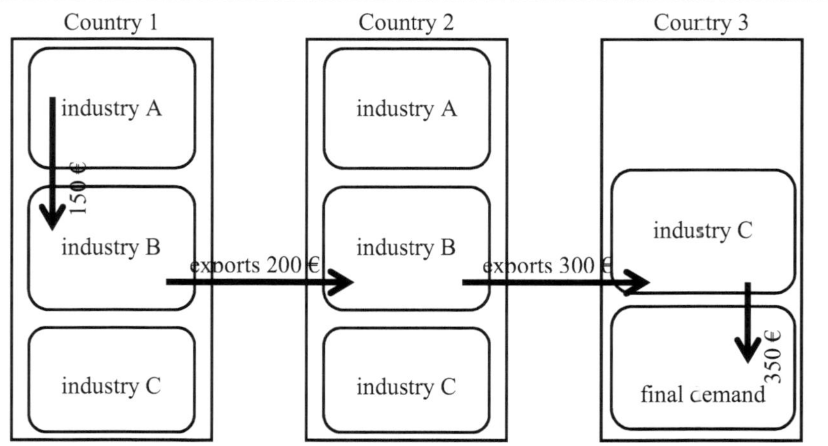

Source: Own depiction

As depicted in figure 25, measuring gross trade would show that country 1 exports goods of industry B with a value of 200€ to country 2 and that country 2 exports goods worth 300€ from industry B to country 3. However, no trade flow is measured between country 1 and 3.

Measuring trade in value added leads to a completely different picture: Country 1 does not export any value to country 2 but a value of 200€ to country 3, whereas country 2 exports a value of only 100€ to country 3. Even though the production of all traded goods is completed in industry B, only 150€ of the overall traded value are actually generated in industry B, whereas another 150€ are contributed by industry A. As it can be seen in this example, parts of the value of imports may originate from third countries or might even be re-imports from the domestic economy. Furthermore, most imports are intermediary goods and may thus contain value added from different sectors.

5.1.1 Methodology

The disentanglement of the embodied values of exports and the differentiation between domestic and foreign value added require a full set of intercountry input-output tables in which all bilateral trade flows are accounted for on a highly disaggregated sectoral level. In other words A world input-output table[116] like the one exemplary depicted in table 17 is required.

Table 17: World input-output table – example

		country 1			country 2			country 3			final demand			exports	output
		A	B	C	A	B	C	A	B	C	1	2	3		
country 1	A	0	150	0	0	0	0	0	0	0	0	0	0	0	150
	B	0	0	0	0	200	0	0	0	0	0	0	0	200	200
	C	0	0	0	0	0	0	0	0	0	1	0	0	0	1
country 2	A	0	0	0	0	0	0	0	0	0	0	1	0	0	1
	B	0	0	0	0	0	0	0	0	300	0	0	0	300	300
	C	0	0	0	0	0	0	0	0	0	0	1	0	0	1
country 3	A	0	0	0	0	0	0	0	0	0	0	0	1	0	1
	B	0	0	0	0	0	0	0	0	0	0	0	1	0	1
	C	0	0	0	0	0	0	0	0	0	0	0	350	0	350
value added		150	50	1	1	100	1	1	1	50					
share		1	0.3	1	1	0.3	1	1	1	0.1					
total input		150	200	1	1	300	1	1	1	350					

Source: Own depiction. The gray shaded areas symbolize areas which are usually shown in national input-output tables. The white cells show imports (columns) and exports (rows). The sums of the exports from a specific industry of a specific country (all white cells in a row) are displayed in the gross exports column.

The values in the input-output table represent the example which is depicted in figure 25.[117] The top left table shows the transaction-matrix (***Z***) which is the heart of the input-output table including the coefficients (z_{ij}^{kl}) that represent the sales from industry i in country k to industry j in country l. Conclusively, z_{ij}^{kl} represents sectoral exchanges within the country if k = l and international exchanges if k ≠ l. In the export column, one can see the export data which would show up in conventional trade statistics.

Similar to the calculation of the Leontief inverse matrix in conventional input-output analysis, the relationship between output and demand in the

116 Again the input-output model is based on the idea that the technical coefficients matrix at least remains stable.

117 I added a final demand of one in the sector home country in which sectors' final demand was zero. This was necessary because I would otherwise be unable to calculate the value added share matrix due to the fact that division by zero is impossible.

input-output framework with g countries and n sectors can be described by:

$$\boldsymbol{X} = \boldsymbol{A} * \boldsymbol{X} + \boldsymbol{Y} \qquad \text{Eq 1}$$

X: is a vector with n*g elements including x_i^k, which represents the gross-output produced by an industry i in country k

A: is a matrix with the dimension n*g x n*g of technical coefficients a_{ij}^{kl}, which represents the ratio of inputs in industry I in country k used in the output of industry j.

Y: is a matrix with the dimension n*g x g of y_i^{kl}, which represents the final goods produced in sector I of country k con sumed in country i

The Leontief inverse matrix (***B***) is calculated:

$$\boldsymbol{B} = (\boldsymbol{I} - \boldsymbol{A})^{-1} \qquad \text{Eq 2}$$

I further define a direct value added coefficient matrix *V* with the dimension n*g x n*g including v_i^k which is the share of value added on total input in industry i in country k, along the diagonal (table 18).118

Table 18: The value added coefficient matrix V – example

The *V* Matrix		country 1			country 2			country 3		
		A	B	C	A	B	C	A	B	C
country 1	A	1	0	0	0	0	0	0	0	0
	B	0	0.25	0	0	0	0	0	0	0
	C	0	0	1	0	0	0	0	0	0
country 2	A	0	0	0	1	0	0	0	0	0
	B	0	0	0	0	0.33	0	0	0	0
	C	0	0	0	0	0	1	0	0	0
country 3	A	0	0	0	0	0	0	1	0	0
	B	0	0	0	0	0	0	0	1	0
	C	0	0	0	0	0	0	0	0	0.13

Source: Own depiction

The multiplication of ***B*** with ***Y*** yields a g*n x g matrix which row sum equals ***X***. The multiplication of *V* with this matrix ***BY*** yields again a g*n x g matrix with the elements vx_i^{kl}. The gray shaded vectors in the diagonal

118 I added a final demand of one in the sector home country in which sectors' final demand was zero (see footnote 117). Accordingly, in these cases the shares equal 100 percent.

of this matrix represent the amount of each sectors' value added which is absorbed at home, whereas the exports of value added are represented in the white vectors on the left (table 19). The trade in value added can now be easily identified. Sector A in country 1 exports 150€ to country 3, sector B of country 1 exports 50€ of value added to country 3, and sector B of country 2 exports 100€ to country 3.

Table 19: The VX matrix – example

The VX Matrix		country 1	country 2	country 3
country 1	A	0	0	150
	B	0	0	50
	C	1	0	0
country 2	A	0	1	0
	B	0	0	100
	C	0	1	0
country 3	A	0	0	1
	B	0	0	1
	C	0	0	50

Source: Own depiction

One intuitively knows from the example that the trade in value added approach leads to a totally different insight into the trade pattern than one would have achieved using conventional trade statistics. The total value added exports of industry i in country k (vt_i^k) can be calculated as follows:

$$vt_i^k = \sum_{\substack{l=1 \\ l \neq k}}^{n} vx_i^{kl} \qquad \text{Eq 3}$$

Again, I used the assumption that the coefficients of the technological matrix $\boldsymbol{A}$ remain the same for the goods which are absorbed (consumed or used for further production) at home versus the goods which are absorbed abroad.119

119 One may allow different production coefficients for exports as done by Koopman et al. (2012), but the OECD & WTO (2012: 16) also points to the need of differentiating the type of companies; e.g., ownership, but especially between exporting and non-exporting companies. The theoretical idea is that companies which produce internationally may also use more advanced technology from abroad than non-exporting firms do.

5.1.2 Dataset

The OECD and WTO have recently published a new dataset on trade in value added.120 The data includes 61 economies but no other African economies besides South Africa. I use the constructed MRIO from chapter 4.3.2 for reasons justified in this chapter.

5.1.3 Results

The main finding of calculating TiVA data is an increasing importance of services in international trade. Figure 26 illustrates that in conventional trade statistics, manufacturing goods account for more than 60 percent of total gross trade. In contrast, manufacturing goods and services each account for 38 percent of value added trade. This is because manufacturing goods include value added from services as well as from primary sectors. African exports consist predominantly of primary products either measured in conventional trade statistics or in value added. The main difference concerning African exports is that the manufacturing share of exports amounts to more than 30 percent in conventional statistics, whereas it is only 18 percent of value added, even exceeded by exports in services value added with 26 percent (see figure 26). Table 20 depicts the gross exports and exports in value added for the major world regions and for single African economies. Indeed, service value added exports exceed manufacturing value added exports in nearly all African economies under examination. Table 21 and 22 shows gross exports and exports in value added for the world and for Africa as a region and 57 sectors. The results suggest that the main differences between gross exports and exports in value added—in the world as well as in Africa—are to be found in market services, such as communication, financial services, and business services.

120 The dataset is based on an OECD-WTO joint initiative "Measuring Trade in Value Added": http://www.oecd.org/sti/ind/measuringtradeinvalue-addedan-oecd-wtojointinitiative.htm (last access: October 6, 2016).

Figure 26: Normal trade and TiVA in comparison

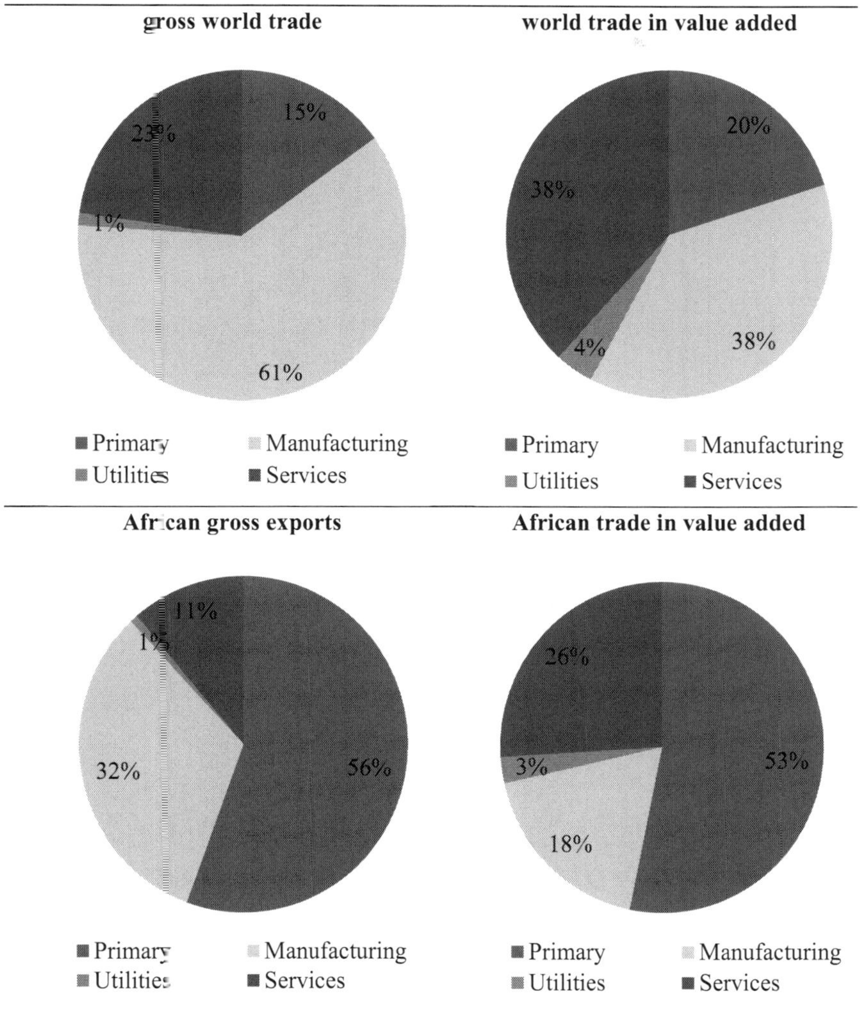

Source: Own calculation based on the GTAP Africa Database 2007[121]

121 The „normal trade" differs slightly from the results when the provided export data from the GTAP Africa Database is used. This is because the TiVA data does not account for intra-regional trade which is accounted for in the GTAP Africa Database. Subsequently, trade within this regions is not counted.

Table 20: Exports and value added exports in world regions and African economies

	exports				tiva exports			
	PRIM	MAN	UTI	SER	PRIM	MAN	UTI	SER
Oceania	31.1%	45.4%	0.4%	23.1%	38.0%	19.9%	4.5%	37.5%
EAsia	0.5%	82.1%	1.0%	16.3%	6.3%	52.4%	3.7%	37.6%
SEAsia	8.8%	69.6%	0.7%	20.9%	21.5%	42.8%	3.1%	32.6%
SouthAsia	6.8%	60.3%	0.4%	32.6%	14.6%	30.9%	4.9%	49.7%
NorthAmerica	6.3%	62.4%	0.8%	30.5%	8.6%	40.0%	3.9%	47.4%
LatinAmerica	30.9%	49.7%	0.4%	19.0%	35.3%	27.0%	3.7%	34.0%
EU27	1.9%	65.7%	1.5%	31.0%	3.5%	47.3%	3.9%	45.3%
RestEurope	24.3%	50.8%	3.1%	21.7%	30.6%	25.4%	7.7%	36.3%
MiddleEast	55.5%	29.1%	0.7%	14.7%	62.3%	17.9%	1.5%	18.3%
SSA	55.6%	32.4%	0.8%	11.2%	53.2%	18.2%	2.6%	26.0%
Northern Africa								
Egypt	15.4%	40.4%	2.7%	41.5%	40.4%	19.7%	3.2%	36.7%
Morocco	14.5%	55.1%	0.1%	30.3%	21.1%	34.4%	2.3%	42.2%
Tunisia	10.8%	66.2%	1.1%	21.8%	20.3%	32.3%	3.2%	44.2%
Western and Central Africa								
Benin	23.2%	46.9%	0.3%	29.6%	50.4%	21.2%	0.5%	27.9%
Burkina Faso	89.1%	6.1%	0.2%	4.6%	79.6%	7.1%	1.6%	11.6%
Cameroon	44.9%	25.5%	0.1%	29.5%	43.6%	10.4%	1.6%	44.4%
Cote d'Ivoire	33.5%	52.7%	1.5%	12.2%	36.0%	19.8%	2.5%	41.7%
Ghana	25.4%	46.2%	0.5%	27.9%	31.2%	28.0%	1.8%	39.0%
Guinea	67.8%	28.0%	1.6%	2.6%	50.0%	12.3%	2.1%	35.7%
Nigeria	94.4%	2.8%	0.1%	2.7%	95.0%	2.1%	0.2%	2.7%
Senegal	9.4%	48.4%	1.9%	40.3%	15.3%	29.4%	2.2%	53.2%
Togo	24.1%	55.5%	0.1%	20.3%	38.2%	23.6%	1.2%	37.1%
Central Africa	81.5%	8.5%	0.3%	9.7%	66.4%	10.5%	1.5%	21.7%
Eastern Africa								
Ethiopia	35.9%	15.8%	0.8%	47.5%	46.1%	3.7%	1.2%	49.0%
Kenya	26.3%	35.3%	0.2%	38.2%	23.3%	32.9%	1.5%	42.3%
Madagascar	41.0%	37.7%	2.9%	18.4%	45.7%	25.8%	1.8%	26.8%
Malawi	68.7%	18.1%	0.9%	12.3%	54.5%	8.3%	1.7%	35.5%
Mauritius	17.0%	44.1%	0.7%	38.2%	21.3%	36.5%	1.6%	40.6%
Mozambique	21.9%	47.3%	21.1%	9.6%	17.6%	17.4%	44.8%	20.1%
Rwanda	70.2%	6.4%	1.4%	22.0%	51.3%	3.4%	3.4%	41.9%
Tanzania	26.6%	39.0%	0.7%	33.7%	33.8%	20.6%	3.8%	41.7%
Uganda	59.2%	22.9%	1.6%	16.2%	56.5%	13.6%	3.4%	26.5%
Zambia	15.6%	78.3%	1.1%	5.0%	13.3%	9.3%	9.9%	67.5%
Zimbabwe	27.1%	64.7%	0.4%	7.9%	32.9%	36.2%	15.1%	15.8%
Southern Africa								
Botswana	57.3%	29.0%	0.3%	13.4%	58.9%	23.8%	1.4%	16.0%
Namibia	28.5%	58.8%	1.0%	11.7%	37.5%	24.5%	2.9%	35.1%
South Africa	16.7%	69.8%	0.6%	12.9%	13.4%	39.0%	2.9%	44.7%

Source: Own calculations; PRIM: primary sectors, MAN: manufacturing sectors, UTI: utilities, SER: services

Table 21: Sector share of exports and TiVA exports in the world and Africa, primary industries and manufacturing

		exports		tiva exports	
		World	Africa	World	Africa
Primary industries	Paddy rice	0.0%	0.0%	0.1%	0.1%
	Wheat	0.2%	0.0%	0.2%	0.1%
	Cereal grains nec	0.2%	0.1%	0.3%	0.3%
	Vegetables, fruit, nuts	0.5%	1.4%	0.7%	1.5%
	Oil seeds	0.3%	0.1%	0.4%	0.2%
	Sugar cane, sugar beet	0.0%	0.0%	0.1%	0.1%
	Plant-based fibers	0.1%	0.4%	0.2%	0.4%
	Crops nec	0.4%	1.5%	0.5%	1.4%
	Cattle,sheep,goats,horses	0.0%	0.1%	0.2%	0.2%
	Animal products nec	0.1%	0.1%	0.3%	0.1%
	Raw milk	0.0%	0.0%	0.1%	0.1%
	Wool, silk-worm cocoons	0.0%	0.0%	0.1%	0.1%
	Forestry	0.2%	0.5%	0.5%	0.6%
	Fishing	0.1%	0.1%	0.2%	0.2%
	Coal	0.5%	0.7%	0.7%	0.7%
	Oil	9.2%	37.9%	11.7%	39.4%
	Gas	1.2%	6.9%	1.7%	8.5%
	Minerals nec	1.8%	4.1%	2.1%	3.5%
Manufacturing	Meat: cattle, sheep, goats, horse	0.2%	0.1%	0.1%	0.1%
	Meat products nec	0.3%	0.1%	0.1%	0.1%
	Vegetable oils and fats	0.5%	0.3%	0.2%	0.1%
	Dairy products	0.3%	0.1%	0.1%	0.1%
	Processed rice	0.1%	0.1%	0.0%	0.0%
	Sugar	0.1%	0.3%	0.1%	0.1%
	Food products nec	1.4%	2.0%	0.9%	0.9%
	Beverages and tobacco products	0.5%	0.4%	0.4%	0.4%
	Textiles	2.0%	1.2%	1.4%	0.8%
	Wearing apparel	1.6%	2.0%	0.7%	0.9%
	Leather products	0.9%	0.5%	0.5%	0.4%
	Wood products	1.2%	0.8%	0.9%	0.5%
	Paper products, publishing	1.1%	0.5%	1.5%	0.6%
	Petroleum coal products	3.5%	4.0%	1.7%	0.7%
	Chemical,rubber,plastic prods	9.0%	3.4%	6.6%	1.7%
	Mineral products nec	0.8%	0.5%	0.9%	0.7%
	Ferrous metals	2.2%	2.3%	2.1%	1.2%
	Metals nec	3.2%	6.8%	1.8%	3.7%
	Metal products	1.6%	0.6%	1.9%	0.6%
	Motor vehicles and parts	5.4%	1.4%	2.4%	0.4%
	Transport equipment nec	2.7%	0.5%	1.5%	0.2%
	Electronic equipment	8.2%	0.6%	3.5%	0.3%
	Machinery and equipment nec	12.3%	2.9%	7.5%	1.1%
	Manufactures nec	2.1%	0.6%	1.4%	0.4%

Source: Own calculations

Table 22: Sector share of exports and TiVA exports in the world and Africa, public utilities and services

		exports		tiva exports	
		World	Africa	World	Africa
Utilities	Electricity	0.2%	0.3%	2.1%	1.3%
	Gas manufacture, distribution	0.3%	0.1%	0.4%	0.3%
	Water	0.0%	0.0%	0.2%	0.1%
	Construction	0.7%	0.4%	1.1%	0.5%
Services	Trade	2.0%	0.7%	7.0%	7.6%
	Transport nec	3.4%	3.7%	4.8%	3.9%
	Sea transport	3.5%	1.1%	1.8%	0.7%
	Air transport	2.5%	1.9%	1.3%	1.1%
	Communication	0.7%	0.7%	1.7%	1.7%
	Financial services nec	1.6%	0.4%	4.0%	1.4%
	Insurance	0.9%	0.4%	1.0%	1.0%
	Business services nec	5.7%	1.8%	12.2%	4.4%
	Recreation and other services	1.0%	0.8%	1.3%	1.0%
	PubAd-min/Defence/Health/Educat	1.7%	1.7%	2.6%	1.6%
	Dwellings	0.0%	0.0%	0.2%	0.0%

5.2 Revealed comparative advantages in Africa

The best known and most influential theory on economic trade is the theory of comparative advantages by David Ricardo (1817). According to this theory, countries do not only profit from trade when a country has an absolute cost advantage but also when they concentrate on the production of goods in which they have their comparative advantage. On the basis of the theory of comparative advantages and the work of Eli Heckscher, Ohlin represents a model which is referred to as the Heckscher-Ohlin theorem (Heckscher et al. 1991). While David Ricardo's model considers only one factor of production, namely labor, the Heckscher-Ohlin model introduces endowments in the factors of production (labor and capital).

Developing countries facing scarce human and physical capital thus exhibit their comparative advantage in labor- and resource-intensive but low technology production activities. The highly developed countries, in contrast, exhibit an endowment structure with abundant human and physical capital. Hence, their comparative advantage is in knowledge and highly capital intensive industries (Lin 2011: 200).

In contrast to the original Ricardian model, it is widely acknowledged that the concept of comparative advantages is a dynamic rather than a static concept (Hiley 1999; Nicolini 2011; Ju et al. 2009). By accumulating capital, educating workers, and acquiring knowledge the developing countries can shift their comparative advantage.

While the neoclassical approach assumes the endowment factors to be causal factors for shifting endowment intensities, economic development, and comparative advantages, quite the reverse is true for the modernization theories and even dependency theories, which prevailed in the 1960s and 1970s (see chapter 2.5). Those theories assumed that the establishment of the industrial sector would lead to self-sustaining economic growth via external effects and virtuous cycle. Structural change is thus the causal factor for economic development and by no means the result. This point of view has been revitalized by several authors such as Ho-Joon Chang or Erik S. Reinert who claimed to re-establish *the Other Canon.122* These opposing views are depicted in the Development Policy Review debate between Justin Yifu Lin and Ha-Joon Chang: *"Should Industrial Policy in Developing Countries Conform to Comparative Advantage or Defy it?"* (Lin & Chang 2009).

The debate was pursued in the African context by Wood & Berge (1997), arguing that Africa has a comparative advantage in land. They modified the Heckscher-Ohlin model in such a way that the relevant endowments are skill and natural resources rather than capital and labor.123 Their main finding is that countries with high skill/land ratios show a revealed comparative advantage in manufacturing, whereas countries with low skill/land ratios show a comparative advantage in agriculture. They conclude that trade policy seems to explain only minor differences in the export ratios (Wood & Berge 1997: 51–53).

Collier (2000: 12) stresses the arguments behind the regression results of Wood & Berge (1997). Accordingly, the African economies only differ to those of Asia due to their natural resource abundance. Subsequently, the African economies would be non-competitive to the Asian economies because their labor would be more expensive than in Asia. Manufacturing would have been crowded out due to its high land and natural resource ratios, such as it is described in the Dutch disease literature. Indeed, there may be some economies in which manufacturing is crowded out, e.g., Botswana. However, in most of the economies, this argument needs to be

122 The Other Canon: http://www.othercanon.org/ (last access: December 30, 2016).

123 They omit labor with the argument that primary production and manufacturing are of equal labor intensity (Wood & Berge 1997: 36), which is a daring hypothesis

challenged as wages are much lower than in several Asian economies, e.g., China (Collier 2000: 13).

5.2.1 Measurement of comparative advantages

Since assessing the real comparative advantages of a nation is difficult124, Balassa (1965: 103) suggests using the "revealed" comparative advantage instead.125 Assuming that trade conforms to the comparative advantages of a nation, a country's relative export performance could be used to measure a country's comparative advantage. This index is widely used in numerous reports of international organizations (OECD 2011; Kowalski 2011) but also in academic publications to identify comparative advantages. Even though it is often stated that the indicator does not reflect the "real" comparative advantage as policy plays a crucial role in this process, it is assumed that the identified trade specialization is driven by factor endowments or intensities (e.g., Kowalski 2011).

The index proposed by Balassa (1965: 106) divides the country's share of exports of a particular good by the world's share of exports of this particular good (equation 4).

$$RCA1_{ij} = [(x_{ij}/x_i)/(x_{wj}/x_w)] \qquad \text{Eq 4}$$

x_{ij}	exports in country i, in industry j.
x_i	total exports in country i
x_{wj}	exports in the world, in industry j
x_w	total exports in the world

Since this version omits imports and is therefore biased especially due to country size (e.g., Laursen 2015), Balassa (1965: 107)also proposes another simple relative export-import measure (equation 5).

$$RCA2_{ij} = [(x_{ij}/x_i)/(m_{ij}/m_i)] \qquad \text{Eq 5}$$

m_{ij}	denotes imports in country i, in industry j
m_i	denotes total imports in country i

However, Balassa emphasizes the export performance as all exporters are subject to the same tariff and the data is thus "not distorted by differences

124 See Balassa (1965: 99–103) for discussion.

125 Balassa (1965) coined the term „revealed comparative advantage". However, Liesner (1958) is probably the first who used the index.

in the degree of tariff protection" (Balassa 1965: 104). Several other indices have been developed and used in the literature. Vollrath (1991) analyzes, compares, and evaluates ten different indices and suggests the following indices (Vollrath 1991: 275):

$$RCA3_{ij} = RXA_{ij} - RMA_{ij} \qquad \text{Eq 6}$$

$$RXA_{ij} = [(x_{ij}/x_{ia})/(x_{wj}/x_{wa})] \qquad \text{Eq 7}$$

$$RMA_{ij} = [(m_{ij}/m_{ia})/(m_{wj}/m_{wa})] \qquad \text{Eq 8}$$

x_{ij}	exports in country i, in industry j.
x_{ia}	total exports in country i, in all commodities except of j
x_{wj}	exports in the world, in industry j
x_{wa}	total exports in the world except of country i, in all commodities except of j
m_{ij}	imports in country i, in industry j
m_{ia}	total imports in country i, in all commodities except of j
m_{wj}	imports in the world except of country i, in industry j
m_{wa}	total imports in the world except of country i, in all commodities except of j

$$RCA4_{ij} = Ln(RXA_{ij}) \qquad \text{Eq 9}$$

$$RCA5_{ij} = Ln(RXA_{ij}) - Ln(RMA_{ij}) \qquad \text{Eq 10}$$

The indices RCA3, RCA4, and RCA5 reveal a positive value when the country has a comparative advantage, and they show a negative value when the country has a comparative disadvantage in the respective commodity. The indices RCA3 and RCA5 both consider the demand and the supply effects. RCA4 similar to RCA1 is preferred to avoid shortcomings due to tariff distortions, which are stressed on the import side. At high levels of commodity aggregation, the RCA5 is preferable to RCA3. However, RCA5 is very sensitive to extreme small values and to the absence of two-way trade.

I use the indices to display Africa's export and import balance and hence its position in the world economy rather than to reveal any comparative advantages in the theoretical sense of the Heckscher-Ohlin trade model. Thus, I do not pay much attention to the distortions due to trade policy. Accordingly, I use the RCA3 which includes imports as well exports and is less sensitive to small values than RCA5.

5.2.2 Results

Table 23 shows RCA3 for normal trade data and the TiVA data. The results for the world regions display the expected pattern. East Asia, followed by the European Union, has the highest revealed comparative advantage in manufacturing. Africa and the Middle East are the major exporters for primary products and the main importer for manufacturing but also services. South Asia and North America are the major exporters for services. In the aggregated data, there are only minor differences between the usual data and the value added trade. The most obvious result is that revealed comparative advantage for primary products in Africa is reduced in favor of a better performance in utilities, which is highly plausible since utilities (especially construction and electricity) are needed to extract the exported primary products. Another aspect is that there is a slightly better performance for SSA in the TiVA data regarding services.

The country specific analysis of the revealed comparative advantage (table 24) in Africa shows that indeed most African economies have their highest values in primary commodities. Detailed sectoral analysis indicates that the revealed comparative advantage in the specific primary commodities is very diverse. While some economies score high in minerals (Botswana, Namibia, Zimbabwe, Rwanda), others score high in crops (Ethiopia, Kenya, Malawi, Togo. Ghana), plant-based fibers (Benin, Burkina-Faso, Cote d'Ivoire), or sugar cane and sugar beets (Madagascar and Mauritius); oil scores especially high in Nigeria and Central Africa. Exceptions to this rule with negative RCA in primary commodities are Senegal and South Africa but also some other countries, such as Zambia, Kenya, or Morocco and Tunisia showing very low positive RCAs in primary commodities. Interestingly, all those economies do not score high in manufacturing, but they show positive values in services. Senegal and Kenya as well as Morocco and Tunisia exhibit especially positive values in communication and air transport. South Africa scores high in insurance, recreation and other services. An exception of this rule is Mozambique which has negative RCAs in all sectors but not in utilities. Indeed, it exports huge amounts of electricity to Zimbabwe and South Africa but also a lot of value added electricity to the EU27 (the exported electricity is mostly embedded in the metals sector). The positive values in the service sectors are of special interest as no African economy shows a positive RCA in manufacturing except for Zimbabwe at a very low level. Zimbabwe manages to process several of its primary products and thus has positive RCAs in several manufacturing sectors including ferrous metals and metals nec. but also sugar, beverages and tobacco, wood products, textiles wearing apparel and leather products. The two second best manufacturing performers are Mauritius followed by South Africa. Mauritius main manufacturing export sectors are sugar as well as textiles and wearing apparel.

Table 23: Revealed comparative advantages for major economic sectors across world regions in normal and TiVA data in 2007

	RCA tiva data				**RCA normal trade data**			
	PRIM	MAN	UTI	SER	PRIM	MAN	UTI	SER
Oceania	1.3	-0.6	0.3	0.0	1.8	-0.4	-0.2	0.0
East Asia	-1.2	0.5	0.0	0.1	-1.8	0.5	0.2	-0.2
South-East Asia	0.2	0.1	-0.2	-0.2	-0.2	0.1	-0.3	-0.1
South Asia	-0.7	-0.1	0.4	0.4	-1.3	0.1	0.0	0.5
North America	-0.5	0.0	0.2	0.3	-0.3	-0.1	0.4	0.4
Latin America	1.1	-0.4	0.0	-0.2	1.6	-0.3	-0.3	-0.3
EU27	-1.0	0.3	-0.1	0.2	-1.0	0.2	-0.1	0.2
Rest of Europe	1.0	-0.6	0.9	-0.1	1.3	-0.3	1.0	0.0
Middle East	2.5	-0.6	-0.9	-0.6	3.3	-0.6	-1.1	-0.4
Sub-Saharan Africa	1.9	-0.6	-0.4	-0.3	3.3	-0.6	-1.1	-0.5

Source: Own calculations from the world input-output table; world regions are according to the GTAP aggregation scheme; PRIM: primary sectors, MAN: manufacturing sectors, UTI: utilities, SER: services

South Africa, which is known as the manufacturing hub in sub-Saharan Africa, is also of special interest as the TiVA data changes the export performing outcome substantially. While the normal trade data shows a positive RCA in primary products and manufacturing (even if it is at a very low level) and a negative RCA in services, the RCAs with TiVA data exhibit the opposite: a negative RCA in primary commodities and manufacturing and a positive value in services. One of the major differences in this data stems from the insurance but also communication sector (which is known to be one of the fastest growing sectors in South Africa). Insurance and communication services are rarely exported directly but serve as an important input in nearly all other sectors. They do not appear in the conventional trade statistics but their performance is exhibited in the trade in value added data. A substantial improvement in the RCAs for services can also be seen in Cote d'Ivoire, Guinea, Central Africa, Rwanda, and Zambia.

To conclude, this analysis suggests that sub-Saharan Africa has a considerable export-surplus in primary products. However, in value-added data, it is not as high as conventional trade statistics suggest. The TiVA data also reveals that economies which are not commodity exporters do not perform well in the manufacturing sector but do so in the services sector.

Table 24: Revealed comparative advantages for major economic sectors in African countries in normal and TiVA data in 2007

	RCA tiva data				RCA normal trade data			
	PRIM	MAN	UTI	SER	PRIM	MAN	UTI	SER
Northern Africa								
Egypt	1.1	-0.5	-0.1	0.0	0.2	-0.4	1.7	0.9
Morocco	0.0	-0.2	-0.4	0.3	-0.1	-0.2	-0.7	0.7
Tunisia	0.2	-0.4	-0.5	0.3	0.2	-0.2	-1.3	0.4
Western and Central Africa								
Benin	1.4	-0.6	-0.9	0.0	1.5	-0.6	-1.0	0.8
Burkina Faso	3.1	-0.9	-0.5	-0.7	5.7	-1.1	-0.3	-0.6
Cameroon	1.4	-0.7	-0.4	0.1	2.4	-0.5	-0.3	-0.1
Cote d'Ivoire	0.6	-0.4	-0.1	0.1	1.1	0.0	1.1	-0.6
Ghana	0.5	-0.3	-0.4	0.1	0.9	-0.4	0.1	0.4
Guinea	1.7	-0.8	-0.6	0.0	4.5	-0.8	-1.3	-0.7
Nigeria	4.1	-0.9	-0.8	-1.1	6.2	-1.0	-0.2	-1.4
Senegal	-0.4	-0.2	-0.3	0.5	-0.2	-0.3	0.9	1.0
Togo	1.0	-0.6	-0.7	0.2	1.3	-0.5	-0.8	0.4
Central Africa	2.8	-0.6	-0.5	-0.8	5.4	-0.7	-0.5	-1.5
Eastern Africa								
Ethiopia	1.5	-1.0	-1.1	0.4	2.3	-0.9	-3.2	1.2
Kenya	0.1	-0.2	-0.5	0.2	1.0	-0.6	0.1	1.0
Madagascar	1.4	-0.4	-0.4	-0.3	2.6	-0.6	1.3	-0.2
Malawi	1.9	-0.8	-0.6	-0.1	4.1	-0.9	0.1	-0.3
Mauritius	0.3	-0.1	-0.4	0.0	0.9	-0.3	0.2	0.3
Mozambique	-0.1	-0.5	10.4	-0.5	1.1	-0.4	14.3	-0.5
Rwanda	1.6	-1.1	-0.1	0.3	4.5	-1.0	0.4	-0.2
Tanzania	0.9	-0.6	0.0	0.1	1.6	-0.6	-0.5	0.6
Uganda	2.0	-0.8	0.0	-0.2	3.8	-0.9	0.9	-0.2
Zambia	0.0	-0.8	0.5	0.7	0.4	0.2	-5.7	-0.5
Zimbabwe	0.8	0.0	1.1	-0.6	1.3	-0.1	-8.6	-0.2
Southern Africa								
Botswana	2.2	-0.3	-0.5	-0.8	3.5	-0.7	-1.2	-0.2
Namibia	1.2	-0.4	-0.4	-0.2	1.7	-0.4	-2.1	0.0
South Africa	-0.2	-0.1	-0.2	0.3	0.2	0.0	-0.6	-0.1

Source: Own calculations from the world input-output table; PRIM: primary sectors, MAN: manufacturing sectors, UTI: utilities, SER: services

Figure 27: Revealed comparative advantage in sub-Saharan Africa, TiVA data (left) vs. convential trade statistics (right)

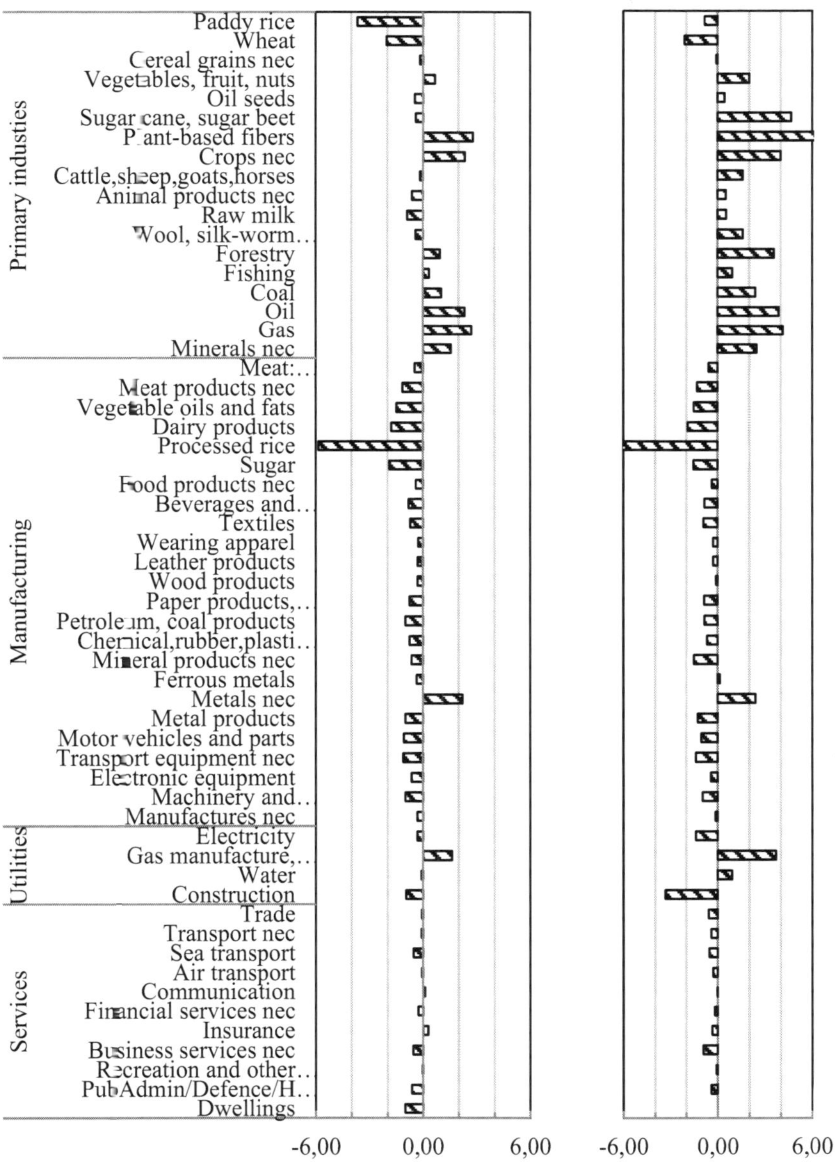

Source: Own calculations from the world input-output table

5.3 Integration into Global Value Chains

The notion of global value chains (GVCs) appeared first in the literature under the denomination global commodity chains (GCCs). The world system theorists Terence Hopkins and Immanuel Wallerstein defined the concept commodity chain as "a network of labor and production processes whose end result is a finished commodity" (Hopkins & Wallerstein 1986: 159). While they analyzed historical commodity chains in the light of historical cycles, the newer paradigm of GCCs may be traced back to Gereffi & Korzeniewicz (1993). In the newer literature, the term GCCs is replaced by GVCs since the latter captures a broader variety of products (Gibbon & Ponte 2005: 77).

The GVC approach assumes that an increasing amount of trade is not only organized in market relations but also takes place within a framework of global buyers and is governed by very few companies. These lead firms (especially their headquarters) are mostly located in developed nations and include either multinational manufacturers or large retailer and brand-name firms (Gereffi et al. 2001: 1). Applying the concept of economic rents, the distribution of margins between producers is found to be strongly influenced by power relationships. Gereffi (1993) shows that commodities produced in developing countries exhibit increasing concentration of global retailers and thus he emphasizes the role of governance in GVCs.

The most prominent prototypical distinction of governance structure is the classification in buyer-driven and producer-driven GVCs by Gereffi (1993): Producer-driven chains are constituted by high barriers of entry due to capital and technology requirement. In sectors of advanced manufacturing as well as with minerals and agricultural commodities, producers therefore retain control and are identified as lead firms in the GVC. In contrast, buyer-driven chains were found in labor-intensive manufacturing. In these chains, barriers of entry are constituted by marketing and branding, information and product design. Lead firms in those GVCs are subsequently large retailers or marketers. Gereffi (1999: 2) argues that the import substitution industrialization applied in Latin America was based on producer-driven value chains which were mainly oriented to domestic markets. In contrast, the export-oriented industrialization strategy—applied in East Asia—was based on the integration into buyer-driven value chains. With this strategy, East-Asian producers managed to gain a lion's share of the European and United States market. Since governance structures are different in economic sectors, different upgrading strategies are needed (OECD 2014: 162–177).

The form of governance is not predetermined and can change once the industry matures. Furthermore, the GVC can be characterized by multiple and interacting governance structures which allow for economic and social upgrading within the chain (Gereffi & Fernandez-Stark 2011: 10). Gibbon & Ponte (2005: 95–124) also have identified a trend toward buyer-driven value chains in the commodity sectors, especially for Africa. A reason for this trend could be the new international trade regime established in 1994 (Gibbon & Ponte 2005: 44–73).

The dichotomy between buyer-driven and producer-driven value chains is questioned from several angles. Gereffi (2001) himself added a new dimension of internet-driven value chains by stating that the service sector provides countless simple opportunities for value chain integration and upgrading.

In contrast to the neoclassical trade theory, the GVC approach takes the organization of trade as well as its institutional framework into account. Furthermore, the concept of governance enables the GVC approach to analyze and discuss power relations while regarding institutions and specific historical processes. Instead of exploring the issue of value creation, the GVC approach rather focuses on the distribution of value. By analyzing factor payments—which vary due to specific chain governances—the GVC approach also takes over the classical theory of uneven exchange, which had been cited under the notion of Dependence Theory (Gibbon et al. 2008: 331).

A main result of the work of Gibbon & Ponte (2005) is that the commodity value chains a turned out to be increasingly buyer-driven. Furthermore, there are evidently no African lead firms and only a few first-tier suppliers. Improvements for African economies, therefore, rely on foreign direct investments in the short term and capacity building of the African states in the long run (Gibbon & Ponte 2005: 201).

While the governance concept is a useful tool to analyze GVCs top-down, the common concept of the bottom-up perspective is upgrading. This notion is widely used, especially in the context of examining the competitiveness of nations (e.g., Porter 1990), but in most cases its application is rather undetermined. Morrison et al. (2008: 51) even question the relevance of the concept after all if the notion of technological capabilities describes the phenomenon considered so much better. Definitions of upgrading are rare; one can be found in Gereffi (2005: 171): "Industrial upgrading refers to the process by which economic actors—nations, firms, and workers—move from low-value to relatively high-value activities in global production networks."

The point of reference for upgrading strategies as indicated by Gereffi is the East-Asian development model. In nearly all cases upgrading is associated with the acquisition of new capabilities, but it also can be a change in the power relationship of the GVC. Several models (e.g. Wortzel & Wortzel 1981) describe stages in which firms (or economies respectively) acquire capabilities, succeedingly find buyers that demand commodities of which production requires those capabilities, and then upgrade into higher value added activities. The process of acquiring capabilities, e.g., workforce development is in fact a process which happens parallel to industrial upgrading and involves a variety of actors, especially from the private sector (Gereffi & Fernandez-Stark 2011).

The strategy of upgrading again is dependent on the type of "governance" under which the value chain operates. In some cases, the lead company might try to protect its core competencies and tries to avoid all kinds of knowledge transfer toward other firms. Unintended knowledge transfer may also play a role in some cases. The reason why lead firms may thus be interested to incorporate developing country producers is the need for long-term contracts for commodities and the need for more standardized inputs. Altenburg (2006: 514) provides a list of conditions under which lead firms will engage in deliberate knowledge transfer (Altenburg 2006: 507–515).

The evolution of the international system of production and trade furthers the transfer of knowledge and technology and thereby brings about new opportunities for developing economies, especially on the African continent. To exploit the advantages of latecomer economies in that respect, the integration into GVCs is required. This also is a necessary condition for reaching international markets and thereby yielding increasing returns to scale.

On the downside, the integration exposes the African companies to challenges of international standards, mostly imposed by multinational companies with their headquarters in the United States or the European Union. Captive governance structures provide not only a risk for unequal division of profits but also hinder technology transfer, prevent African producers from upgrading, and increase the risk of confining African economies to specialize in primary products.126 Any case of forward par-

126 According to the African Economic Outlook expert interviews, the greatest threats associated with global value chains and resulting new trade patterns are firstly: being locked in low value-added stages of GVCs, and secondly: foreign

ticipation in GVCs should be considered carefully and against the background of the rise of buyer-driven chains. The OECD (2014: 145) even argues that backward participation has positive effects on diversification and structural transformation, whereas the forward participation causes the opposite. These conclusions derive from the correlations between strong forward linkages of primary commodities and strong backward linkages of manufacturing sectors.

The correlations of the OECD (2014: 145) stress the importance of revealing the sectoral differences in GVC participation. Thus, it is crucial to analyze the integration into GVCs from both the angles, i.e., the backward and the forward participation.

Since the participation in GVCs is seen to enhance productivity, sophistication, and diversification of exports, a recent OECD paper (Kowalski et al. 2015) addresses the issue of what drives GVC participation in developing countries. According to their findings, the main determining factors in that respect are the level of development, which is positively correlated with the extend of integration into GVCs, market size, which is positively correlated with the forward and negatively correlated with the backward participation index, and location. The larger the distance to main manufacturing hubs located in Europe, North America, and Asia, the lower the backward participation index. Due to its distance to all manufacturing hubs, I expect African backward participation into GVCs, especially in sub-Saharan Africa, to be generally lower than in other regions. Kowalski et al. (2015: 82) also have identified another positive relationship between the size of the manufacturing sector and the backward participation index.

It therefore appears obvious that entering GVCs will not automatically lead to positive effects. The central weakness of this approach is the lack of reliable and comparable data to measure the supposed influences on African economic activity (Asche 2012: 399). The purpose of this section of the work at hand is to fill this gap.

5.3.1 Methodology

With the measurement of trade in value added, the OECD-WTO joint initiative published indices on the participation in GVCs. Applying the Eora

investors operate in isolation with limited spillovers to domestic economy (OECD 2014: 132).

MRIO Database, these indices were used in several publications to measure the participation of African economies in GVCs (UNCTAD 2013; ECA 2015; AfDB et al. 2014; Foster-McGregor et al. 2015; Pfeiffer 2015; Kowalski et al. 2015). Until now, this dataset as well as the used indicators are the only source for measuring the integration of African economies into GVCs.

As I will show in the next section, the OECD data which is based on the methodology explained by Kowalski et al. (2015) and De Backer & Miroudot (2013) (section 5.3.1.1) suffers from important shortcomings (section 5.3.1.2). Conclusively, I will propose a different indicator to measure the extent to which different sectors are integrated into GVCs (section 5.3.1.3).

Due to the aforementioned shortcomings of the Eora MRIO Database (see chapter 4.3.2), the proposed methodology will be applied for the multiregional input-output table which is constructed from the GTAP Africa Database.

Section 5.3.2 presents the results using these indicators.

5.3.1.1 OECD indicators

According to the OECD, participation in GVCs is defined as the share of imported inputs in the overall exports of a country and of its exported goods and services used as imported inputs to produce other countries' exports. The higher the foreign value-added embodied in a given country's gross exports and the higher the value of inputs exported to third countries used in their respective exports are, the greater is that country's participation in the value chain.

This index is based on Koopman et al. (2010). The starting point is the decomposition of gross exports into value added shares by source country. The following matrix is calculated:

$$\boldsymbol{VBE} = \boldsymbol{V}\,(\boldsymbol{I} - \boldsymbol{A})^{-1}\,\boldsymbol{E} \qquad \text{Eq 11}$$

$\boldsymbol{V}$ and $\boldsymbol{B}$ are already defined above, and $\boldsymbol{E}$ is the diagonal of a vector of gross exports. Table 25 shows the $\boldsymbol{VBE}$ matrix for the example which is depicted in figure 25.

Table 25: The VBE matrix – example

VBE		country 1			country 2			country 3		
		A	B	C	A	B	C	A	B	C
country 1	A	0	150	0	0	150	0	0	0	0
	B	0	50	0	0	50	0	0	0	0
	C	0	0	0	0	0	0	0	0	0
country 2	A	0	0	0	0	0	0	0	0	0
	B	0	0	0	0	100	0	0	0	0
	C	0	0	0	0	0	0	0	0	0
country 3	A	0	0	0	0	0	0	0	0	0
	B	0	0	0	0	0	0	0	0	0
	C	0	0	0	0	0	0	0	0	0

Source: Own depiction

Summing over rows (and omitting domestic industries, thus exclude the gray shaded area), one can calculate the contribution of domestically produced intermediates to exports in third countries (VS1). Dividing the VS1 by gross exports gives an index which is interpreted as the forward participation index (FPI) (Kowalski et al. 2015: 151).

When adding values in the columns of the ***VBE*** matrix (without the contribution of domestic industries, thus excluding the gray shaded area), one obtains the contribution of foreign industries to exports (the import content of exports (VS)) which, divided by gross exports in each country, is interpreted by the OECD as the backward participation index (BPI) (Kowalski et al. 2015: 151). The total GVC participation index (PI) simply adds the BPI and FPI.

Table 26 shows the results for our example economies. Comparing these results with our example picture (see figure 25) will provide an idea of what is measured in the index of backward and forward participation.

Country 1 has gross exports of 200€, industry A adds 150€ of value, and industry B adds 50€ of value, which is finally consumed in country 3. All exports are domestically produced intermediates which are exported in third countries and thus measured as forward participation. The forward participation index thus shows 100 percent. In country 2, industry B adds 100€ value which is exported into country 3. Since this value added crosses only one border, it is not counted as forward participation. Hence, country 2 and 3 show a forward participation index of zero.

Table 26: GVC participation according to the OECD – example

		VS	VS1	exports	BPI	FPI	PI	BPI	FPI	PI
	A	0	150		0%	75%	75%			
country 1	B	0	50	200	0%	25%	25%	0%	100%	100%
	C	0	0		0%	0%	0%			
	A	0	0		0%	0%	0%			
country 2	B	200	0	300	67%	0%	67%	67%	0%	67%
	C	0	0		0%	0%	0%			
	A	0	0		0%	0%	0%			
country 3	B	0	0	0	0%	0%	0%	0%	0%	0%
	C	0	0		0%	0%	0%			

Source: Own depiction

The backward participation index measures the import content of exports. Country 1 has no imports and thus a backward participation index of zero. Country 3 has no exports and thus also a backward participation index of zero. Country 2 exports 300€ to country 3 from which 200€ are value added from country 1. The import content of these exports is consequently two thirds, and the backward participation index shows 66.6 percent.127

5.3.1.2 Critique on the OECD indicators

It is important to note that by definition the sum of VS and VS1 are equivalent (as can be seen in table 26), indicating that I measure one phenomenon out of two directions. The two indices measure to which extend value added in exports are re-exported again. The sector in which the value is actually added is the one showing up in the FPI. In contrast, the sectors through which the value is being passed are the sectors appearing in the BPI. The index value, therefore, is high in those sectors in which pro-

127 To analyze sectoral differences in the participation indices, it is useful to divide the import content of exports by the exports in the corresponding sector (and not by total exports as it is done in the OECD procedure). Dividing the contribution of domestically produced intermediates to exports in third countries (VS1) by exports of the corresponding sector may be misleading unless the exporting sector is the sector in which the value added is produced. It is, in contrast, more useful to divide the contribution of domestically produced intermediates to exports in third countries by their exports in value added.

cessing trade plays a major role.128 However, the BPI does not measure the value that is added in processing trade sectors.

Reconsidering the definition of Hopkins & Wallerstein (1986: 159), a GVC (GCC) is "a network of labor and production processes whose end result is a finished commodity". According to this definition, country 3 in the example (figure 25) is clearly integrated in the GVC. However, the indicators of the OECD do not consider the final economy of the GVC.

Figure 28: Trade in value added – example 2

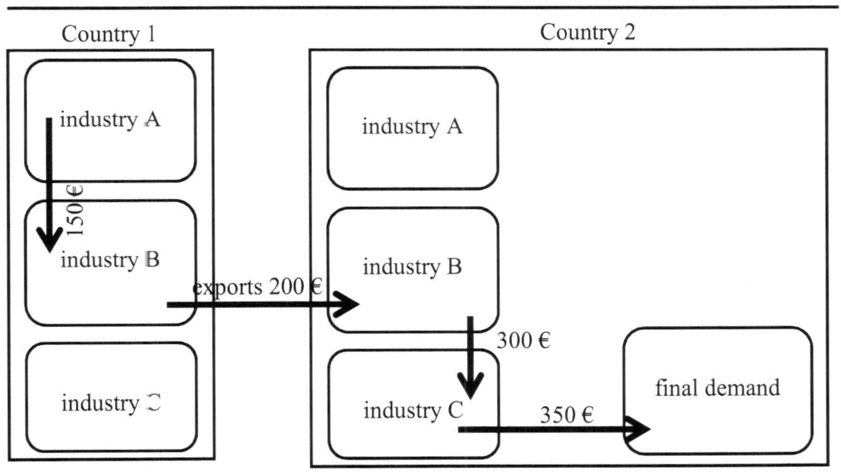

Source: Own depiction

In general, the indicators do not relate the trade to value added which is produced in the corresponding sector. In contrast, the indicators implicitly differentiate between two types of trade. Common trade takes place between two economies, the other trade, in which at least three economies are integrated, is defined as trade within a GVC. Accordingly, the trade

128 The concept of processing trade is mainly discussed in the context of the Chinese economy; according to the EU SME Centre (2011: 1) processing trade refers to the "business activity of importing all, or part of, the raw and auxiliary materials, components and parts, accessories and packaging materials from enterprises abroad to enterprises within China to carry out the manufacturing process The finished products after processing or assembly by the enterprises within China will be re-exported to the foreign enterprises that are responsible for selling them."

between more than two economies as share of total trade is defined as the participation in GVCs, whereas the economic meaning of this differentiation remains unclear.

The problem is illustrated by another value chain depicted in figure 28; the only difference to example 1 in figure 25 is that the last production process and the consumption is carried out in country 2 rather than in country 3. In this example both the forward and the backward indices show a value of zero. However, there is no change in the production process, which should be of relevance to country 1. Nevertheless, the forward participation index changes dramatically from 100 to 0. While both indicators depend on the size of the economy, the forward participation index is also heavily dependent on the size of the economy to which it exports.

5.3.1.3 The share of international linkages

As chapter 4.3.1.7 illustrates, the importance of GVC lies in linkages. In contrast to the OECD indicators which are built upon the rather questionable distinction between normal trade and trade in GVCs, I propose to measure the participation in GVCs as the share of international linkages on total linkages. Reconsidering section 4.3.1.6, a world input-output table allows to measure world linkages (WBL) as well as domestic linkages (DBL). Accordingly, it allows calculating international backward (IBL) and forward linkages (IFL) as follows:

if k ≠ l: $$IBL_j^l = \sum_{i=1}^{n} \sum_{k=1}^{g} b_{ij}^{kl}$$ Eq 12

if l ≠ l: $$IFL_i^k = \sum_{j=1}^{n} \sum_{l=1}^{g} d_{ij}^{kl}$$ Eq 13

Dividing the international linkages with the world linkages equals the international share of linkages which is used as an indicator for the integration into GVCs. In analogy to the OECD indicators, the procedure differentiates between backward (BII) and forward integration (FII) into GVCs.

$$BII_j^l = {IBL_j^l}/{WBL_j^l}$$ Eq 14

$$FII_k^i = {IFL_k^i}/{WFL_k^i} \qquad \text{Eq 15}$$

Both indicators measure to what extend a sector is integrated into the global production network. As discussed earlier, the integration may have advantages as well as disadvantages. Economies may benefit from the integration into the global production network by technology transfer and the exploitation of increasing returns to scale. Regarding the backward linkages, the advantages are obvious: Foreign machinery but also foreign services may enhance domestic productivity. Forward integration opens foreign markets and allows the exploitation of increasing returns to scale. On the other hand, international lead firms may have a detrimental influence by setting higher standards and enforcing long-term contracts. For those reasons, especially multinational companies may allow for knowledge transfer. Additionally, as Altenburg (2006: 515) emphasizes, cooperation may lead to non-intended knowledge transfer. Whether and to what extend firms and economies profit from knowledge and technology transfer depends on several factors, such as the governance type.

As discussed in section 4.3.1.6, large shares of international linkages have merely positive effects. In contrast, especially in resource sectors, the essential problem of developing economies is increasing the local content and thus domestic value added and employment.

The issue of increasing content is of special relevance for several African economies. Examples for backward production linkages may be found in the Nigerian oil sector, whereas the attempts to increase local content in the forward linkages are exemplified in the construction of gold refinery in Ghana (Bloch & Owusu 2012: 439) and the establishment of a diamond polishing industry in Botswana (Mbayi 2011).

It is important to note that increasing local content does not contradict the presence of international companies. On the contrary, economic policy of the respective economy even seeks to build consortia with multinational firms to benefit from technology and knowledge transfer. However, the presence of international companies is not measured with this indicator.

5.3.2 Results

In a first step, I divide the BII and FII into four major economic sectors and show the integration between the big world regions (see figure 29). I therefore use an aggregated version of the world input-output table with the corresponding regions to construct this data. It should be noted that the data is not comparable with country specific data on GVCs since the regions are treated as single entity so that intra-regional trade is not counted. In general, the country-specific data need to be higher than the one of aggregated regions (chapter 5.3.2.1). In a second step, I will examine which industries specifically show high or low integration indices (chapter 5.3.2.2). Finally, country specific data on GVCs participation is presented (chapter 5.3.2.3).

5.3.2.1 Comparing world regions

Figure 29 illustrates enormous differences between the large regions of the world. Especially the big manufacturing hubs North America, the EU, and East Asia stand out with the lowest values. In comparison to economically less developed regions, they show a considerably smaller share of international linkages because the respective economies and their major trade partners are located within the same region. Again, it should be noted that regions are treated as single entities, meaning that data for single economies differs substantially in those aforementioned regions. For example, 69 percent of EU exports are sent to other countries within the EU. The corresponding value for East Asia is 48 percent, whereas the intra-regional exports of sub-Saharan African nations add up to only 14 percent. Thus, the data points out a severe lack of regional integration on the African continent (e.g., Hartzenberg 2011; Kayizzi-Mugerwa et al. 2014). African economies are part of GVCs which are dominated by companies in the industrialized North but remain loosely integrated within the continent. These findings support the conclusions drawn by trade policy analysis of Asche (2015b).

Concerning the BII, the manufacturing sector shows the highest values across all world regions. However, this is not true for sub-Saharan Africa and the Middle East, for which manufacturing is outscored by utilities. Especially electricity and construction show considerably high shares of international linkages. The primary commodity sectors and services show generally lower backward linkages. However, the example of South East Asia demonstrates that even in services, high backward integration is possible: The sectors with the highest indices are sea and air transport but also business services nec.

Figure 29: Backward (BII) and forward (FII) integration indices for aggregated sectors in world regions

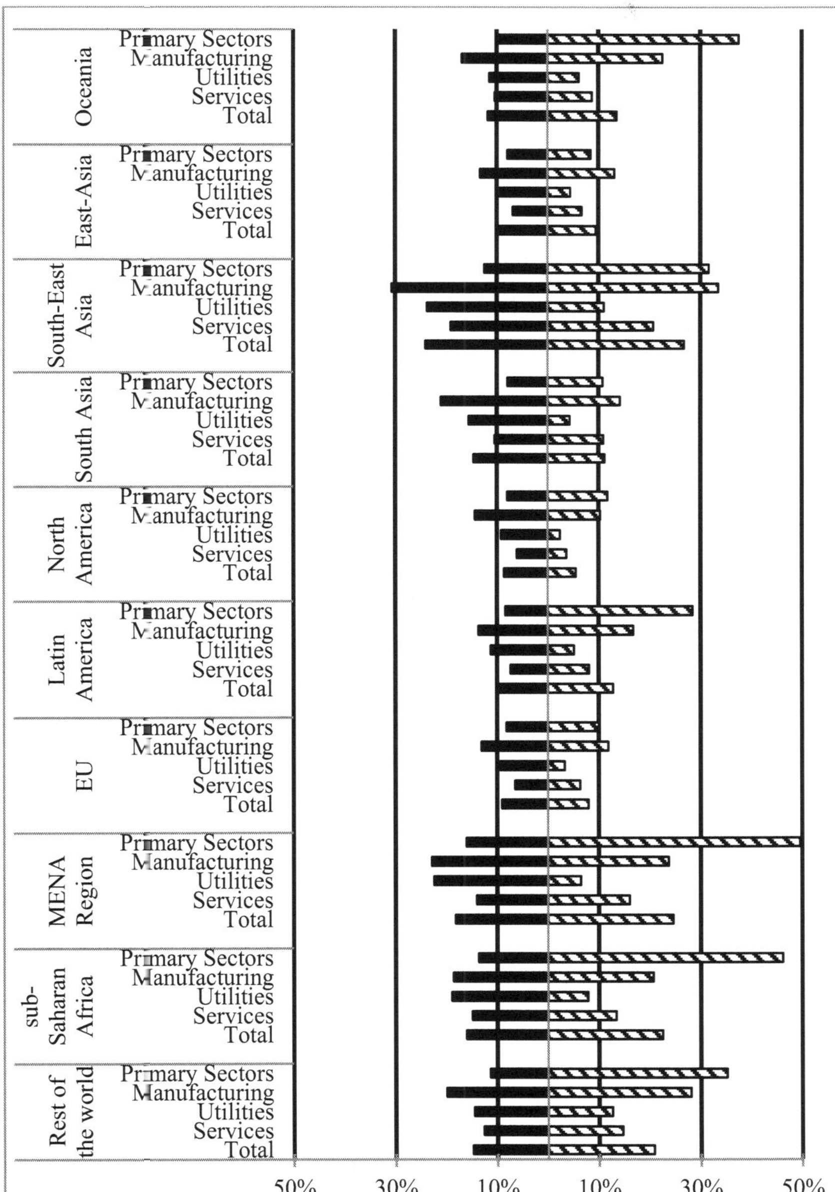

Source: Own calculation based on the GTAP Africa Database 2007; the value for the whole region (total) is calculated as the output weighted average of all four sectors.

Concerning the FII, primary products evidently show the highest indices, most narrowly followed by manufacturing. In South-Asia, the manufacturing sector's value even outscores the value of primary products. In Oceania, sub-Saharan Africa, and the MENA region, the values are especially high for the primary sectors.

According to the data, the service sector in general shows the lowest backward and forward participation and thus seems to be much less integrated into GVCs. The opposite is true for manufacturing, which scores high in both backward and forward participation, whereas primary commodities show only high forward participation indices.

5.3.2.2 Detailed sectoral analysis

Figure 30 clarifies to what extent sectors differ substantially concerning their integration into GVCs. Regarding primary commodities, backward integration in general is relatively low. The only sector in which the share of international linkages is higher than 20 percent is plant-based fibers exhibiting a backward integration index value of 24 percent. Concerning the forward linkage, there are huge differences between the sectors. The mineral sectors but also plant-based fibers and crops show a high forward integration. In the oil and gas sectors, the international share of forward linkages even exceeds 50 percent.

Indeed, most African economies are unable to process their primary products. The mineral sectors seem to be highly integrated into GVCs showing the most potential for technology transfer and upgrading in the sense of adding value within the economy. This is best exemplified by Nigeria's oil sector in which the international share of linkages is 74 percent. A case study on the Nigerian economy examining the reason for such linkages and pondering options to enhance local content in the oil sector is provided by Oyejide & Adewuyi (2012).

With regard to the literature (Kowalski et al. 2015: 82; OECD 2014: 142), a positive correlation between the size of the manufacturing sector and the backward integration index should be present. Accordingly, I expect high backward integration index values in those sectors. However, not all manufacturing sectors show a high BII.

Figure 30: Average backward (BII) and forward integration (FII) indices in Africa

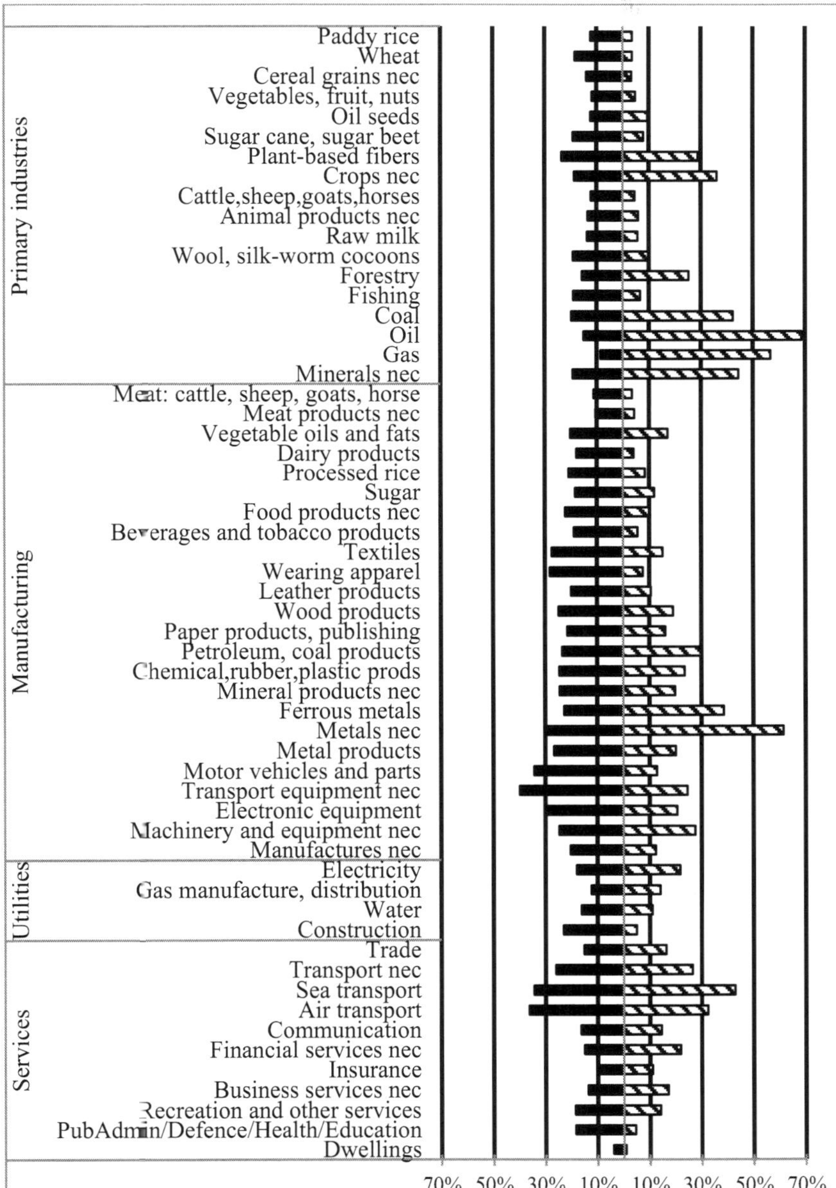

Source: Own depiction

In fact, nearly all low-technology sectors[129] such as food and beverages but also textiles as well as paper and wood products exhibit relatively low backward and forward integration indices.

The sectors showing the highest backward and forward integration indices are indeed the medium and high technology sectors, such as motor vehicles and parts, transport, machinery and electronic equipment, petroleum and coal products, as well as several metal producing sectors. In particular, the metals nec. sector—which is the only manufacturing sector with a positive RCA—shows the highest forward participation index across all other sectors.

These results are of special interest as Fagerberg (2000: 399) found that low-technology industries have a higher market-power in the sense of keeping rewards of productivity growth entirely within the industry so that these are not shared by price reductions. The sectors connected to electronic industries are, in contrast, highly competitive, and technological progress is passed on through lower prices.

Concerning the service sector, the BII and FII differs substantially between sectors. The transport sectors show considerably high values comparable to high technology manufacturing sectors. All other service sectors exhibit a very low share of international linkages. Insurance and dwellings are the only sectors in which the BII is below 10 percent.

5.3.2.3 Country specific integration into GVCs

The BII and the FII for 27 African economies and four aggregated sectors are shown in table 27. There are large differences between African economies. Cameroon shows the lowest BII of 12 percent, whereas Togo exhibits an extraordinary high backward integration into GVCs of 44 percent.

In terms of GDP, Togo is the smallest economy in the sample and without surprise the economy with the largest share of international backward linkages. The case of Togo confirms the results of Kowalski et al. (2015:

129 See Hatzichronoglou (1997) for a common definition of low, medium-low, medium-high, and high technology manufacturing sectors in ISIC industries. There is not a clear concordance table between the low and high technology sectors and the GTAP sector classification yet. However, the sectors are roughly comparable.

82) who propose that market size matters and is negatively correlated with the backward integration into GVCs.130

However, Togo still has extraordinary high values in the BII, especially in utilities and the service sectors, of above 40 percent. The other economies showing a high BII above 30 percent are Egypt, Mauritius, and Zimbabwe. In Egypt, the sectors with the highest BII (above 60 percent) are high-technology manufacturing sectors, such as motor vehicles and transport equipment. In contrast, the highest international share of backward linkages in Mauritius is in low technology manufacturing sectors, such as dairy products, processed rice but also agricultural sectors such as wheat, plant-based fibers, raw milk as well as wool and silk-worm cocoons. However, also textiles and wearing apparal, which are the main products of the successful Mauritian export processing zone, show relatively high values above 40 percent. In Zimbabwe the highest shares are also in agricultural products, such as paddy rice and wheat.

A generally low backward integration into GVCs is found in Cameroon (12 percent), followed by Nigeria (15 percent), Burkina Faso (16 percent), Rwanda (16 percent), Tanzania (16 percent), and South Africa (17 percent). The case of Nigeria—Africa's largest economy—deserves special attention because 84 percent of its exports is oil. The inputs to the oil sector were predominantly produced within the country (except for chemicals originating from East Asia) so that this sector shows a comparably low BII of 11.5 percent. Apart from that, Nigeria's low BII is a result of the successful promotion of local content (Morris et al. 2012: 87ff).

Another interesting example is Tanzania which has a considerable share of manufacturing exports. According to the usual export data, manufacturing is the largest sector accounting for 39 percent; this share is reduced to 21 percent in value added data. Tanzania's manufacturing exports predominantly originate from the metals nec. sector, which might be mainly gold. The sector usually exhibits a considerable high BII since to produce metals, minerals (the primary commodity) need to be imported. However, Tanzania—with a production capacity of 50 tons of gold in 2009—is a significant gold producer, and the corresponding sector shows a relatively low BII of only 19 percent in the data, suggesting that Tanzania would be

130 The hypothesis seems plausible regardless of the fact that Kowalski et al. (2015) use a different indicator. Their supporting argument: The smaller the economy, the lower the probability that inputs are produced within the economy. A counter example is Rwanda, the second smallest economy in the sample, with only 16 percent of international backward linkages.

able to provide most inputs for their mining industry on its own. This is in contrast to the case study of Mjimba (2011) which concludes: The GVC of Tanzania's mineral sector is dominated by multinational companies which source high complex value added from external producers and local content is limited to lowly critical products, such as food and beverages. If this is correct, the BII should show considerably higher values. The differences between the results of the case studies and the data used here need further examination.131

In principle, the highest BII is present in either manufacturing or utilities. Primary commodities, followed by services, show the lowest share of international linkages. Nonetheless, there are some exceptions in the primary sectors. In Guinea, Rwanda, and Zimbabwe, the primary commodities sector shows the highest international share of linkages.

Zimbabwe exhibits the highest BII value in primary commodities with 41 percent. Its main primary products are minerals nec. (especially platinum, iron ore, gold, and diamonds), crops and coal. Interestingly, all those sectors exhibit a high international share in backward and forward linkages. As a matter of fact, Zimbabwe is very well integrated due to its vicinity to South Africa, the largest manufacturing producer in sub-Saharan Africa. According to the data, 36 percent of its manufacturing exports and 30 percent of its primary commodity exports are delivered to South Africa.132

The other economy with high international backward linkages in primary commodities is Guinea. Its largest primary commodity sector is also minerals nec. (especially iron, gold, diamond, and bauxite), followed by cereal grains, paddy rice, and forestry. While the latter sectors show moderate values of about 15 percent in the BII, the minerals nec. sector shows a comparably high value of 30 percent.

The third example is Rwanda with generally weak international backward linkages. Its main primary commodities are vegetables and fruits which also show only small shares of international linkages of 6 percent. Again, relatively high values can be found in the mineral sector which shows a share of international linkages of nearly 50 percent.

---

131 Meanwhile the GTAP 9 Database is released with an update of the Tanzanian input-output tables. A comparison with this data should give more information.

132 A detailed analysis of the linkages in the mineral sector of Zimbabwe and the minerals policy can be found in Jourdan (2014).

The examples suggest that some economies such as Nigeria are capable (due to local content policies) to increase the domestic linkages of the mineral sectors, whereas some others are not.

The FII total value for the economies examined ranges from 10 to 40 percent. The differences in the broad sectors are much larger, ranging from 1 percent in utilities in Benin to 62 percent in primary commodities in Botswana

Table 27 demonstrates that the primary sector in nearly all countries reaches the highest values. Exceptions are Tunisia, Ghana, Senegal, Mozambique, Tanzania, and Zambia, in which the manufacturing sector ranks highest in FII. Much smaller values are found in utilities and the service sector. The economies with the highest FII total of above 30 percent are Mozambique, Nigeria, Zimbabwe, Botswana, Mauritius, and Guinea.

In general, the FII value seems to be dependent on the production and exports of the mineral sectors. As mentioned above, Nigeria's main export product is oil which generally has a high forward participation. In contrast to the relatively successful local content policy concerning the backward linkages of the oil sector, Nigeria is still an importer of petroleum as it is represented by the relatively high FII. In fact, Nigeria's downstream oil industry is made up of four refineries which often operate at less than 40 percent of full capacity due to fire, sabotage, poor management, or corruption (Morris et al. 2012: 87). Guinea's exports mainly consist of minerals such as bauxite, iron, diamond, and gold exhibiting a relatively high FII because these goods are exported as primary rather than processed metal products.

Analyzing the FII in that respect, a major difference emerges between mineral commodities, which are mostly exported as raw materials, and other minerals such as gold and copper, which are directly processed at the mines.

This is best exemplified by Ghana, the second largest gold producer after South Africa on the continent. In contrast to Nigeria (3 percent) and Guinea (28 percent), for examples, 46 percent of Ghana's exports are manufacturing goods. Interestingly, nearly 90 percent of Ghana's goods exported from the metals nec. sector (accounting for more than 60 percent of Ghana's manufacturing exports) are sold to South Africa where they are further processed and then re-exported. Thus, the FII of the manufacturing sector for non-ferrous metals (which includes gold) takes the value of 72 percent in Ghana. However, compared among the national economies, it is by far the sector with the highest FII in manufacturing (see figure 30).

Table 27: Backward and forward integration into GVCs, four aggregated sectors in African countries

		backward integration					forward integration				
		PRI	MA	UTI	SER	SU	PRI	MA	UTI	SER	SU
North Africa	Egypt	14%	36%	28%	27%	30%	19%	18%	7%	19%	18%
	Morocco	15%	27%	24%	17%	22%	18%	16%	4%	12%	14%
	Tunisia	18%	35%	30%	21%	28%	27%	32%	10%	21%	26%
Western Africa	Benin	12%	32%	38%	30%	29%	17%	15%	1%	9%	12%
	Burkina Faso	14%	18%	24%	14%	16%	41%	7%	4%	7%	22%
	Cameroon	10%	12%	15%	12%	12%	30%	16%	6%	16%	19%
	Cote d'Ivoire	13%	20%	22%	12%	16%	29%	27%	11%	17%	23%
	Ghana	13%	24%	28%	18%	20%	21%	30%	6%	16%	20%
	Guinea	31%	18%	28%	17%	22%	52%	30%	10%	20%	33%
	Nigeria	10%	18%	24%	23%	15%	52%	10%	4%	12%	39%
	Senegal	12%	35%	35%	23%	28%	15%	23%	4%	15%	17%
	Togo	31%	47%	51%	45%	44%	35%	27%	4%	21%	26%
Eastern Africa	Ethiopia	8%	19%	24%	21%	18%	13%	8%	1%	10%	10%
	Kenya	23%	28%	31%	22%	25%	21%	11%	5%	15%	13%
	Madagascar	14%	23%	27%	20%	22%	27%	12%	6%	16%	17%
	Malawi	19%	27%	30%	27%	25%	41%	19%	15%	15%	24%
	Mauritius	28%	35%	34%	27%	31%	50%	33%	9%	30%	34%
	Mozambique	24%	33%	31%	32%	30%	41%	53%	44%	25%	40%
	Rwanda	19%	15%	17%	13%	16%	36%	9%	5%	12%	20%
	Tanzania	8%	16%	21%	18%	16%	25%	30%	7%	18%	21%
	Uganda	15%	22%	25%	15%	18%	42%	17%	5%	10%	21%
	Zambia	21%	21%	28%	18%	21%	30%	41%	15%	21%	28%
	Zimbabwe	41%	33%	30%	31%	34%	43%	48%	24%	25%	39%
Southern Africa	Botswana	15%	26%	31%	23%	24%	62%	42%	7%	15%	35%
	Namibia	27%	25%	38%	23%	26%	44%	38%	9%	17%	28%
	South Africa	16%	21%	16%	12%	17%	37%	25%	9%	12%	19%

Source: Own calculation based on the GTAP Africa Database 2007; PRI: primary sectors, MA: manufacturing sectors, UTI: utilities, SER: services; see also footnote 108; the value for the whole region (SU) is calculated as the output weighted average of all four sectors.

This being said, there are in fact several other economies in which metals nec. accounts for a huge share of exports pushing the FII in the whole economy. Those are Tanzania (also with its gold sector), Zambia as the largest copper producer in Africa (Fessehaie 2012) as well as Zimbabwe and Mozambique. Another perfect example is Botswana with its diamond industry.133 These are the economies which also display a high FII in the manufacturing sector.

Mozambique is a special case since it additionally shows a high FII value in utilities which mainly derives from the electricity sector with a FII of 60 percent. The manufacturing sector in Mozambique accounts for 47 percent of all exports which are dominated by the metals sector. Besides other minerals, the largest share of those metals is constituted by aluminum which is entirely produced in the smelter Mozal near the capital Maputo for exporting purposes. Regarding trade in value added data, Mozambique's manufacturing sector accounts only for 17 percent, whereas the electricity sector accounts for 44 percent of exports. The input-output data reveals that the metals sector uses 41 percent of value added from the electricity sector as inputs, while another huge part is exported directly to South Africa and Zimbabwe. It is thus not the availability of bauxite134 but the cheap supply of energy which is the decisive factor for the production of aluminum in Mozambique.

5.4 Interim conclusion

Technological developments as well as trade and investment liberalization allow for the increasing fragmentation of production activities across the globe. Accordingly, GVCs, which are dominated by large multinational companies, are considered to be the defining feature of the current wave of globalization. As a result, developing economies nowadays face a growing competitive pressure and a reduction of policy space for industry protection compared to previous decades.

Due to the increasing fragmentation of the production process, goods and services contain inputs from many countries, which are not represented in conventional statistics on gross trade. The chapter introduces the concept of trade in value added and questions the differentiation between tradable and non-tradable goods. I have revealed that the manufacturing share of total world trade is reduced from 61 to 38 percent in trade in value added. In contrast, the share of services in trade in value added accounts for 38 percent rather than 23 percent in gross trade. In Africa, more

133 Today, about 60 percent of the global diamond polishing industry is in India (Mbayi 2011: 11).

134 A large part of bauxite is imported from Australia (Yager 2006).

than half of the exports in value added (53 percent) and gross exports (56 percent) are amounted by primary commodities. The share of manufacturing in exports in value added is only 18 percent in contrast to gross exports of 32 percent. Services, which are generally regarded as non-tradable goods, exceed the share of manufacturing exports in value added data (26 percent), whereas they only account for 11 percent in gross exports.

Despite a huge share of services in the GDP, primary commodities and manufacturing remain the dominant trading sectors. Conventional trade statistics underestimate the role of services in international trade. Nonetheless, the share of service content in exports is lower than the share of services in GDP.

In the light of the new trade data, I re-evaluate the revealed comparative advantage of African economies. African economies show a considerable export-surplus in primary products. However, in value-added data, it is not as high as conventional trade statistics suggest. I can furthermore demonstrate that those economies which have no revealed comparative advantage in commodities perform well in the services rather than in manufacturing.

The question for African economies remains whether the integration into GVCs has a positive or negative impact. Indeed, there is a growing divergence among researchers regarding the topic of GVCs. Some focus on the organization and governance structures of GVCs which determine the distribution within the chain. Their data is mostly based on case studies, and they take the role of the international trade system into account. Thus, they seem to be aligned with the tradition of world system theorists while arguing that the involvement of low development countries in intra-industry trade poses risks for an uneven distribution of profits. They are opposed by a growing number of scholars whose research roots in new datasets by international organizations in which governance structures as well as the international trade system play only a minor role. This group of scientists largely focuses on the influence of the nation state and its economic policy and emphasizes chances as well as opportunities of the integration into GVCs while providing several strategies for upgrading within those chains. From their point of view, the integration of developing countries into GVCs provides not only the opportunity to specialize in their (dynamic) comparative advantage but also is a chance to exploit increasing returns to scale and benefit from intended or unintended knowledge and technology transfer.

According to the literature, the integration of African economies into GVCs is a unique opportunity for industrialization. However, this statement mainly counts on case studies. Only recently, with the provision of international input-output tables, there have been attempts to provide an empirical assessment of African economies into GVCs. As to the respective publications, the Eora MRIO Database which includes input-output tables for only two African economies has been used to the present day. The GTAP Africa Database with national input-output tables from 27 African economies is suggested at this point to provide better data for such an analysis. I further propose to use the international share of linkages as an indicator for measuring the extent to which different sectors are integrated into GVCs.

As a result, I find that Africa possesses a considerable share of international linkages comparable to other regions, such as South Asia. African economies participate in GVCs which are dominated by companies in the industrialized North while remaining loosely integrated within the continent.

Concerning backward linkages, especially the manufacturing sectors and utilities are integrated into GVCs, whereas the primary sectors display the highest share of international forward linkages. Accordingly, the mineral sector plays the major role in Africa's integration into GVCs. Oil and gas but also other minerals and the corresponding manufacturing for non-ferrous metals are the sectors which are mainly integrated into GVCs. The economies with the highest forward integration into GVCs are economies with large mineral resources, such as Nigeria, Botswana, Zimbabwe, and Mozambique. These results confirm the findings of case studies, which suggest an increasing importance of multinational companies, especially in mineral commodities. While this phenomenon provides a wide range of upgrading opportunities, it also jeopardizes perpetuated international dependence. Interestingly, several of those resource-rich economies managed to increase their local content of backward linkages (e.g., Nigeria) but were not able to process the minerals yielded on their own. However, there have been attempts to also increase the local content of the forward linkage (e.g., the gold industry in Ghana or the diamond polishing industry in Botswana).

The literature suggests a relationship between a large manufacturing sector and a high participation in GVCs. Indeed, I have shown that overall the African manufacturing sector scores the highest BII. The sectors with the highest backward integration into GVCs are high-technology manufacturing sectors, such as the production of motor vehicles, transport, and electronic equipment. Similarly, high values can be found for the service sectors sea and air transport. However, these are not the only sectors with a high international share of backward linkages. In several African economies, also agricultural sectors and low-tech manufacturing sectors are highly integrated into GVCs. The economies showing the highest backward integration in that regard are Togo, followed by Egypt, Mauritius, and Zimbabwe.

The service sector generally scores relatively low in the FII and BII. It is only the transport sectors showing relatively high degrees of forward and backward participation. Business services (communication, financial services, insurance, and business nec.) rank low on BII and FII and generally seem to be less integrated into GVCs, especially in Africa. These results suggest that offshoring in services is not yet as developed as in manufacturing.135 If technology transfer in services is also dependent on the integration in GVCs (measured by FII und BII), this would be no good indication for a successful service-led growth model in African economies. On the other hand, there is some evidence suggesting that services are less dominated by large multinational firms than manufacturing, meaning that market access is much easier. Especially for landlocked economies with fewer natural resources, the service sector may provide opportunities for economic development.

Future research should be first and foremost directed to the improvement of data quality and availability. Special actions should be taken to the provision of current input-output tables for single African economies. Accordingly, further research should carefully differentiate between integration into GVCs defined as foreign production linkages and the presence of international firms. Research questions should focus on how and under which conditions integration into GVCs influence technology transfer and productivity changes in single economic sectors. Most case studies focus on the role of hierarchical governance structures. Up to date, there is no international comparable data available to empirically measure the influence of differing governance types.

135 The low integration of services might be a result of trade barriers in services. Especially poor regulatory systems are considered to be a special problem for the benefits of trade liberalization in services (Majluf & Zarrilli 2007).

6 Résumé

Africa is often said to be the enclave of the economic world system stagnating in the stage of traditional economy. In contrast to this presumption, the continent was already integrated in the international economic system since the period of Islamic trade when Muslims dominated the commercial world between the 11th and the 16th century. The opening of the Atlantic sea route to West Africa and the establishment of the European mercantile trade system are turning points in the African history. Since then, African economies were heavily influenced by its outside relations with the European imperial powers. Colonization was only the culmination point of a long-lasting period of imperial exploitation of resources with a disastrous economic and political record. Traditional agriculture and the production of cheap raw materials were the major economic activities when African economies reached independence. After decolonization, the goal of the newly established governments was to become politically and economically independent of their former colonial masters. The quest for industrial self-sufficiency became apparent, especially since the former colonies served as markets for industrial goods only and exported solely raw materials and food. Thus, early development theories were characterized by export pessimism and recommended policies of import substitution industrialization.

The data sources for the time between 1960 and 1980 are ambiguous. However, the industrial and manufacturing sector in most African economies rose during this period. Nevertheless, only few industries became competitive so that the economic outcomes of this industrialization remain negligible. The African world share of manufacturing remained at 2.3 percent in 1980. Despite the early industrialization efforts after its political independence, Africa has never managed to become economically independent and has remained vulnerable to external developments.

The African continent experienced a disastrous economic crisis at the beginning of the 1980s. The neoclassical explanation of the African crisis focused on government debt as a result of high state consumption, corruption, and inefficient allocation. The Washington Consensus, suggesting a minimalist government including the achievement of balance-of-payments as well as fiscal deficit equilibrium, became the main feature of the new development paradigm of the 1980s and early 1990s. The following recommendations of privatization, deregulation, and liberalization gained supremacy in important development institutions. During this time, the manufacturing share in whole Africa rose from 11.5 to 14.8 percent, whereas in the developing Africa it fell from 12.6 percent in 1980 to 8.2 percent in 1995. Most of the developing countries needed to go through a painful adjustment process, and it became clear that the overall situation has become one of stagnation.

Since 1995, in the period of the Post Washington Consensus Consensus, the African economic growth rate has been as high as in the time of import substitution industrialization. Sub-Saharan Africa has even outscored these growth rates. However, the growth is not associated with an increasing share of manufacturing value added. In contrast, the share fell from 14.8 to 10.4 percent in 2010.

The rise of East Asian economies as well as the establishment of the New Development Economics paved the way for a new interest in industrialization and industrial policy not only in the literature but also in African government institutions. The goal of industrialization was even implemented in the new United Nation Sustainable Development Goals.

6.1 Premature deindustrialization

The historical evidence for the importance of industrialization is overwhelming. It is often stated that each developed country had gone through a process of industrialization. Industrialization describes the transformation from an economy based on agriculture toward one based on industry and especially manufacturing. Indeed, there are some examples of economies which managed to develop without a significant share of the manufacturing sector. However, these examples are either extraordinarily small or resource-rich or both. For all other economies, industrialization was an inevitable process which they needed to go through.

Since the works of Kuznets and Chenery (Kuznets 1967; Chenery 1960; Chenery & Syrquin 1975; Chenery 1982; Syrquin & Chenery 1989), structural change can thus be regarded as one of the stylized facts of economic development. The share of agriculture in GDP and employment falls as economies grow richer; the share of manufacturing shows a hub, and services rise unambiguously when economies grow richer. However, these patterns have changed over time. The manufacturing hub in employment has been much smaller in recent years than it was in 1960. Instead, services show higher shares of employment at earlier levels of development. If manufacturing is an important engine of growth, this trend is no good signs for Africa's latecomer economies. The trend may also suggest that services will take the role of manufacturing in developing countries.

However, the reduction in the manufacturing hub can only be found in employment shares but not in value added shares. Global manufacturing employment has decreased substantially in the last decades. However, these decreases were mainly due to labor-saving technological progress so that value added shares have remained relatively stable. The declining manufacturing employment share which Rodrik calls "premature deindustrialization" can thus be attributed to increases in global manufacturing productivity.

African economies deviate substantially from the development paths of the early industrializers but also from those of Asian and Latin American economies. They show comparably high shares of agriculture in value added and employment, respectively, and corresponding low shares of manufacturing.

In contrast to the global development, African manufacturing experienced no increases in relative productivity. As a result, African economies display value added shares that are significantly lower than expected judging from their income levels.

In the service sector, the opposite is the case. Relative productivity of services decreased in the rest of the world but not in African economies. Consequently, African economies exhibit by far lower employment shares but higher value added shares in services than expected by their income level.

Thus, it seems that the history of industrialization has by-passed the continent. In early development theories, industrialization was seen as synonymous with technological development, economic wealth, and political dominance. In the same vein, a bulk of literature implies that manufacturing is the engine of economic growth, and thus structural change is responsible for economic development, especially in developing economies.

In economic theory, however, it is not clear whether industrialization is the key for economic growth or is merely a by-product of economic development. African economies may follow a different development path than the early industrializers or the East-Asian economies. Services have already significantly increased in importance on a global scale, not least because of the steady rise of information and communication technologies. It is thus likely to become the key sector for economic development in the twenty-first century, especially in the African economies.

If, however, manufacturing is still the main engine of economy, what makes the manufacturing sector unique? The literature emphasizing the role of the manufacturing sector draws mainly on three arguments: the structural bonus hypothesis, increasing returns to scale, and the relevance of backward and forward linkages. All three arguments were tested for African economies.

6.2 Structural bonus hypothesis

Productivity gaps between economic sectors are generally present but are particularly large in African economies. Agriculture has by far the lowest productivity while maintaining the by far largest sector in employment shares. Manufacturing only accounts for 7.5 percent of total employment and shows productivity slightly above the average productivity. The sectors with the highest productivity are mining, followed by public utilities and financial and business services, respectively. Thus, it is argued, that if one could shift labor or output from the agricultural to the higher productivity sectors such as manufacturing, productivity in the whole economy would rise immediately. In recent empirical literature the concept has become prominent again under the notion of the structural change bonus.

Using a shift-share analysis, it was shown that during the period of import substitution industrialization, economic growth in Africa was mainly driven by structural change. During the time of policies, the positive static effect of structural change was exceeded by the negative dynamic shift effect. From 1995 to 2010, the positive static shift effect outweighed the negative dynamic shift effect.

A negative dynamic shift effect means that labor productivity decreases in the high productivity sector which experiences labor inflows. The negative dynamic shift effect is attributed to adjustment frictions or problems in organizational restructuring. As I have shown in section 4.2, the negative dynamic effect is a result of a more general problem of labor surplus in most of the economic sectors.

6.3 Increasing returns to scale or labor surplus?

The structural bonus hypothesis assumes that all sectors exhibit constant returns to scale, meaning that productivity is not influenced by the amount of resources employed in the sector. In contrast to this assumption, the manufacturing sector is supposed to exhibit increasing returns to scale. In agricultural sector and services, one generally assumes decreasing rather than increasing returns to scale.

The extent of increasing returns is usually measured by the relationship between output and productivity growth. The relationship, which is known by the name of Verdoorn's law, has been subject of several long-lasting controversies.

Kaldors demand-side version is the most common interpretation of this law. According to him, the Verdoorn coefficient measures the extent to which productivity growths if the growth of output rises; the higher the Verdoorn coefficient, the higher the returns to scale. However, a high Verdoorn coefficient is a double-edged sword. A high Verdoorn coefficient near to unity shows independence between employment and output growth. In the supply-side interpretation, shifting employment to a sector with a Verdoorn coefficient near to unity would not increase output at all. A simultaneous decrease in labor productivity is the statistical result. The phenomenon can be interpreted as surplus labor. Reconsidering the structural bonus hypothesis, this phenomenon is depicted in the negative dynamic shift effect.

The results presented in this thesis clearly refute the hypothesis that the manufacturing sector is important because it shows the highest returns to scale. In contrast, manufacturing and construction can be regarded as the sectors with the highest output elasticity on employment, thus providing the most opportunities for jobs. However, the tests for different periods demonstrate that the results are not very robust over time.

In the three African economies under consideration, I found indication for surplus labor in the majority of sectors. The only sectors with a positive output-elasticity on employment in Mauritius and South Africa are manufacturing and construction. In Kenya, the only sector with a positive relationship between output and labor is the service sector for wholesale and retail trade.

It seems that there is no clear classification of industries according to decreasing, constant and increasing returns to scale. Measuring the extent of increasing returns for single sectors might be misleading due to theoretical reasons. A common theoretical explanation for increasing returns to scale, provided by Adam Smith, is the division of labor itself which relates to the extent of the market. Services may help manufacturing firms to be more productive by efficiency gains in logistics, management, and coordination but also by absorbing frontier technologies (Lodefalk 2015: 1). Former in-house production of services is outsourced and, by consequence, shows up in recent statistics as services value added whereas it has formerly been counted as manufacturing value added. Hence, services are, to some degree, a result of the increasing segmentation of manufacturing production and the differentiation between services and manufacturing becomes increasingly blurred. Increasing returns to scale and the servicification of the economy can be interpreted as the results of the same phenomenon.

6.4 Tradable versus non-tradable goods

Increasing returns can only unfold their strength if the demand is large enough. Opening the economy offers the opportunity to exploit the advantages of increasing returns to scale. However, this is only possible if the produced goods can be traded worldwide. Thus, the distinction between tradable and non-tradable goods is an important element of international economics. In conventional sector classifications, service industries are characterized as non-tradables.

By applying an international input-output table, it is possible to disentangle exports and to differentiate between domestic and foreign value added. The resulting data for trade in value added reveals an increasing importance of services in international trade. According to conventional trade statistics, the manufacturing goods account for more than 60 percent of international trade. Services account for only 23 percent. Measuring trade in value added, manufacturing goods and services each account for 38 percent of international trade. In nearly all African economies, service value added exports exceed manufacturing value added exports.

6.5 Linkages

The third major argument in favor of the manufacturing sector is that linkage effects are stronger than in agriculture and services. The concept of linkages was originally introduced by Albert Hirschman but is widely used to identify the key sectors for economic development. It distinguishes backward linkages from forward linkages. Backward linkages are the interrelations of an economic sector along the whole upstream supply chain. Forward linkages are the interrelations of an economic sector along the whole downstream supply chain.

African linkages generally conform to the values found in other regions of the world. Acknowledging the superior importance of the backward linkage, I confirm the hypothesis that the manufacturing sector shows the strongest backward linkages. Regarding the forward linkages, the primary sectors show the highest value, followed by manufacturing. I further demonstrate that in primary sectors, it is not agriculture but the mineral sectors which show the strongest linkages.

Sectors showing both strong backward and forward linkages can be defined as lead sectors. These sectors are found in the intermediary manufactures such as metal, chemical, paper or coal industries, as already suggested by Chenery & Watanabe (1958: 493).

6.6 Global Value Chains

Hirschman (1958: 105–110) argued that due the large interdependences to other sectors, the promotion of these lead sectors can spur economic growth in the whole economy. However, the linkages can exert their influence beyond the limits of national economy. African economies reveal huge gaps between the domestic and the world linkage, especially in the mineral sectors.

Technological developments as well as trade and investment liberalization allow for an increasing fragmentation of production activities across the globe. The proliferation of GVCs is seen as a defining feature in trade during the new century.

Integration into GVCs provides an enormous chance for the industrialization of Africa. Market access allows the exploitation of increasing returns to scale and economies and firms can profit from technology and knowledge transfer.

On the downside, the integration into GVCs displaces a loss of domestic linkages. Especially in resource sectors, the challenge of developing economies is to increase the local content and thus domestic value added and employment, respectively. Furthermore, the integration into GVCs obliges the African companies to captive governance structures and international standards by international companies which may hinder technology transfer and increase the risk of unequal division of profits.

I reveal that the sectors with the highest backward integration in GVCs are high-technology manufacturing sectors, such as motor vehicles, transport, and electronic equipment. Similar high values are shown by the service sectors sea and air transport. However, these are not the only sectors with a high international share of backward linkages. In several economies, also agricultural sectors and low-tech manufacturing sectors are highly integrated into GVCs. The economies showing the highest backward integration into GVCs are Togo, followed by Egypt, Mauritius, and Zimbabwe.

Oil and gas but also other minerals and the corresponding manufacturing sector for non-ferrous metals are the sectors with the highest share of international forward linkages, which are mostly integrated into GVCs. Accordingly, the large mineral exporters Nigeria, Botswana, Zimbabwe, and Mozambique are the economies with the highest forward integration into GVCs.

In contrast to commonplace preconceptions, African economies are well integrated into the global economy. In many cases, however, they are mostly integrated by providing mineral commodities which are exported without further processing. The challenge those economies are facing is how to increase the local content of the forward and backward linkages to spread the economic benefit throughout the domestic economy as a whole. Unfortunately, the forward linkages in commodities are much stronger than the backward linkages, and it seems even more difficult to increase the local content of the forward linkage. The service sectors are not yet as integrated into GVCs as manufacturing sectors are. Service industries are less dominated by multinational firms and provide easier market access also for latecomer economies. The service sector may thus provide development opportunities especially for landlocked economies with fewer natural resources.

6.7 Summing up

The influence of the East Asian Development Model has spurred a renewed commitment to industrialization and the manufacturing sector in Africa. From an economic perspective, there seems no need for a continent-wide goal of industrialization. Nevertheless, concrete policy recommendations and the identification of key sectors for single African economies are vital for further development, and more detailed research is needed to account for single country characteristics and the related challenges.

Future research should be first and foremost directed to the provision of a broader and more reliable database. Comparable data on the sectoral is still rare and, if available, at a low quality. Especially data on a more disaggregated level is needed to give insight into the negative deviation of African manufacturing. Sectoral data on education or human capital but also reliable sectoral data of the capital stock would allow determing how to cope with labor surplus in the majority of sectors in African economies. Finally, special attention should be given to the provision of current input-output tables for single African economies. Research questions should focus on how and under which conditions the integration into GVCs influence technology transfer and productivity changes in single economic sectors.

Nevertheless, the research conducted in this thesis reveals that the African economies are characterized by a development which shows a significantly lower share of manufacturing than if they had followed the "normal" development path. The global shift toward services and the African economic history indicate that industrialization has by-passed the continent. Meaning that the majority of economies will never achieve the same share of manufacturing as the early industrializers and the East Asian economies.

The global environment has dramatically changed in the last decades and still is. Especially the production of manufacturing spreads worldwide and, thus, is increasingly organized in GVCs which are dominated by large companies. The increasing prevalence of GVCs has several impacts on African economies. African economies can profit from technology and knowledge transfer and do not need to create entire industries to be competitive but may focus on specialized production processes.

Accordingly, premature deindustrialization is not necessarily a bad sign for the African economies. Services might be a good compensation for the manufacturing sector. Service sectors show similar or even higher labor productivity than manufacturing. Additionally, there are no signs that manufacturing exhibits higher returns to scale than services. In contrast to the conventional view, services may also be traded either directly or indirectly when embedded in primary or manufacturing goods. However, I found evidence that manufacturing is the sector with the highest employment elasticity to output, indicating that the manufacturing sector provides the best opportunities for employment creation. Regarding the provision of jobs for the huge amounts of young people growing up in the African economies, the rise of services is no good sign.

Furthermore, the manufacturing sector is the sector with the strongest linkages. In line with the unbalanced growth hypothesis by Albert Hirschman, promoting the manufacturing sector seems to be the best way for inducing economic growth in the total economy. Services show by far weaker production linkages. Thus, the linkages hypothesis provides the best argument for industrial policy in the manufacturing sector.

To conclude, the manufacturing sector remains an important engine of growth and is not only a by-product of economic development. Conclusively, the lack of manufacturing in the African economies is a severe constraint for the development prospects of these economies. The service-led growth model, however, might be a good alternative for resource scarce or landlocked economies with low chances to compete in global manufacturing.

Table a1: Regression results for equation 1; value added share as dependent variable; sample: benchmark economies

dep. var:	AGR	MIN	MAN	CON	PU	WRT	TSC	FIRE	GCSP	SER
C	-2.94 (-1.7)	-22.6 (3.4)**	-13.5 (0.9)**	-12.0 (0.9)**	-19.7 (1.6)**	-4.75 (0.6)**	-5.6 (0.7)**	-7.93 (2.0)**	-6.92 (0.8)**	-5.11 (0.4)**
LG(RGDPC)	1.13 (0.4)**	4.99 (0.8)**	2.68 (0.2)**	2.04 (0.2)**	3.27 (0.4)**	0.59 (0.1)**	0.46 (0.2)**	1.00 (0.5)*	2.38 (0.2)**	0.8 (0.1)**
LG(RGDPC)^2	-0.12 (0.0)**	-0.32 (0.0)**	-0.15 (0.0)**	-0.11 (0.0)**	-0.17 (0.0)**	-0.03 (0.0)**	-0.02 0.00	-0.05 0.00	-0.13 (0.0)**	-0.03 (0.0)**
Obs.	1297	1297	1297	1297	1297	1297	1297	1297	1297	1001
R^2	0.64	0.19	0.17	0.12	0.28	0.07	0.23	0.03	0.24	0.63
F-stat.	1144	150.8	134.8	87.4	256.3	49.37	198.3	20.55	201.1	852.6
				period fixed effects						
Year	AGR	MIN	MAN	CON	PU	WRT	TSC	FIRE	GCSP	SER
1960	-0.31	-0.60	0.06	0.16	-0.46	0.08	-0.25	-0.34	0.04	0.01
1970	-0.22	-0.35	0.08	0.20	-0.20	0.04	-0.23	-0.29	-0.04	-0.07
1980	-0.05	-0.09	0.06	0.12	-0.06	0.00	-0.06	-0.16	-0.01	-0.05
1990	0.07	0.13	0.00	-0.02	0.15	0.00	0.04	0.07	0.00	0.00
2000	0.16	0.27	-0.06	-0.20	0.21	-0.02	0.21	0.28	-0.02	0.03
2010	0.18	0.29	-0.26	-0.28	0.13	-0.06	0.32	0.31	-0.01	0.09

Source: Own calculations using E-Views 9.0, standard errors in parentheses

Table a2: Regression results for equation 2; employment share as dependent variable; sample: benchmark economies

dep. var:	AGR	MIN	MAN	CON	PU	WRT	TSC	FIRE	GCSP	SER
C	-14.5	-29.9	-15.6	-24.1	-25.3	-15.2	-12.1	-16.7	-10.4	-10.3
	(1.2)**	(2.0)**	(0.8)**	(0.6)**	(0.9)**	(0.8)**	(0.7)**	(1.1)**	(0.6)**	(0.5)**
LG(RG DPC)	4.09	6.18	2.94	4.47	4.3	2.72	1.76	2.2	3.19	1.73
	(0.3)**	(0.5)**	(0.2)**	(0.1)**	(0.2)**	(0.2)**	(0.2)**	(0.3)**	(0.1)**	(0.1)**
LG(RG DPC)^2	-0.29	-0.38	-0.15	-0.23	-0.23	-0.13	-0.08	-0.08	-0.17	-0.07
	(0.0)**	(0.0)**	(0.0)**	(0.0)**	(0.0)**	(0.0)**	(0.0)**	(0.0)**	(0.0)**	(0.0)**
Obs.	1275	1275	1275	1275	1274	1275	1275	1275	1274	1029
R^2	0.77	0.36	0.39	0.73	0.36	0.62	0.51	0.72	0.55	0.81
F-stat.	2129	362.3	401.9	1711	362.0	1041	660.5	1662	764.6	2239
				period fixed effects						
Year	AGR	MIN	MAN	CON	PU	WRT	TSC	FIRE	GCSP	SER
1960	0.30	0.01	0.23	0.06	-0.03	-0.34	-0.10	-0.30	-0.18	-0.20
1970	0.17	-0.08	0.13	0.03	-0.01	-0.26	-0.08	-0.26	-0.16	-0.19
1980	0.07	0.06	0.09	0.01	0.04	-0.12	-0.08	-0.16	0.01	-0.07
1990	-0.10	-0.02	0.04	-0.02	0.06	0.07	0.00	0.01	0.04	0.04
2000	-0.22	-0.09	-0.12	0.00	-0.06	0.25	0.16	0.25	0.05	0.14
2010	-0.24	0.17	-0.33	0.04	-0.07	0.35	0.20	0.36	0.10	0.21

Source: Own calculations using E-Views 9.0, standard errors in parentheses

Table a3: Regression results for equation 3; relative productivity as dependent variable; sample: benchmark economies

dep. var:	AGR	MIN	MAN	CON	PU	WRT	TSC	FIRE	GCSP	SER
C	32.91	779.2	-24.2	178.1	116.7	9.09	57.60	-123	-12.0	-23.5
	(3.2)**	(98)**	(6.3)**	(31)**	(33)**	(8.1)	(8.2)**	(35)**	(9.1)	(6.1)**
LG(RG DPC)	-10.5	-248	8.96	-56.7	-40.4	-0.80	-18.1	45.59	5.52	10.06
	(1.1)**	(88)**	(2.1)**	(11)**	(11)**	(2.8)	(2.7)**	(12)**	(3.1)	(2.1)**
LG(RG DPC)^2	1.13	26.34	-1.06	6.03	4.82	-0.15	1.93	-5.36	-0.67	-1.29
	(0.1)**	(9.7)**	(0.2)**	(1.2)**	(1.3)**	(0.3)	(0.3)**	(1.3)**	(0.3)	(0.2)**
Obs.	1267	1267	1267	1267	1266	1267	1267	1267	983	983
R^2	0.72	0.63	0.9	0.73	0.81	0.85	0.82	0.79	0.83	0.87
F-stat.	38.1	25.84	133.9	41.24	64.43	86.95	69.19	57.5	61.8	82.9
				period fixed effects						
Year	AGR	MIN	MAN	CON	PU	WRT	TSC	FIRE	GCSP	SER
1960	-0.20	-4.42	-0.14	0.42	-1.96	0.58	-0.17	0.31	0.32	0.29
1970	-0.13	-2.63	-0.04	0.39	-1.00	0.46	-0.20	0.11	0.06	0.20
1980	-0.05	-0.79	-0.04	0.16	-0.78	0.14	-0.04	0.06	-0.08	0.01
1990	0.05	0.17	-0.04	-0.08	0.05	-0.12	0.01	0.36	-0.11	-0.06
2000	0.12	3.88	0.08	-0.33	1.24	-0.38	0.09	-0.42	-0.05	-0.19
2010	0.15	1.43	0.15	-0.44	1.59	-0.56	0.20	-0.67	0.03	-0.14

Source: Own calculations using E-Views 9.0, standard errors in parentheses

Table a4: Regression results for equation 2; employment share as dependent variable; sample: Africa

dep. var:	AGR	MIN	MAN	CON	PU	WRT	TSC	FIRE	GCSP	SER
C	-5.59	-16.9	-4.96	-17.8	-11.5	-0.9	-3.77	-3.24	-7.09	-4.96
	(0.8)**	(2.4)**	(1.2)**	(1.8)**	(1.8)**	-1.2	(0.9)**	(1.0)**	(1.2)**	(1.0)**
LG(RG	1.52	3.03	0.28	3.42	1.37	-0.58	-0.16	-0.62	1.89	0.81
DPC)	(0.2)**	(0.6)**	(0.3)	(0.5)**	(0.5)**	(0.3)	(0.2)	(0.3)*	(0.3)**	(0.2)**
LG(RG	-0.11	-0.20	0.00	-0.20	-0.08	0.05	0.02	0.05	-0.11	-0.05
DPC)^2	(0.0)**	(0.0)**	(0.0)	(0.0)**	(0.0)*	(0.0)*	(0.0)	(0.0)**	(0.0)**	(0.0)**
Obs.	628	628	628	628	628	628	628	628	628	478
R^2	0.95	0.83	0.91	0.9	0.83	0.88	0.93	0.95	0.92	0.94
F-stat.	152.0	41.6	86.22	81.01	41.71	61.47	116.0	164.7	95.34	103.0
				period fixed effects						
Year	AGR	MIN	MAN	CON	PU	WRT	TSC	FIRE	GCSP	SER
1960	0.20	-0.31	-0.20	-0.37	-0.43	-0.54	-0.28	-0.59	-0.53	-0.44
1970	0.14	-0.24	-0.09	-0.18	-0.17	-0.41	-0.16	-0.50	-0.14	-0.26
1980	0.01	0.03	-0.04	-0.02	0.12	-0.16	-0.01	-0.19	0.03	-0.07
1990	-0.04	0.05	0.07	0.02	0.20	0.04	0.00	0.12	0.04	0.04
2000	-0.07	0.02	0.08	0.18	0.01	0.28	0.04	0.32	0.14	0.19
2010	-0.16	0.12	0.11	0.34	-0.14	0.53	0.32	0.72	0.17	0.36

Source: Own calculations using E-Views 9.0, standard errors in parentheses

Table a5: Regression results for equation 2; employment share as dependent variable; sample: Latin America

dep. var:	AGR	MIN	MAN	CON	PU	WRT	TSC	FIRE	GCSP	SER
C	-8.6	-4.75	-17	-11.6	-11.3	-18.5	-6.24	-11.8	-21.7	-11.7
	(2.0)**	-6.8	(3.3)**	(3.6)**	-6.8	(2.7)**	(2.7)*	-6.2	(2.6)**	(2.2)**
LG(RG	1.69	0.16	3.69	2.13	1.71	4.02	1.08	1.91	2.3	2.59
DPC)	(0.5)**	(1.6)	(0.8)**	(0.8)*	(1.6)	(0.6)**	(0.6)	(1.4)	(0.6)**	(0.5)**
LG(RG	-0.1	-0.02	-0.23	-0.13	-0.11	-0.24	-0.08	-0.11	-0.14	-0.15
DPC)^2	(0.0)**	(0.1)	(0.0)**	(0.0)**	(0.1)	(0.0)**	(0.0)*	(0.1)	(0.0)**	(0.0)**
Obs.	466	466	466	466	466	466	466	466	466	208
R^2	0.97	0.9	0.71	0.7	0.82	0.91	0.79	0.85	0.7	0.96
F-stat.	237.7	59.37	16.04	15.58	30.49	63.78	25.04	38.52	15.61	67.28
				period fixed effects						
Year	AGR	MIN	MAN	CON	PU	WRT	TSC	FIRE	GCSP	SER
1960	0.57	0.17	-0.11	-0.34	-0.29	-0.57	-0.41	-0.56	-0.13	-0.34
1970	0.39	0.07	0.04	-0.12	-0.11	-0.38	-0.24	-0.38	-0.09	-0.23
1980	0.07	0.12	0.07	0.14	0.13	-0.13	-0.06	-0.22	0.05	-0.04
1990	-0.08	-0.02	0.04	-0.01	0.04	0.07	-0.03	0.02	0.11	0.07
2000	-0.36	-0.23	-0.03	0.08	0.04	0.37	0.26	0.47	0.04	0.21
2010	-0.60	0.02	-0.05	0.31	0.07	0.54	0.50	0.73	0.02	0.31

Source: Own calculations using E-Views 9.0, standard errors in parentheses

Table a6: Regression results for equation 2; employment share as dependent variable; sample: Asia

dep. var:	AGR	MIN	MAN	CON	PU	WRT	TSC	FIRE	GCSP	SER
C	-14.7	-31.5	-19.2	-21.5	-19.1	-11.1	-11.0	-7.11	-9.53	-8.1
	(0.7)**	(1.2)**	(1.0)**	(0.8)**	(1.0)**	(0.6)**	(0.4)**	(1.5)**	(0.7)**	(0.5)**
LG(RG	3.59	6.83	3.76	3.97	3.08	2.01	1.8	0.19	3.53	1.36
DPC)	(0.2)**	(0.3)**	(0.2)**	(0.2)**	(0.2)**	(0.1)**	(0.1)**	(0.3)	(0.2)**	(0.1)**
LG(RG	-0.24	-0.44	-0.2	-0.21	-0.17	-0.11	-0.1	0.02	-0.19	-0.06
DPC)^2	(0.0)**	(0.0)**	(0.0)**	(0.0)**	(0.0)**	(0.0)**	(0.0)**	(0.0)	(0.0)**	(0.0)**
Obs.	504	504	504	504	503	504	504	504	503	413
R^2	0.99	0.95	0.81	0.94	0.89	0.97	0.97	0.95	0.9	0.97
F-stat.	569.1	144.1	28.84	118.7	57.76	214.1	199.9	125.1	64.27	218.3
				period fixed effects						
Year	AGR	MIN	MAN	CON	PU	WRT	TSC	FIRE	GCSP	SER
1960	0.16	-0.15	0.22	-0.11	-0.20	-0.14	-0.17	0.58	0.05	0.01
1970	0.09	-0.01	-0.04	-0.27	-0.14	-0.19	-0.12	-0.13	0.03	-0.08
1980	0.04	0.07	0.11	-0.11	-0.01	-0.13	-0.11	-0.10	0.01	-0.07
1990	-0.11	0.03	0.07	0.03	0.11	0.05	0.05	-0.06	-0.01	0.00
2000	-0.26	-0.11	-0.08	0.22	0.07	0.19	0.21	0.19	0.05	0.12
2010	-0.18	0.11	-0.27	0.23	0.06	0.27	0.29	0.26	0.06	0.18

Source: Own calculations using E-Views 9.0, standard errors in parentheses

Table a7: Regression results for equation 2; employment share as dependent variable; sample: Europe and USA

dep. var:	AGR	MIN	MAN	CON	PU	WRT	TSC	FIRE	GCSP	SER
C	34.59	1.06	-33.2	-12.6	-32.2	-13.4	-28.8	-19.7	-37.9	-21.6
	(5.7)**	-12.2	(2.3)**	(5.6)*	(4.6)**	(1.8)**	(2.2)**	(4.7)**	(2.7)**	(1.8)**
LG(RG	-7.44	-2.25	6.21	1.98	5.94	2.03	5.37	3.11	5.20	4.32
DPC)	(1.2)**	(2.6)	(0.5)**	(1.2)	(1.0)**	(0.4)**	(0.5)**	(1.0)**	(0.6)**	(0.4)**
LG(RG	0.37	0.16	-0.3	-0.1	-0.32	-0.09	-0.28	-0.14	-0.25	-0.22
DPC)^2	(0.1)**	(0.1)	(0.0)**	(0.1)	(0.1)**	(0.0)**	(0.0)**	(0.1)*	(0.0)**	(0.0)**
Obs.	408	408	408	408	408	408	408	408	408	408
R^2	0.97	0.85	0.94	0.76	0.63	0.91	0.97	0.97	0.94	0.98
F-stat.	164.9	34.71	98.74	19.05	10.02	56.9	212.1	211.2	90.26	251.1
				period fixed effects						
Year	AGR	MIN	MAN	CON	PU	WRT	TSC	FIRE	GCSP	SER
1960	0.63	1.55	0.53	0.15	-0.11	0.14	0.06	-0.40	-0.58	-0.24
1970	0.39	0.71	0.33	0.19	-0.07	0.04	-0.02	-0.31	-0.39	-0.19
1980	0.18	0.27	0.10	0.02	0.04	-0.02	-0.03	-0.18	-0.10	-0.07
1990	-0.12	-0.24	-0.11	-0.08	0.08	-0.02	-0.03	0.14	0.13	0.06
2000	-0.46	-1.03	-0.30	-0.14	0.02	-0.08	0.05	0.32	0.41	0.19
2010	-0.67	-1.22	-0.59	-0.11	0.02	-0.09	0.03	0.44	0.59	0.28

Source: Own calculations using E-Views 9.0, standard errors in parentheses

Table a8: Comparison of 13 economies in the GGDC 10-Sector Database

country	population	GDP per capita	GDP per capita growth	GDP	natural resource rents	share of mining value added
Botswana	2.03	13021	2.97%	26 443	4.00	18.60%
Ethiopia	84.73	979	5.81%	82 973	17.92	0.60%
Egypt	82.54	5547	2.79%	457 792	14.00	13.30%
Ghana	24.97	1652	4.31%	41 252	19.45	2.90%
Kenya	41.61	1510	1.52%	62 814	3.32	0.60%
Morocco	32.27	4448	3.57%	143 538	4.60	1.60%
Mauritius	1.29	12733	3.21%	16 376	0.00	0.40%
Malawi	15.38	789	2.44%	12 134	7.96	3.10%
Nigeria	162.47	2237	4.23%	363 423	21.56	29.70%
Senegal	12.77	1737	1.11%	22 179	5.00	1.30%
Tanzania	46.22	1296	4.05%	59 902	9.26	3.30%
South Africa	50.59	9678	2.32%	489 587	12.80	6.50%
Zambia	13.47	1431	3.12%	19 284	21.77	13.50%

Source: World Development Indicators, population and GDP in million, GDP and GDP per capita in PPP constant 2005 international Dollar, GDP per capita growth is the average growth rate of GDP per capita within the last 10 years, share of mining value added (in constant prices) is from the GGDC 10-Sector Database

Table a9: Control variables: other general factors

abbreviation	variable	source
log(vaks_min)	share of mining value added (in constant prices) in logarithms	GGDC 10-Sector Database
log(alp)	arable land (hectares per person) in logarithms	WDI
log(pop)	population (in millions) in logarithms	PENN World Tables
island	island economy dummy	
trade	trade is the sum of exports and imports of goods and services measured as a share of gross domestic product.	WDI
cs	share of capital stock on GDP (ck/cgdpo)	PENN World Tables
hc	Index of human capital per person, based on years of schooling (Barro/Lee, 2012) and returns to education (Psacharopoulos, 1994)	PENN World Tables

Source: Own compilation

Table a10: Regression results for equation 5; employment share as dependent variable; sample: all

dep. var:	AGR	MIN	MAN	CON	PU	WRT	TSC	FIRE	GCSP	SER
C	-16.5	-17.0	-15.1	-24.9	-26.4	-16.1	-9.60	-18.8	-5.18	-8.38
	(0.9)**	(1.8)**	(0.6)**	(0.7)**	(1.1)**	(0.8)**	(0.7)**	(1.4)**	(0.7)**	(0.5)**
LG(RG	4.43	3.11	2.66	4.69	4.53	3.02	1.30	2.77	0.60	1.47
DPC)	(0.2)**	(0.4)**	(0.1)**	(0.2)**	(0.2)**	(0.2)**	(0.2)**	(0.3)**	(0.2)**	(0.1)**
LG(RG	-0.31	-0.19	-0.13	-0.25	-0.24	-0.16	-0.06	-0.11	-0.01	-0.06
DPC)^2	(0.0)**	(0.0)**	(0.0)**	(0.0)**	(0.0)**	(0.0)**	(0.0)**	(0.0)**	(0.0)	(0.0)**
LOG(P	0.08	0.07	0.04	-0.01	-0.03	-0.04	-0.07	-0.04	-0.10	-0.07
OP)	(0.0)**	(0.0)**	(0.0)**	(0.0)*	(0.0)**	(0.0)**	(0.0)**	(0.0)**	(0.0)**	(0.0)**
LOG(A	0.19	-0.07	-0.04	0.01	-0.01	0.03	-0.05	-0.02	0.09	0.04
LP)	(0.0)**	(0.0)**	(0.0)**	(0.0)	(0.0)	(0.0)**	(0.0)**	(0.0)	(0.0)**	(0.0)**
LOG(V	-0.06	0.38	-0.03	-0.01	-0.05	0.02	0.06	-0.02	0.07	0.04
AKS_MIN)	(0.0)**	(0.0)**	(0.0)**	(0.0)*	(0.0)**	(0.0)**	(0.0)**	(0.0)	(0.0)**	(0.0)**
IS-	0.01	-0.26	-0.08	0.10	-0.21	0.34	0.18	-0.06	0.12	0.20
LAND	(0.0)	(0.1)**	(0.0)**	(0.0)**	(0.0)**	(0.0)**	(0.0)**	(0.1)	(0.0)**	(0.0)**
Obs.	1248	1248	1248	1248	1247	1248	1248	1248	1247	1247
R^2	0.85	0.65	0.66	0.72	0.48	0.74	0.6	0.75	0.75	0.85
F-stat.	118.7	40.4	41.41	54.85	20.31	60.86	32.96	65.74	66.07	125.5

				period fixed effects						
Year	AGR	MIN	MAN	CON	PU	WRT	TSC	FIRE	GCSP	SER
1960	-0.06	0.45	0.23	0.00	0.08	-0.20	0.00	0.01	-0.14	-0.14
1970	-0.08	0.29	0.18	-0.01	0.03	-0.17	0.00	-0.16	-0.08	-0.12
1980	0.00	0.16	0.10	0.01	0.10	-0.08	-0.03	-0.14	0.01	-0.04
1990	-0.05	-0.08	0.02	-0.02	0.06	0.04	-0.02	0.01	0.06	0.04
2000	0.06	-0.35	-0.16	0.03	-0.10	0.16	0.05	0.20	0.04	0.10
2010	0.10	-0.09	-0.38	0.09	-0.20	0.21	0.07	0.25	0.00	0.12

Source: Own calculations using E-Views 9.0, standard errors in parentheses

Table a11: Regression Results for Equation 4; value added share as dependent variable; sample: all

dep. var:	AGR	MIN	MAN	CON	PU	WRT	TSC	FIRE	GCSP	SER
C	-0.12 (1.3)		-13.5 (0.7)**	-15.9 (0.8)**	-19.0 (1.3)**	-7.13 (0.6)**	-3.77 (0.7)**	-12.9 (2.2)**	-3.83 (0.7)**	-5.20 (0.4)**
LG(RGDPC)	0.52 (0.3)		2.64 (0.1)**	2.68 (0.2)**	3.22 (0.3)**	1.17 (0.1)**	0.24 (0.2)	2.09 (0.5)**	0.15 (0.2)	0.82 (0.1)**
LG(RGDPC)^2	-0.09 (0.0)**		-0.15 (0.0)**	-0.14 (0.0)**	-0.18 (0.0)**	-0.07 (0.0)**	-0.01 (0.0)	-0.11 (0.0)**	0.01 (0.0)	-0.04 (0.0)**
LOG(POP)	0.07 (0.0)**		0.03 (0.0)**	0.12 (0.0)**	0.04 (0.0)**	-0.03 (0.0)**	-0.05 (0.0)**	0.14 (0.0)**	-0.05 (0.0)**	0.00 (0.0)
LOG(ALP)	0.26 (0.0)**		0.02 (0.0)**	0.07 (0.0)**	0.07 (0.0)**	0.01 (0.0)	0.02 (0.0)**	-0.29 (0.0)**	0.07 (0.0)**	0.06 (0.0)**
LOG(VAKS_MIN)	-0.05 (0.0)**		-0.06 (0.0)**	-0.03 (0.0)**	-0.16 (0.0)**	-0.10 (0.0)**	-0.05 (0.0)**	0.11 (0.0)**	-0.08 (0.0)**	-0.06 (0.0)**
ISLAND	-0.17 (0.0)**		0.21 (0.0)**	0.01 (0.0)	-0.33 (0.1)**	0.06 (0.0)**	-0.01 (0.0)	-0.17 (0.1)*	-0.02 (0.0)	-0.01 (0.0)
Obs.	1274		1274	1274	1274	1274	1274	1274	924	924
R^2	0.79		0.44	0.5	0.45	0.39	0.49	0.23	0.78	0.77
F-stat.	79.63		16.84	21.91	17.48	13.77	20.91	6.5	56.67	54.29
				period fixed effects						
Year	AGR	MIN	MAN	CON	PU	WRT	TSC	FIRE	GCSP	SER
1960	-0.49		-0.27	0.22	-0.67	-0.06	-0.36	-0.23	0.35	0.10
1970	-0.30		-0.11	0.21	-0.33	-0.03	-0.30	-0.23	0.13	-0.02
1980	-0.10		0.02	0.13	-0.06	-0.03	-0.07	-0.14	0.05	-0.02
1990	0.08		0.06	-0.05	0.20	0.02	0.07	0.03	-0.02	0.00
2000	0.30		0.13	-0.24	0.28	0.05	0.26	0.22	-0.19	-0.02
2010	0.36		0.04	-0.34	0.26	0.03	0.43	0.38	-0.30	0.01

Source: Own calculations using E-Views 9.0, standard errors in parentheses

Table a12: Structural deviation of employment shares; for African economies in the years 1970 and 1980

country	AGR	MIN	MAN	CON	PU	WRT	TSC	FIRE	GSPS	SER
year					1970					
Botswana	45%	1.1%	-2.2%	-0.5%	2.2%	-2.3%	-1.5%	0.8%	-3.2%	-5.0%
Egypt	11%	-1.0%	7.7%	-0.5%	2.6%	3.6%	-0.1%	0.5%	11%	15%
Ethiopia	34%	-0.1%	-2.6%	-0.6%	0.2%	0.1%	-1.1%	-0.1%	-3.9%	-5.3%
Ghana	17%	-0.1%	-0.4%	-3.7%	2.0%	4.1%	-1.4%	-1.3%	-4.5%	-3.8%
Kenya	22%	-0.2%	-4.8%	-2.0%	0.6%	-0.8%	-1.2%	0.1%	-3.1%	-5.6%
Morocco	0.4%	0.9%	0.8%	-2.6%	4.2%	1.1%	0.0%	-0.5%	0.8%	0.9%
Mauritius	12%	-0.5%	-2.4%	-4.4%	7.4%	-9.9%	-0.7%	-1.2%	5.7%	-7.3%
Malawi	36%	-0.1%	-2.0%	-0.8%	1.9%	-1.8%	-1.2%	-0.2%	-4.3%	-7.7%
Nigeria	11%	-2.2%	-2.9%	-2.7%	0.8%	7.4%	-2.1%	-0.7%	-3.4%	1.0%
Senegal	14%	-0.3%	-3.1%	-2.3%	1.0%	-0.1%	-1.2%	-0.8%	-3.6%	-6.0%
Tanzania	29%	-0.4%	-6.1%	-1.8%	0.4%	-3.8%	-1.7%	-0.5%	-7.3%	-14%
South Africa	12%	7.0%	-4.5%	-6.4%	5.2%	-1.8%	-1.1%	-1.0%	-7.3%	-12%
Zambia	15%	2.3%	-5.9%	-2.4%	3.7%	-4.6%	-1.2%	0.3%	0.5%	-4.9%
Africa	13%	0.5%	-3.8%	-2.7%	2.4%	-1.2%	-1.1%	-0.4%	-1.6%	-4.7%
year					1980					
Botswana	19%	2.6%	-6.6%	-2.6%	4.9%	-7.3%	-3.3%	0.4%	2.0%	-8.1%
Egypt	1.6%	-1.1%	5.8%	-1.1%	5.9%	3.5%	3.5%	0.9%	11%	18%
Ethiopia	21%	-0.1%	-3.0%	-0.8%	0.2%	0.3%	-1.1%	-0.2%	-1.7%	-3.1%
Ghana	7.7%	-0.1%	4.0%	-3.1%	1.6%	5.4%	-1.5%	-0.9%	-4.2%	-2.0%
Kenya	17%	-0.2%	-6.1%	-2.7%	0.7%	-2.8%	-0.6%	-0.2%	-1.9%	-6.3%
Morocco	-13%	0.7%	3.3%	-3.6%	6.9%	2.6%	-0.5%	-0.5%	1.9%	2.8%
Mauritius	2.1%	-0.5%	7.5%	-5.8%	12%	-12%	-1.4%	-1.0%	-3.5%	-19%
Malawi	32%	-0.1%	-1.6%	-0.9%	2.1%	-2.2%	-1.3%	0.0%	-5.6%	-9.4%
Nigeria	-7.3%	-1.9%	-3.1%	-2.7%	2.3%	12%	0.1%	-0.7%	1.9%	13%
Senegal	7.6%	-0.3%	-2.5%	-2.1%	1.3%	1.7%	-1.1%	-0.7%	-2.5%	-3.2%
Tanzania	18%	0.3%	-6.2%	-2.1%	0.5%	-1.9%	-1.6%	-0.5%	-6.4%	-11%
South Africa	4.0%	8.0%	-1.1%	-6.9%	4.6%	-1.5%	-0.6%	-0.7%	-6.3%	-9.8%
Zambia	17%	2.6%	-2.7%	-1.5%	2.0%	-1.8%	-0.3%	0.6%	-1.7%	-3.2%
Africa	5.2%	0.8%	-2.7%	-3.3%	3.4%	-0.8%	-0.7%	-0.3%	-1.0%	-3.5%

Table a12: Structural deviation of employment shares; for African economies in the years 1995 and 2010

country	AGR	MIN	MAN	CON	PU	WRT	TSC	FIRE	GSPS	SER
year					1995					
Botswana	22%	1.8%	-6.9%	-5.5%	7.9%	-11%	-4.8%	0.0%	-6.3%	-24%
Egypt	2.7%	-0.9%	0.1%	-3.5%	7.6%	-3.9%	1.2%	0.5%	10%	6.9%
Ethiopia	30%	0.1%	-1.3%	-0.5%	0.2%	0.9%	-1.2%	-0.2%	-1.1%	-2.3%
Ghana	0.9%	0.8%	3.1%	-2.3%	1.8%	6.6%	-0.6%	-0.3%	-3.3%	1.2%
Kenya	-1.7%	-0.1%	-0.5%	-2.3%	1.5%	1.9%	-0.4%	0.1%	1.2%	1.8%
Morocco	-5.4%	0.3%	2.1%	-4.7%	7.1%	-1.2%	-0.9%	-1.6%	1.2%	-3.3%
Mauritius	5.5%	0.1%	15%	-7.7%	9.9%	-16%	-2.7%	-4.0%	-15%	-40%
Malawi	28%	-0.1%	-1.4%	-0.8%	1.2%	-0.2%	-1.4%	0.1%	-3.9%	-6.3%
Nigeria	29%	-0.3%	2.2%	0.2%	0.8%	22%	1.5%	0.5%	4.6%	29%
Senegal	2.0%	-0.2%	-0.3%	-2.0%	1.6%	6.1%	-1.3%	-0.9%	-3.6%	-0.8%
Tanzania	25%	0.3%	-2.5%	-0.7%	0.5%	1.6%	-1.1%	-0.2%	-3.3%	-3.7%
South Africa	-5.2%	5.6%	-1.6%	-5.4%	5.7%	-0.5%	0.0%	2.3%	-0.9%	0.0%
Zambia	21%	1.2%	-1.8%	-0.8%	1.1%	-2.4%	-0.9%	0.6%	-0.3%	-3.6%
Africa	7.6%	0.6%	-2.5%	-3.8%	3.5%	-1.8%	-1.2%	-0.4%	-1.9%	-6.3%
year					2010					
Botswana	32%	1.1%	-4.8%	-5.8%	1.9%	-7.1%	-5.8%	-3.2%	-16%	-36%
Egypt	2.3%	-1.2%	-0.8%	-3.8%	12%	-5.2%	3.1%	-1.2%	8.9%	4.2%
Ethiopia	1.9%	0.2%	1.8%	-1.1%	1.9%	4.0%	-1.7%	-0.3%	-2.5%	-2.0%
Ghana	-10%	0.5%	2.9%	-3.0%	2.6%	10%	-0.6%	-0.2%	-1.4%	5.9%
Kenya	-18%	0.3%	6.4%	-2.0%	2.5%	6.7%	0.4%	-0.3%	4.6%	9.7%
Morocco	-14%	-0.2%	3.3%	-4.3%	11%	0.4%	-0.1%	-1.8%	4.7%	1.5%
Mauritius	-1.1%	0.0%	7.3%	-6.5%	9.2%	-13%	-0.7%	-0.2%	-7.0%	-25%
Malawi	2.9%	-0.3%	0.4%	-1.0%	4.4%	5.6%	-0.5%	-0.2%	-0.9%	2.3%
Nigeria	5.1%	-1.4%	-3.5%	-2.9%	1.3%	3.3%	-1.0%	0.6%	-3.4%	-2.1%
Senegal	-14%	-0.2%	3.9%	-2.3%	3.5%	9.9%	0.0%	-1.1%	-3.1%	3.8%
Tanzania	2.3%	0.3%	-1.7%	-1.2%	1.2%	1.2%	-1.0%	-0.4%	-0.2%	-2.1%
South Africa	-2.5%	1.3%	-0.4%	-5.5%	6.5%	-2.5%	-0.7%	4.3%	3.3%	2.4%
Zambia	19%	1.5%	-2.9%	-2.4%	1.1%	-2.3%	-2.2%	-0.8%	-9.0%	-16%
Africa	8.7%	0.1%	-1.4%	-4.4%	4.4%	-1.7%	-1.0%	-0.7%	-1.8%	-6.8%

Source: Own calculations using E-Views 9.0, standard errors in parentheses

Table a13: Structural deviation of employment shares; for African economies in the years 1970 and 1980

country	AGR	MIN	MAN	CON	PU	WRT	TSC	FIRE	GSPS	SER
year					1970					
Botswana	19%	19%	3.6%	0.8%	25%	15%	1.6%	1.6%	14%	32%
Egypt	28%	19%	23%	1.1%	1.4%	13%	3.0%	3.1%	8.3%	28%
Ethiopia	74%	0.2%	3.2%	1.0%	4.4%	12%	1.9%	0.9%	2.9%	17%
Ghana	38%	5.4%	19%	0.7%	9.9%	11%	8.4%	1.2%	6.9%	28%
Kenya	38%	0.6%	7.0%	1.7%	8.7%	11%	8.5%	3.4%	21%	44%
Morocco	29%	3.2%	16%	1.4%	7.6%	15%	3.0%	8.1%	16%	43%
Mauritius	13%	3.0%	18%	1.7%	7.9%	23%	9.9%	5.3%	19%	57%
Malawi	34%	1.2%	11%	0.9%	6.2%	18%	5.9%	1.8%	21%	47%
Nigeria	36%	48%	1.7%	0.1%	1.8%	11%	0.6%	0.4%	1.0%	13%
Senegal	29%	1.6%	15%	2.0%	1.5%	23%	8.0%	2.0%	19%	51%
Tanzania	36%	1.5%	11%	1.2%	9.9%	19%	8.4%	3.4%	8.7%	40%
South Africa	3.5%	23%	20%	1.4%	4.7%	14%	6.1%	5.3%	22%	47%
Zambia	15%	28%	12%	1.1%	19%	10%	4.7%	1.7%	8.0%	25%
Africa	30%	12%	12%	1.1%	8.3%	15%	5.4%	3.0%	13%	36%
year					1980					
Botswana	9.2%	33%	6.5%	1.2%	12%	22%	1.5%	3.3%	12%	38%
Egypt	19%	26%	18%	0.9%	1.7%	13%	9.6%	4.4%	6.8%	34%
Ethiopia	69%	0.1%	3.9%	1.3%	4.2%	12%	2.5%	2.0%	4.9%	21%
Ghana	40%	2.7%	15%	1.4%	9.1%	8.9%	9.4%	1.9%	12%	32%
Kenya	32%	0.7%	13%	2.7%	5.9%	12%	9.7%	3.9%	21%	46%
Morocco	20%	2.8%	17%	1.8%	8.7%	16%	3.5%	11%	19%	50%
Mauritius	15%	2.7%	19%	1.4%	6.0%	19%	9.5%	4.0%	24%	57%
Malawi	28%	0.8%	10%	1.1%	6.4%	24%	7%	5%	17%	54%
Nigeria	18%	63%	3.5%	0.1%	2.8%	9.6%	0.8%	0.7%	1.4%	13%
Senegal	23%	1.6%	15%	2.1%	2.2%	22%	7.2%	5.5%	22%	56%
Tanzania	31%	0.9%	12%	2.3%	8.2%	15%	9.1%	4.5%	17%	46%
South Africa	3.7%	15%	24%	2.0%	4.4%	14%	7.6%	6.9%	23%	52%
Zambia	12%	23%	12%	5.0%	11%	14%	5.1%	6.2%	12%	37%
Africa	25%	13%	13%	1.8%	6.4%	15%	6.4%	4.6%	15%	41%

Table a13: Structural deviation of employment shares; for African economies in the years 1995 and 2010

country	AGR	MIN	MAN	CON	PU	WRT	TSC	FIRE	GSPS	SER
year					1995					
Botswana	3.8%	37%	6.2%	1.6%	7.3%	12%	4.6%	8.7%	20%	44%
Egypt	15%	15%	25%	1.4%	3.6%	13%	9.1%	5.7%	12%	40%
Ethiopia	58%	0.5%	5.1%	2.2%	3.4%	14%	4.0%	3.7%	9.7%	31%
Ghana	35%	3.0%	11%	2.0%	5.4%	10%	15%	4.9%	14%	43%
Kenya	27%	0.6%	14%	2.5%	4.5%	12%	9.4%	7.2%	23%	52%
Morocco	12%	1.7%	18%	2.4%	5.4%	15%	4.2%	19%	23%	60%
Mauritius	9.2%	2.1%	24%	1.7%	5.8%	21%	9.8%	7.9%	18%	57%
Malawi	27%	0.9%	12%	1.6%	3.6%	19%	6.6%	7.9%	21%	55%
Nigeria	26%	51%	3.5%	0.1%	1.7%	12%	0.7%	2.1%	1.8%	17%
Senegal	23%	1.4%	18%	2.3%	3.1%	23%	6.8%	6.9%	17%	53%
Tanzania	40%	1.4%	8.3%	2.4%	6.7%	16%	7.1%	5.2%	13%	41%
South Africa	2.9%	11%	22%	2.8%	2.8%	14%	8.2%	9.0%	27%	59%
Zambia	29%	7.3%	11%	3.9%	5.8%	18%	5.0%	8.8%	11%	43%
Africa	24%	10%	14%	2.1%	4.6%	15%	6.9%	7.5%	16%	46%
year					2010					
Botswana	2.8%	19%	8.0%	1.3%	7.9%	21%	6.0%	12%	23%	61%
Egypt	[illegible]3%	13%	16%	1.5%	5.8%	15%	14%	7.8%	13%	50%
Ethiopia	42%	0.6%	5.2%	1.8%	5.7%	19%	5.7%	6.1%	14%	44%
Ghana	30%	2.9%	8.8%	1.9%	8.6%	12%	17%	5.9%	14%	48%
Kenya	24%	0.6%	12%	2.3%	5.3%	14%	14%	8.1%	20%	56%
Morocco	[illegible]6%	1.6%	14%	3.1%	7.0%	13%	7.4%	17%	21%	58%
Mauritius	5.2%	0.4%	19%	1.9%	7.2%	20%	16%	12%	19%	67%
Malawi	30%	3.1%	10%	1.9%	5.3%	19%	9.4%	8.4%	13%	49%
Nigeria	38%	30%	3.5%	0.1%	2.2%	20%	2.0%	2.2%	2.3%	27%
Senegal	[illegible]8%	1.3%	15%	2.7%	5.2%	20%	15%	8.2%	15%	59%
Tanzania	30%	3.3%	10%	2.5%	10%	17%	8.5%	4.7%	13%	44%
South Africa	2.7%	6.5%	18%	2.2%	3.8%	15%	11%	18%	23%	66%
Zambia	9.4%	14%	8.7%	1.8%	7.2%	22%	13%	8.8%	15%	59%
Africa	20%	7.3%	12%	1.9%	6.3%	17%	11%	9.1%	16%	53%

Source: Own calculations using E-Views 9.0, standard errors in parentheses

Table a14: Employment shares for economic sectors in world regions in 2010

	AGR	MIN	MAN	CON	PU	WRT	TSC	FIRE	GSPS	SER
Africa	54%	0.6%	7.5%	0.4%	4.1%	15%	3.4%	2.5%	8.7%	4.3%
Asia	40%	0.9%	16%	0.4%	7.3%	13%	4.6%	2.7%	6.4%	9.3%
Latin America	[illegible]5%	0.8%	12%	0.4%	8.0%	23%	5.7%	9.5%	11%	15%
Europe & USA	2.2%	0.4%	11%	0.4%	6.2%	22%	5.6%	16%	29%	7.2%

Source: Own calculation using the GGDC 10-Sector Database; Africa, Asia Latin America and Europe & United States are the average values of the economies included in the dataset

Table a15: Labor productivity for major economic sectors African economies in 2010

	AGR	MIN	MAN	PU	CON	WRT	TSC	FIRE	GSPS	SUM
Botswana	3.3	418.6	54.9	97.1	129.4	47.3	84.6	74.2	49.4	44.3
Ethopia	1.2	2.5	1.7	38.2	5.9	3.8	23.3	28.8	6.0	2.1
Ghana	4.7	17.8	5.4	33.1	18.8	3.2	31.3	17.0	7.4	6.7
Kenya	2.2	4.2	4.2	52.7	8.4	3.8	18.5	29.8	6.1	4.5
Malawi	1.2	66.3	6.2	15.9	3.1	3.9	11.1	30.5	3.6	2.7
Mauritius	23.5	64.9	32.0	61.5	23.4	30.7	61.9	39.7	26.5	32.5
Nigeria	5.0	1038	6.9	5.2	10.9	9.6	5.4	6.6	1.8	8.1
Senegal	1.8	29.9	7.7	332.1	7.2	5.0	22.7	83.6	8.2	5.2
South Africa	6.2	106.4	53.1	124.6	17.8	25.1	70.7	54.7	29.5	34.3
Tanzania	1.2	12.5	9.3	16.4	22.4	5.2	13.2	21.1	4.0	3.0
Zambia	1.0	41.3	19.5	51.4	37.4	15.6	49.7	59.3	17.2	7.5
Morrocco	8.0	71.4	15.3	108.7	8.6	10.2	24.2	126.5	14.2	14.4
Egypt	12.1	2264	33.2	24.0	10.6	25.0	35.3	48.1	11.5	22.4

Source: Own calculation using the GGDC 10-Sector Database

Table a16: Employment shares for major economic sectors African economies in 2010

	AGR	MIN	MAN	PU	CON	WRT	TSC	FIRE	GSPS
Botswana	38%	2%	6%	1%	3%	19%	3%	7%	21%
Ethopia	75%	0%	6%	0%	2%	10%	1%	0%	5%
Ghana	42%	1%	11%	0%	3%	24%	4%	2%	13%
Kenya	48%	1%	13%	0%	3%	16%	3%	1%	14%
Malawi	65%	0%	4%	0%	5%	13%	2%	1%	9%
Mauritius	7%	0%	19%	1%	10%	21%	8%	10%	23%
Nigeria	61%	0%	4%	0%	2%	17%	3%	3%	10%
Senegal	51%	0%	10%	0%	4%	21%	3%	1%	10%
South Africa	15%	2%	12%	1%	7%	20%	5%	11%	26%
Tanzania	72%	1%	3%	0%	1%	10%	2%	1%	10%
Zambia	72%	2%	3%	0%	1%	11%	2%	1%	7%
Morrocco	29%	0%	13%	0%	12%	18%	4%	2%	21%
Egypt	24%	0%	11%	1%	12%	14%	9%	4%	25%

Source: Own calculation using the GGDC 10-Sector Database

Table a17: Decomposition Results for single African economies from 1960-1980 and 1980-1995

country	period	within	static	dynamic	productivity growth
Egypt	1960-1980	3.5%	0.4%	0.7%	4.7%
Morrocco	1960-1980	0.6%	1.4%	-0.2%	1.8%
Botswana	1964-1980	3.1%	4.4%	1.9%	9.3%
Ethiopia	1961-1980	-0.6%	1.3%	-0.7%	0.0%
Ghana	1960-1980	-1.1%	-0.3%	-0.1%	-1.5%
Kenya	1969-1980	-0.4%	1.1%	-0.4%	0.3%
Mauritius	1970-1980	4.7%	2.1%	-1.5%	5.2%
Malawi	1966-1980	1.4%	-0.4%	-0.4%	0.6%
Nigeria	1961-1980	2.0%	0.2%	2.3%	4.5%
Senegal	1970-1980	-3.3%	0.7%	-0.3%	-2.9%
Tanzania	1960-1980	-0.2%	5.2%	-3.7%	1.3%
South Africa	1960-1980	1.7%	1.3%	0.7%	3.7%
Zambia	1966-1980	-0.5%	-1.1%	0.0%	-1.6%
Egypt	1980-1995	1.7%	0.0%	0.0%	1.7%
Morrocco	1980-1995	0.1%	0.5%	0.1%	0.7%
Botswana	1980-1995	3.5%	3.7%	-2.4%	4.7%
Ethiopia	1980-1995	-1.6%	0.4%	-0.1%	-1.3%
Ghana	1980-1995	0.5%	0.5%	0.0%	0.9%
Kenya	1980-1995	-1.5%	2.7%	-1.4%	-0.2%
Mauritius	1980-1995	2.0%	1.1%	-0.6%	2.6%
Malawi	1980-1995	-1.5%	2.3%	-1.7%	-0.8%
Nigeria	1980-1995	9.2%	-3.3%	-6.7%	-0.8%
Senegal	1980-1995	-2.1%	1.1%	-0.6%	-1.5%
Tanzania	1980-1995	-0.6%	0.2%	-0.1%	-0.5%
South Africa	1980-1995	-1.3%	0.5%	-0.4%	-1.2%
Zambia	1980-1995	1.0%	-1.9%	0.2%	-0.7%

Source: Own calculation using the GGDC 10-Sector Database

Table a17: Decomposition Results for single African economies from 1995-2010 and 1960-2010

country	period	within	static	dynamic	productivity growth
Egypt	1995-2010	3.9%	-0.2%	-1.3%	2.3%
Morrocco	1995-2010	1.3%	0.7%	-0.4%	1.7%
Botswana	1995-2010	3.1%	-0.3%	-1.0%	1.8%
Ethiopia	1995-2010	1.8%	2.7%	-1.2%	3.3%
Ghana	1995-2010	2.2%	0.8%	-0.2%	2.8%
Kenya	1995-2010	-0.5%	1.2%	-0.6%	0.1%
Mauritius	1995-2010	3.4%	0.8%	-0.4%	3.8%
Malawi	1995-2010	0.0%	4.7%	-2.6%	2.1%
Nigeria	1995-2010	2.1%	2.6%	-1.7%	2.9%
Senegal	1995-2010	1.5%	1.6%	-1.9%	1.3%
Tanzania	1995-2010	0.2%	3.8%	-1.2%	2.8%
South Africa	1995-2010	2.8%	0.1%	-0.6%	2.4%
Zambia	1995-2010	3.0%	1.7%	-0.8%	3.9%
Egypt	1960-2010	3.2%	0.0%	-0.2%	3.1%
Morrocco	1960-2010	0.9%	1.0%	-0.4%	1.4%
Botswana	1964-2010	1.5%	2.2%	1.7%	5.3%
Ethiopia	1961-2010	-0.2%	1.9%	-1.0%	0.6%
Ghana	1960-2010	0.4%	0.3%	-0.2%	0.5%
Kenya	1969-2010	-0.6%	2.0%	-1.3%	0.0%
Mauritius	1970-2010	3.1%	1.0%	-0.5%	3.7%
Malawi	1966-2010	-0.1%	2.2%	-1.5%	0.6%
Nigeria	1961-2010	2.5%	0.0%	-0.1%	2.4%
Senegal	1970-2010	-1.0%	1.7%	-1.5%	-0.8%
Tanzania	1960-2010	0.0%	4.6%	-3.4%	1.2%
South Africa	1960-2010	1.3%	0.6%	0.0%	1.8%
Zambia	1966-2010	1.7%	-0.4%	-0.7%	0.5%

Source: Own calculation using the GGDC 10-Sector Database

Table a18: Regression results for equation 17; cross section; period 1970-1980

dep. var:	AGR	MIN	MAN	CON	PU	WRT	TSC	FIRE	GSPS	SUM
constant	0.023	-0.027	-0.015	-0.022	-0.019	-0.032	-0.009	-0.034	-0.009	-0.006
	(0.0)	(0.0)	(0.0)	(0.0)	(0.0)	(0.0)**	(0.0)	(0.0)*	(0.0)	(0.0)
output	1.050	0.905	0.465	0.010	0.498	0.674	0.400	0.666	0.581	0.718
	(0.1)**	(0.2)**	(0.2)*	(0.1)	(0.2)*	(0.2)**	(0.1)**	(0.1)**	(0.2)*	(0.1)**
p-gap	-0.004	0.000	0.000	0.000	0.000	0.000	-0.000	0.000	-0.000	-0.000
	(0.0)**	(0.0)	(0.0)	(0.0)	(0.0)	(0.0)	(0.0)	(0.0)*	(0.0)	(0.0)
capital	0.272	0.031	0.200	0.087	0.143	0.034	0.231	-0.348	-0.079	0.078
	(0.1)*	(0.4)	(0.3)	(0.2)	(0.3)	(0.2)	(0.2)	(0.2)*	(0.2)	(0.1)
Obs.	37	37	37	37	37	37	37	37	27	37
R^2	0.69	0.53	0.52	0.09	0.3	0.52	0.47	0.59	0.24	0.76
F-stat.	25.05	12.23	12.16	1.12	4.83	12.11	9.85	15.91	2.38	34.55

Source: Own calculations using E-Views 9.0, standard errors in parentheses

Table a19: Regression results for equation 17; cross section; period 1980-1990

dep. var:	AGR	MIN	MAN	CON	PU	WRT	TSC	FIRE	GSPS	SUM
constant	0.025	-0.009	-0.008	0.004	0.006	-0.031	-0.004	-0.052	-0.016	-0.005
	(0.0)**	(0.0)	(0.0)	(0.0)	(0.0)	(0.0)**	(0.0)	(0.0)**	(0.0)*	(0.0)
output	0.375	0.701	0.243	0.506	0.719	0.720	0.517	0.826	0.818	0.911
	(0.2)*	(0.1)**	(0.2)	(0.1)**	(0.2)**	(0.2)**	(0.1)**	(0.1)**	(0.1)**	(0.1)**
p-gap	-0.002	0.000	0.000	-0.000	-0.000	-0.000	-0.000	0.000	-0.000	-0.000
	(0.0)**	(0.0)	(0.0)	(0.0)	(0.0)	(0.0)	(0.0)	(0.0)	(0.0)	(0.0)**
capital	0.345	0.628	0.230	-0.168	-0.070	-0.007	0.048	-0.091	-0.040	-0.003
	(0.1)**	(0.3)	(0.3)	(0.2)	(0.3)	(0.2)	(0.1)	(0.2)	(0.1)	(0.1)
Obs.	41	41	41	41	41	41	41	41	30	41
R^2	0.49	0.48	0.2	0.38	0.41	0.52	0.49	0.79	0.72	0.85
F-stat.	11.85	11.2	3.06	7.71	8.42	13.12	11.74	45.13	22.16	69.9

Source: Own calculations using E-Views 9.0, standard errors in parentheses

Table a20: Regression results for equation 17; cross section; period 1990-2000

dep. var:	AGR	MIN	MAN	CON	PU	WRT	TSC	FIRE	GSPS	SUM
constant	0.022	0.012	0.010	-0.003	0.012	-0.029	-0.014	-0.048	-0.009	-0.005
	(0.0)**	(0.0)	(0.0)	(0.0)	(0.0)	(0.0)**	(0.0)	(0.0)**	(0.0)	(0.0)
output	0.909	0.379	0.619	0.659	0.761	0.903	0.928	0.898	0.701	0.977
	(0.1)**	(0.2)	(0.2)**	(0.2)**	(0.3)*	(0.3)**	(0.2)**	(0.1)**	(0.1)**	(0.1)**
p-gap	-0.001	0.000	-0.001	-0.000	0.000	-0.001	-0.000	0.000	-0.000	-0.000
	(0.0)**	(0.0)	(0.0)	(0.0)	(0.0)	(0.0)*	(0.0)	(0.0)	(0.0)	(0.0)**
capital	0.318	0.748	0.211	-0.019	0.012	-0.017	-0.106	-0.338	0.020	-0.054
	(0.1)**	(0.4)	(0.2)	(0.2)	(0.4)	(0.2)	(0.2)	(0.2)	(0.1)	(0.1)
Obs.	41	41	41	41	41	41	41	41	30	41
R^2	0.59	0.17	0.41	0.26	0.36	0.42	0.4	0.74	0.65	0.75
F-stat.	17.9	2.49	8.51	4.29	6.79	9.1	8.1	34.74	16.16	37.73

Source: Own calculations using E-Views 9.0, standard errors in parentheses

Table a21: Regression results for equation 17; cross section; period 2000-2010

dep. var:	AGR	MIN	MAN	CON	PU	WRT	TSC	FIRE	GSPS	SUM
constant	0.025	-0.015	0.019	-0.018	0.016	-0.012	0.001	-0.021	-0.020	-0.008
	(0.0)*	(0.0)	(0.0)	(0.0)	(0.0)	(0.0)	(0.0)	(0.0)	(0.0)	(0.0)
output	0.838	0.394	0.047	0.277	0.912	0.713	0.838	0.101	0.931	0.938
	(0.1)**	(0.2)*	(0.2)	(0.3)	(0.3)**	(0.2)**	(0.2)**	(0.2)	(0.3)**	(0.1)**
p-gap	-0.001	0.000	-0.001	-0.000	0.000	-0.000	-0.001	0.000	-0.000	-0.000
	(0.0)	(0.0)	(0.0)**	(0.0)	(0.0)	(0.0)	(0.0)*	(0.0)	(0.0)	(0.0)**
capital	0.099	0.405	0.579	0.851	-0.391	-0.147	0.082	0.416	0.159	0.125
	(0.2)	(0.6)	(0.2)*	(0.4)*	(0.4)	(0.2)	(0.3)	(0.3)	(0.3)	(0.1)
Obs.	34	34	34	34	34	34	34	34	23	34
R^2	0.6	0.28	0.3	0.26	0.27	0.36	0.46	0.1	0.52	0.78
F-stat.	15	3.81	4.33	3.46	3.74	5.72	8.6	1.1	6.84	34.53

Source: Own calculations using E-Views 9.0, standard errors in parentheses

Table a22: Regression results for equation 17; panel regression including all four periods

dep. var:	AGR	MIN	MAN	CON	PU	WRT	TSC	FIRE	GSPS	SUM
constant	0.007	-0.004	-0.003	-0.004	0.002	-0.028	-0.007	-0.043	-0.012	-0.009
	(0.0)	(0.0)	(0.0)	(0.0)	(0.0)	(0.0)**	(0.0)	(0.0)**	(0.0)**	(0.0)**
output	0.634	0.569	0.311	0.391	0.535	0.741	0.567	0.772	0.680	0.852
	(0.1)**	(0.1)**	(0.1)**	(0.1)**	(0.1)**	(0.1)**	(0.1)**	(0.1)**	(0.1)**	(0.1)**
p-gap	-0.001	0.000	-0.000	-0.000	0.000	-0.000	-0.000	0.000	-0.000	-0.000
	(0.0)**	(0.0)*	(0.0)	(0.0)	(0.0)	(0.0)	(0.0)	(0.0)	(0.0)	(0.0)**
capital	0.238	0.376	0.307	0.010	0.015	-0.023	0.047	-0.178	-0.038	0.011
	(0.1)**	(0.2)	(0.1)*	(0.1)	(0.1)	(0.1)	(0.1)	(0.1)	(0.1)	(0.1)
Obs.	153	153	153	153	153	153	153	153	110	153
R^2	0.37	0.29	0.3	0.2	0.25	0.44	0.43	0.6	0.46	0.75
F-stat.	29.23	20.63	20.97	12.35	16.69	39.53	37.64	73.04	29.64	148.4

Source: Own calculations using E-Views 9.0, standard errors in parentheses

Table a23: Regression results for equation 18; panel regression including all four periods

variable	coefficient	std. error	t-statistic	prob.
constant	0.009015	0.003056	2.949736	0.0037
output	0.899517	0.062073	14.49120	0.0000
R-squared		0.578506		
adjusted R-squared		0.575751		

Source: Own calculations using E-Views 9.0, standard errors in parentheses

Table a24: Regression Results and the Verdoorn coefficient for all four models, panel regression with a sample over all four periods and all countries

variable dep. variable	model 1 p	model 2 e	model 3 p	model 4 q
constant	-0.0168 (0.002)**	0.0174 (0.002)**	0.0056 (0.003)	0.0053 (0.003)
q	0.7558 (0.063)**	0.2225 (0.063)**	-	-
e	-	-	-0.6585 (0.095)**	0.3433 (0.097)**
c	0.0667 (0.053)	-0.0661 (0.53)	0.5962 (0.043)**	0.6093 (0.044)**
adj. R^2	0.72	0.10	0.59	0.60
Verdoorn coefficient	0.76	0.78	-4.19	-4.23

Source: Own calculations using E-Views 9.0, standard errors in parentheses

Table a25: Regression results for Kenya, sample 1977-2010, p-values in parentheses

	model 1a, dependent variable p									
	AGR	MIN	MAN	CON	PU	WRT	TSC	FIRE	GSPS	SUM
c	-0.02	-0.07	-0.10	-0.07	-0.02	-0.05	-0.06	-0.02	-0.05	-0.04
	(0.00)	(0.13)	(0.00)	(0.00)	(0.29)	(0.00)	(0.04)	(0.27)	(0.00)	(0.00)
q	1.01	0.69	1.11	0.99	1.14	0.47	1.28	0.45	0.92	1.03
	(0.00)	(0.13)	(0.00)	(0.00)	(0.00)	(0.04)	(0.00)	(0.01)	(0.00)	(0.00)
k	0.59	-0.19	0.53	0.26	-0.81	0.93	-0.27	0.10	-0.07	0.06
	(0.00)	(0.90)	(0.01)	(0.70)	(0.04)	(0.01)	(0.47)	(0.68)	(0.74)	(0.57)
R^2	0.98	0.07	0.73	0.74	0.73	0.29	0.34	0.20	0.61	0.89
	model 1b, dependent variable p									
	AGR	MIN	MAN	CON	PU	WRT	TSC	FIRE	GSPS	SUM
C	0.00	-0.02	-0.04	-0.06	-0.03	-0.07	-0.01	-0.01	-0.05	-0.03
	(0.39)	(0.66)	(0.05)	(0.00)	(0.21)	(0.00)	(0.57)	(0.68)	(0.00)	(0.00)
Q	1.01	0.44	0.63	0.98	1.17	0.45	0.87	0.67	0.96	1.00
	(0.00)	(0.38)	(0.00)	(0.00)	(0.00)	(0.06)	(0.00)	(0.00)	(0.00)	(0.00)
q(-1)	-0.86	-0.84	-0.23	-0.08	-0.04	0.25	-0.34	-0.59	0.16	-0.31
	(0.00)	(0.09)	(0.28)	(0.71)	(0.86)	(0.31)	(0.29)	(0.00)	(0.44)	(0.11)
p(-1)	0.83	0.29	0.62	0.08	0.17	-0.17	0.63	0.11	0.05	0.32
	(0.00)	(0.14)	(0.00)	(0.68)	(0.36)	(0.42)	(0.00)	(0.48)	(0.79)	(0.07)
K	0.16	0.74	0.24	0.24	-0.67	0.93	-0.37	0.15	-0.25	-0.37
	(0.10)	(0.65)	(0.20)	(0.75)	(0.11)	(0.04)	(0.25)	(0.49)	(0.27)	(0.88)
R^2	1.00	0.19	0.84	0.74	0.75	0.25	0.65	0.45	0.63	0.91
e	0.86	-0.56	1.06	0.98	1.36	0.61	1.43	0.08	1.18	1.02
	model 4a, dependent variable q									
	AGR	MIN	MAN	CON	PU	WRT	TSC	FIRE	GSPS	SUM
c	0.04	0.03	0.04	0.03	0.04	0.02	0.04	0.02	0.01	0.04
	(0.13)	(0.07)	(0.07)	(0.38)	(0.14)	(0.16)	(0.02)	(0.25)	(0.53)	(0.08)
e	-0.77	0.05	-0.14	0.04	-0.26	0.29	-0.09	0.46	0.12	-0.23
	(0.55)	(0.48)	(0.47)	(0.89)	(0.28)	(0.02)	(0.38)	(0.00)	(0.59)	(0.64)
k	-0.17	-0.20	0.39	-1.92	0.34	0.40	0.22	0.22	0.54	0.20
	(0.88)	(0.74)	(0.09)	(0.08)	(0.55)	(0.15)	(0.28)	(0.31)	(0.04)	(0.47)
R^2	0.0[illegible]	0.02	0.17	0.09	0.04	0.16	0.05	0.27	0.14	0.03
	model 4b, dependent variable lnQ									
	AGR	MIN	MAN	CON	PU	WRT	TSC	FIRE	GSPS	SUM
c	-16.76	0.25	0.18	7.22	4.27	1.79	4.66	4.67	6.44	3.41
	(0.02)	(0.95)	(0.80)	(0.14)	(0.01)	(0.11)	(0.00)	(0.00)	(0.00)	(0.00)
lne	1.54	0.24	0.04	0.07	0.27	0.50	0.11	0.62	0.46	0.59
	(0.00)	(0.00)	(0.47)	(0.26)	(0.11)	(0.00)	(0.04)	(0.00)	(0.00)	(0.00)
lnk	1.63	1.06	1.15	0.34	0.54	0.73	0.62	0.42	0.25	0.43
	(0.00)	(0.05)	(0.00)	(0.55)	(0.03)	(0.00)	(0.00)	(0.00)	(0.01)	(0.00)
R^2	0.96	0.57	0.95	0.32	0.91	0.98	0.94	0.99	0.97	0.99
	Engle-Granger cointegration test									
tau-s	-2.58	-1.48	-2.27	-3.10	-2.93	-2.86	-2.90	-3.14	-2.66	-2.17
prob.	(0.46)	(0.90)	(0.62)	(0.24)	(0.31)	(0.33)	(0.32)	(0.23)	(0.43)	(0.66)

Source: Own calculations using E-Views 9.0, p-values in parentheses

Table a25: Regression results for Kenya, error correction model, sample 1977-2010, p-values in parentheses

	error correction model (dependend variable q)									
	AGR	MIN	MAN	CON	PU	WRT	TSC	FIRE	GSPS	SUM
c	0.03	0.04	0.03	0.04	0.03	0.01	0.04	-0.03	0.00	0.03
	(0.31)	(0.03)	(0.21)	(0.23)	(0.37)	(0.33)	(0.01)	(0.06)	(0.98)	(0.30)
q(-1)	0.05	-0.14	0.55	0.11	0.02	0.45	-0.15	0.37	-0.12	-0.04
	(0.82)	(0.40)	(0.00)	(0.55)	(0.90)	(0.01)	(0.47)	(0.06)	(0.57)	(0.84)
e	-0.53	0.10	0.40	0.03	-0.27	0.33	0.14	0.59	0.15	0.20
	(0.83)	(0.15)	(0.05)	(0.91)	(0.26)	(0.01)	(0.34)	(0.00)	(0.55)	(0.73)
e(-1)	0.38	-0.12	-0.62	-0.23	0.10	-0.24	-0.31	0.30	0.22	-0.27
	(0.88)	(0.08)	(0.00)	(0.40)	(0.68)	(0.07)	(0.02)	(0.04)	(0.33)	(0.62)
k	0.50	-0.17	0.05	-1.59	0.55	-0.13	0.23	0.44	0.51	0.25
	(0.70)	(0.79)	(0.78)	(0.13)	(0.35)	(0.68)	(0.31)	(0.03)	(0.09)	(0.41)
resi4b	-0.29	-0.11	-0.03	-0.45	-0.37	-0.29	-0.12	-0.81	-0.16	-0.15
	(0.07)	(0.17)	(0.67)	(0.01)	(0.04)	(0.01)	(0.27)	(0.00)	(0.21)	(0.27)
R^2	0.14	0.21	0.60	0.31	0.24	0.44	0.24	0.61	0.24	0.09

Source: Own calculations using E-Views 9.0, p-values in parenthese

Table a26: Regression results for Mauritius, sample 1977-2010, p-values in parentheses

	AGR	MIN	MAN	CON	PU	WRT	TSC	FIRE	GSPS	SUM
model 1a, dependent variable p										
c	0.00		0.04	0.01	0.01	-0.01	0.02	-0.04	-0.02	-0.02
	(0.98)		(0.08)	(0.49)	(0.79)	(0.66)	(0.52)	(0.06)	(0.33)	(0.21)
q	0.95		0.25	0.44	0.85	0.43	0.39	0.91	0.87	0.88
	(0.00)		(0.30)	(0.03)	(0.01)	(0.15)	(0.19)	(0.00)	(0.14)	(0.00)
k	-0.61		-0.46	-0.11	-0.03	-0.11	-0.06	-0.38	-0.02	-0.02
	(0.39)		(0.19)	(0.89)	(0.80)	(0.74)	(0.78)	(0.07)	(0.96)	(0.95)
R^2	0.89		0.07	0.14	0.20	0.07	0.06	0.81	0.10	0.61
model 1b, dependent variable p										
	AGR	MIN	MAN	CON	PU	WRT	TSC	FIRE	GSPS	SUM
C	0.00		0.05	0.03	0.05	0.00	0.01	-0.04	-0.02	-0.01
	(0.98)		(0.06)	(0.10)	(0.16)	(0.92)	(0.76)	(0.22)	(0.50)	(0.53)
Q	0.93		0.27	0.76	0.65	0.47	0.41	0.84	0.88	0.91
	(0.00)		(0.35)	(0.00)	(0.04)	(0.13)	(0.21)	(0.00)	(0.15)	(0.00)
q(-1)	-0.16		-0.10	-0.62	-0.69	-0.25	0.04	-0.11	-0.27	-0.37
	(0.39)		(0.74)	(0.01)	(0.03)	(0.42)	(0.88)	(0.56)	(0.33)	(0.07)
p(-1)	0.11		-0.12	0.06	0.31	-0.17	0.07	0.22	0.26	0.20
	(0.54)		(0.54)	(0.70)	(0.09)	(0.35)	(0.73)	(0.28)	(0.16)	(0.27)
K	-0.59		-0.53	0.44	-0.04	-0.06	-0.04	-0.25	0.00	-0.04
	(0.42)		(0.19)	(0.55)	(0.66)	(0.86)	(0.84)	(0.28)	(0.99)	(0.79)
R^2	0.89		0.10	0.32	0.33	0.14	0.06	0.82	0.16	0.66
e	0.86		0.15	0.15	-0.06	0.19	0.48	0.92	0.81	0.67
model 4a, dependent variable q										
	AGR	MIN	MAN	CON	PU	WRT	TSC	FIRE	GSPS	SUM
c	0.00		0.04	0.04	0.05	0.05	0.06	0.13	0.02	0.04
	(0.96)		(0.00)	(0.00)	(0.00)	(0.00)	(0.00)	(0.00)	(0.00)	(0.02)
e	0.45		0.32	0.38	0.05	0.19	0.20	0.26	0.01	0.23
	(0.40)		(0.00)	(0.01)	(0.63)	(0.06)	(0.05)	(0.39)	(0.83)	(0.37)
k	-0.54		0.03	0.10	0.08	-0.05	-0.03	-1.08	0.42	-0.02
	(0.80)		(0.91)	(0.88)	(0.15)	(0.80)	(0.78)	(0.00)	(0.00)	(0.97)
R^2	0.02		0.26	0.22	0.08	0.11	0.12	0.29	0.39	0.03
model 4b, dependent variable lnQ										
	AGR	MIN	MAN	CON	PU	WRT	TSC	FIRE	GSPS	SUM
c	10.90		-0.47	23.17	2.86	4.90	1.32	3.04	1.82	-4.82
	(0.00)		(0.09)	(0.00)	(0.00)	(0.00)	(0.00)	(0.17)	(0.00)	(0.00)
lne	0.06		0.28	1.06	0.07	0.97	1.43	0.98	0.30	0.76
	(0.69)		(0.00)	(0.00)	(0.87)	(0.00)	(0.00)	(0.01)	(0.00)	(0.00)
lnk	-0.24		1.10	-2.48	0.62	0.12	0.38	0.37	0.84	1.13
	(0.04)		(0.00)	(0.00)	(0.00)	(0.18)	(0.01)	(0.32)	(0.00)	(0.00)
R^2	0.27		0.98	0.94	0.81	0.98	0.97	0.94	0.99	0.99
Engle-Granger cointegration test										
tau-s	-5.32	-2.29	-2.74	-2.75	-2.32	-1.93	-2.96	-1.97	-1.34	-2.96
prob.	(0.00)	(0.61)	(0.39)	(0.38)	(0.59)	(0.76)	(0.30)	(0.75)	(0.93)	(0.29)

Source: Own calculations using E-Views 9.0, p-values in parentheses

Table a26: Regression results for Mauritius, error correctio model, sample 1977-2010, p-values in parentheses

	error correction model (dependend variable q)									
	AGR	MIN	MAN	CON	PU	WRT	TSC	FIRE	GSPS	SUM
c	-0.01		0.03	0.02	0.07	0.06	0.06	0.10	0.03	0.03
	(0.83)		(0.09)	(0.24)	(0.00)	(0.00)	(0.00)	(0.01)	(0.00)	(0.24)
q(-1)	0.39		0.24	0.55	-0.25	-0.18	0.05	0.33	0.04	0.18
	(0.04)		(0.19)	(0.01)	(0.13)	(0.46)	(0.72)	(0.04)	(0.50)	(0.39)
e	0.09		0.24	0.24	0.17	0.03	0.20	0.45	-0.02	0.28
	(0.82)		(0.03)	(0.15)	(0.11)	(0.80)	(0.05)	(0.11)	(0.77)	(0.33)
e(-1)	-0.48		0.16	-0.13	-0.14	0.18	0.09	-0.74	0.04	-0.01
	(0.18)		(0.19)	(0.36)	(0.18)	(0.12)	(0.41)	(0.01)	(0.53)	(0.97)
k	-0.04		-0.04	-0.05	0.09	-0.29	-0.05	-0.35	0.27	0.22
	(0.98)		(0.90)	(0.94)	(0.11)	(0.23)	(0.68)	(0.34)	(0.04)	(0.69)
resi4b	-1.33		-0.09	-0.15	-0.06	0.29	-0.04	-0.07	0.15	-0.19
	(0.00)		(0.45)	(0.19)	(0.07)	(0.11)	(0.32)	(0.20)	(0.08)	(0.20)
R^2	0.58		0.42	0.40	0.27	0.23	0.21	0.49	0.47	0.09

Source: Own calculations using E-Views 9.0, p-values in parentheses

Table a27: Regression Results for South Africa, sample 1960-2010, p-values in parentheses

	model 1a, dependent variable p									
	AGR	MIN	MAN	CON	PU	WRT	TSC	FIRE	GSPS	SUM
c	0.01	0.05	0.00	-0.02	0.01	-0.03	-0.03	-0.06	-0.02	-0.02
	(0.48)	(0.00)	(0.91)	(0.22)	(0.54)	(0.01)	(0.00)	(0.00)	(0.02)	(0.00)
q	0.99	0.50	0.72	0.50	0.25	0.87	0.93	1.01	0.42	0.96
	(0.00)	(0.03)	(0.00)	(0.00)	(0.42)	(0.00)	(0.00)	(0.00)	(0.12)	(0.00)
k	0.55	-1.15	-0.26	0.20	-0.02	0.30	0.08	0.15	0.19	0.30
	(0.40)	(0.00)	(0.02)	(0.39)	(0.91)	(0.36)	(0.66)	(0.85)	(0.17)	(0.13)
R^2	0.80	0.28	0.61	0.26	0.01	0.49	0.54	0.69	0.18	0.63
	model 1b, dependent variable p									
	AGR	MIN	MAN	CON	PU	WRT	TSC	FIRE	GSPS	SUM
C	0.01	0.03	0.00	-0.01	0.02	-0.02	-0.03	-0.03	-0.01	-0.02
	(0.28)	(0.02)	(0.71)	(0.37)	(0.39)	(0.06)	(0.01)	(0.13)	(0.23)	(0.01)
Q	1.02	0.55	0.73	0.61	0.81	0.90	0.83	0.95	0.37	0.94
	(0.00)	(0.02)	(0.00)	(0.00)	(0.02)	(0.00)	(0.00)	(0.00)	(0.16)	(0.00)
q(-1)	0.60	-0.45	-0.18	-0.39	-0.77	-0.38	0.21	-0.40	-0.13	-0.10
	(0.00)	(0.07)	(0.22)	(0.03)	(0.02)	(0.09)	(0.30)	(0.04)	(0.64)	(0.60)
p(-1)	-0.59	0.36	0.05	0.51	0.36	0.38	0.02	0.44	0.38	0.09
	(0.00)	(0.02)	(0.78)	(0.00)	(0.02)	(0.01)	(0.90)	(0.01)	(0.01)	(0.57)
K	1.1[illegible]	-0.81	-0.16	0.20	-0.05	0.30	-0.02	0.00	0.12	-0.02
	(0.05)	(0.04)	(0.25)	(0.35)	(0.74)	(0.44)	(0.90)	(1.00)	(0.44)	(0.20)
R^2	0.85	0.40	0.63	0.46	0.17	0.56	0.55	0.74	0.29	0.63
e	1.02	0.17	0.58	0.46	0.07	0.84	1.06	1.00	0.39	0.92
	model 4a, dependent variable q									
	AGR	MIN	MAN	CON	PU	WRT	TSC	FIRE	GSPS	SUM
c	0.02	0.02	0.01	0.01	0.03	0.01	0.04	0.02	0.01	0.02
	(0.29)	(0.05)	(0.25)	(0.27)	(0.00)	(0.51)	(0.00)	(0.38)	(0.00)	(0.01)
e	0.05	0.19	0.66	0.48	0.15	0.12	0.09	-0.02	0.16	0.06
	(0.36)	(0.03)	(0.00)	(0.00)	(0.02)	(0.40)	(0.59)	(0.93)	(0.03)	(0.72)
k	0.31	-0.38	0.37	0.25	0.11	0.88	0.21	2.43	0.29	0.52
	(0.31)	(0.10)	(0.04)	(0.27)	(0.15)	(0.00)	(0.31)	(0.03)	(0.00)	(0.02)
R^2	0.00	0.11	0.40	0.25	0.16	0.18	0.03	0.10	0.37	0.10
	model 4b, dependent variable lnQ									
	AGR	MIN	MAN	CON	PU	WRT	TSC	FIRE	GSPS	SUM
c	34.79	11.53	1.33	4.06	2.26	0.35	-1.87	-33.12	3.87	-1.71
	(0.00)	(0.00)	(0.01)	(0.00)	(0.00)	(0.21)	(0.01)	(0.00)	(0.00)	(0.00)
lne	-2.21	0.03	1.25	0.69	0.67	0.11	0.83	-0.08	0.49	0.40
	(0.00)	(0.30)	(0.00)	(0.00)	(0.00)	(0.05)	(0.00)	(0.37)	(0.00)	(0.00)
lnk	-0.69	-0.02	0.15	0.17	0.59	1.05	0.70	3.65	0.39	0.87
	(0.18)	(0.44)	(0.27)	(0.14)	(0.00)	(0.00)	(0.00)	(0.00)	(0.00)	(0.00)
R^2	0.59	0.05	0.97	0.69	0.91	0.98	0.95	0.98	0.99	0.97
	Engle-Granger cointegration test									
tau-s	-2.03	-4.26	-1.34	-2.05	-1.27	-1.24	-2.29	-2.12	-2.42	-1.71
prob.	(0.72)	(0.02)	(0.93)	(0.72)	(0.94)	(0.94)	(0.60)	(0.68)	(0.54)	(0.84)

Source: Own calculations using E-Views 9.0, p-values in parentheses

Table a27: Regression Results for South Africa, error correction model, sample 1960-2010, p-values in parentheses

	error correction model (dependend variable q)									
	AGR	MIN	MAN	CON	PU	WRT	TSC	FIRE	GSPS	SUM
c	0.03	0.01	0.01	-0.01	0.02	-0.02	0.02	-0.02	0.01	0.02
	(0.16)	(0.16)	(0.45)	(0.52)	(0.00)	(0.20)	(0.05)	(0.54)	(0.03)	(0.13)
q(-1)	-0.23	0.31	0.17	0.53	0.15	0.34	0.45	0.34	0.27	0.46
	(0.13)	(0.02)	(0.31)	(0.00)	(0.31)	(0.04)	(0.01)	(0.03)	(0.13)	(0.00)
e	-0.24	0.20	0.59	0.42	0.03	0.09	0.18	-0.02	0.20	0.07
	(0.50)	(0.01)	(0.01)	(0.00)	(0.64)	(0.52)	(0.26)	(0.94)	(0.02)	(0.67)
e(-1)	-0.09	-0.09	-0.43	-0.18	0.12	-0.07	-0.12	-0.39	-0.11	-0.35
	(0.80)	(0.27)	(0.09)	(0.21)	(0.10)	(0.59)	(0.45)	(0.11)	(0.19)	(0.04)
k	-0.98	-0.21	0.55	0.55	0.16	1.37	0.01	4.63	0.20	0.27
	(0.51)	(0.32)	(0.01)	(0.06)	(0.03)	(0.00)	(0.96)	(0.01)	(0.02)	(0.40)
resi4b	-0.20	-0.31	-0.16	-0.14	-0.06	-0.41	-0.01	-0.25	-0.02	-0.05
	(0.07)	(0.00)	(0.04)	(0.01)	(0.03)	(0.00)	(0.73)	(0.03)	(0.73)	(0.36)
R^2	0.19	0.47	0.47	0.55	0.42	0.38	0.20	0.26	0.40	0.32

Source: Own calculations using E-Views 9.0, p-values in parentheses

References

Acemoglu, D., Johnson, S., & Robinson, J. A. (2001): The Colonial Origins of Comparative Development: An Empirical Investigation. In: The American Economic Review, 91 (5), 1369–1401.

Acemoglu, D., Johnson, S., & Robinson, J. A. (2002): Reversal of Fortune: Geography and Institutions in the Making of the Modern World Income Distribution. In: *The Quarterly Journal of Economics*, *117* (4), 1231–1294.

African Development Bank (AfDB) (2013): Situational Analysis of the Reliability of Economic Statistics in Africa: Special Focus on GDP Measurement.

African Development Bank (AfDB) (2014): In-Depth Situational Analysis of the Reliability of Economic Statistics in Africa: With a Special Focus on GDP Measurement & Methodological Requirements.

African Development Bank (AfDB), Organisation for Economic Co-operation and Development (OECD), & United Nations Development Programme (UNDP) (2014): Global Value Chains and Africa's Industrialisation. African Economic Outlook. Paris: OECD Publishing.

African Development Bank (AfDB), Organisation for Economic Co-operation and Development (OECD), United Nations Development Programme (UNDP), & Economic Commision for Africa (ECA) (2013): Structural Transformation and Natural Resources. African Economic Outlook. Paris: OECD Publishing.

African Union (AU) (2000): Constitutive Act of the African Union.

Aguiar, A. Narayanan, B., & McDougall, R. (2016): "An Overview of the GTAP 9 Data Base.". In: *Journal of Global Economic Analysis*, *1* (1), 181–208.

Ajayi, A. (1969): Colonialism: an episode in African history. In: L. H. Gann, & P. Duignan (Eds.), *Volume 1: The History and Politics of Colonialism in Africa 1870–1914* (pp. 497–509). Cambridge: University Press.

Ajayi, A. (1989): Africa at the beginning of the nineteenth century: issues and prospects. In: A. Ajayi (Ed.), *General history of Africa* (pp. 1–22). London: Heinemann.

Ajayi, A. (1989): Conclusion: Africa on the eve of the European conquest. In: A. Ajayi (Ed.), *General history of Africa* (pp. 773–791). London: Heinemann.

Alesina, A., Easterly, W., & Matuszeski, J. (2011): Artificial States. In: *Journal of the European Economic Association*, *9* (2), 246–277.

Alexiadis, S., & Tsagdis, D. (2010): Is cumulative growth in manufacturing productivity slowing down in the EU12 regions? In: *Cambridge Journal of Economics*, *34* (6), 1001–1017.

Altenburg, T. (2006): Governance Patterns in Value Chains and their Development Impact. In: *The European Journal of Development Research*, *18* (4), 498–521.

Altenburg, T. (2013): Can Industrial Policy Work under Neopatrimonial Rule? In: A. Szirmai, L. Alcorta, & W. Naudé (Eds.), *Pathways to industrialization in the twenty-first century: New challenges and emerging paradigms* (pp. 345–372). Oxford: Oxford University Press.

Amin, S. (1972): Underdevelopment and Dependence in Black Africa: Origins and Contemporary Forms. In: *The Journal of Modern African Studies*, *10* (04), 503–524.

Amin, S. (1974): Accumulation and Development: A Theoretical Model. In: *Review of African Political Economy* (1), 9–26.

Amsden, A. H. (1989): Asia's next giant. South Korea and late industrialization. New York [u.a.]: Oxford University Press.

Angeriz, A., McCombie, J., & Roberts, M. (2008): New Estimates of Returns to Scale and Spatial Spillovers for EU Regional Manufacturing, 1986—2002. In: *International Regional Science Review*, *31* (1), 62–87.

Aoki, M., Kim, H.-k., & Okuno-Fujiwara, M. (Eds.) (1997): The role of government in East Asian economic development: comparative institutional analysis. Oxford: Clarendon.

Ark, B. v., & Timmer, M. (2003): Asia's Productivity Performance and Potential: The Contribution of Sectors and Structural Change. Groningen: University of Groningen & Conference Board.

Artadi, E. V., & Sala-i-Martin, X. (2003): The Economic Tragedy of the XXth Century: Growth in Africa. In: *National Bureau of Economic Research Working Paper Series*, *9865* .

Asche, H. (2012): Die Wirtschaft Afrikas seit 1960. In: T. Bierschenk, & E. Spies (Eds.), *50 Jahre Unabhängigkeit in Afrika: Kontinuitäten, Brüche, Perspektiven* (pp. 371–411). Köln: Rüdiger Köppe Verlag.

Asche, H. (2015a): Down to Earth Again: The Third Stage of African Growth Perceptions. In: *Africa Spectrum*, *50* (3), 123–138.

Asche, H. (2015b): Europe, Africa, and the Transatlantic: The North - South Challenge for Development-Friendly Trade Policy. Berlin: Heinrich Böll Stiftung.

Austen, R. A. (1987): African economic history: Internal development and external dependency. London: Currey.

Austin, G. (2008): The 'reversal of fortune' thesis and the compression of history: Perspectives from African and comparative economic history. In: *Journal of International Development*, *20* (8), 996–1027.

Bach, D. (2012): Neopatrimonial and developmental the emerging states' syndrome. In: D. Bach, & M. Gazibo (Eds.), *Neopatrimonialism in Africa and beyond* (pp. 221–224). New York: Routledge.

Bah, E.-h. M. (2011): Structural Transformation Paths Across Countries. In: *Emerging Markets Finance and Trade*, *47* (sup2), 5–19.

Balassa, B. (1965): Trade Liberalisation and "Revealed" Comparative Advantage. In: *The Manchester School*, *33* (2), 99–123.

Bauer, P. T. (1954): West African trade. A study of competition, oligopoly and monopoly in a changing economy. Cambridge: University Press.

Bayart, J.-F., & Ellis, S. (2000): Africa in the World: A History of Extraversion. In: *African Affairs, 99* (395), 217–267.

Berlemann, M., & Wesselhöft, J.-E. (2014): Estimating Aggregate Capital Stocks Using the Perpetual Inventory Method: A Survey of Previous Implementations and New Empirical Evidence for 103 Countries. In: *Review of Economics, 65* (1), 1–34.

Bernard, A. B., & Jones, C. I. (1996): Comparing Apples to Oranges: Productivity Convergence and Measurement Across Industries and Countries. In: *The American Economic Review, 86* (5), 1216–1238.

Berthémely, J.-C., & Söderling, L. (2002): Emerging Africa. Development Centre Studies. Paris: OECD Publishing and OECD Development Centre.

Beyers, W. B. (1976): Empirical identification of key sectors: some further evidence. In: *Environment and Planning A, 8* (2), 231–236.

Bhaduri, A. (2006): Structural Change and Economic Development: On the Relative Roles of Effective Demand and the Price Mechanism in a 'Dual' Economy. In: H.-J. Chang (Ed.), *Rethinking development economics* (pp. 219–234). London: Anthem Press.

Bhagwati, J. (1993): Protectionism. In: *The Concise Encyclopedia of Economics.* Library of Economics and Liberty. http://www.econlib.org/library/Enc1/Protectionism.html. Accessed 25.06.2016.

Bhorat, H., & Oosthuizen, M. (2008): Employment shifts and the 'jobless growth' debate. In: A. Kraak, & K. Press (Eds.), *Human resources development review 2008: Education, employment and skills in South Africa* (pp. 50–68). Cape Town: HSRC Press.

Bielschowsky, R. (2009): Sixty years of ECLAC: structuralism and neo-structuralism. In: *CEPAL Review* (97), 171–192.

Bienefeld, M. (1988): Dependency Theory and the Political Economy of Africa's Crisis. In: *Review of African Political Economy* (43), 68–87.

Bloch, R., & Owusu, G. (2012): Linkages in Ghana's gold mining industry: Challenging the enclave thesis. In: *Resources Policy - Making the Most of Commodities: The Determinants of Linkages in Africa, 37* (4), 434–442.

Block, S. A. (2001): Does Africa grow differently? In: *Journal of Development Economics, 65* (2), 443–467.

Boahen, A. A. (1985): Africa and the colonial challenge. In: A. A. Boahen (Ed.), *Africa under colonial domination 1880 - 1935* (pp. 1–18). London: Heinemann.

Boahen, A. A. (1985): Colonialism in Africa: its impact and significance. In: A. A. Boahen (Ed.), *Africa under colonial domination 1880 - 1935* (pp. 782–809). London: Heinemann.

Boeke, J. H. (1942): Economics and economic policy of dual societies. Haarlem: Tjeenk Willnik.

Brett, E. A. (1973): Colonialism and underdevelopment in East Africa: The politics of economic change 1919-1939. London: Heinemann.

Brunnschweiler, C. N., & Bulte, E. H. (2008): The resource curse revisited and revised: A tale of paradoxes and red herrings. In: *Journal of Environmental Economics and Management*, *55* (3), 248–264.

Bujra, A. (2004): Pan-African Political and Economic Visions of Development From the OAU to the AU: From the Lagos Plan of Action (LPA) to the New Partnership for African Development (NEPAD). DPMF Occasional Paper, 13. Addis Ababa:

Bulmer-Thomas, V. (1978): Trade, structure and linkages in Costa Rica: An input-output approach. In: *Journal of Development Economics*, *5* (1), 73–86.

Cai, J., & Leung, P. (2004): Linkage Measures: a Revisit and a Suggested Alternative. In: *Economic Systems Research*, *16* (1), 63–83.

Cantore, N., Michele, C., Soare, C., & Lavopa, A. (2014): Manufacturing as an engine of growth: Which is the best fuel? Development Policy, Statistics and Research Branch Working Paper, 01/2014. Vienna: United Nations Industrial Development Organization (UNIDO).

Caselli, F. (2005): Chapter 9 Accounting for Cross-Country Income Differences. In: Philippe Aghion and Steven N. Durlauf (Ed.), *Handbook of Economic Growth* (pp. 679–741). New York [u.a.]: Elsevier.

Castellacci, F., Los, B., & Vries, G. J. (2014): Sectoral productivity trends: convergence islands in oceans of non-convergence. In: *Journal of Evolutionary Economics*, *24* (5), 983–1007.

Castiglione, C. (2011): Verdoorn-Kaldor's Law: an empirical analysis with time series data in the United States. In: *Advances in Management & Applied Economics*, *1* (3), 135–151.

Cella, G. (1984): The Input-Output Measurement of Interindustry Linkages. In: *Oxford Bulletin of Economics and Statistics*, *46* (1), 73–84.

Chang, H. (2002): Breaking the mould: an institutionalist political economy alternative to the neo-liberal theory of the market and the state. In: *Cambridge Journal of Economics*, *26* (5), 539–559.

Chang, H.-J. (2006): Kicking away the ladder. Development strategy in historical perspective. (Repr). Anthem studies in development and globalization. London: Anthem Press.

Chang, H.-J. (2013): Is industrial policy neccessary and feasible in Africa?: Theoretical considerations and historical lessons. Working paper prepared for JICA/IPD Africa Task Force Meeting. Cambridge: University of Cambridge.

Chang, H.-J. (2015): Is industrial policy necessary and feasible in Africa?: Theoretical considerations and historical lessons. In: A. Noman, & J. E. Stiglitz (Eds.), *Industrial Policy and Economic Transformation in Africa* (pp. 30–52). New York: Columbia University Press.

Chenery, H., & Syrquin, M. (1975): Patterns of development, 1950-1970. New York: Oxford University Press.

Chenery, H. B. (1960): Patterns of Industrial Growth. In: *The American Economic Review*, *50* (4), 624–654.

Chenery, H. B. (1982): Industrialization and Growth: The Experience of Large Countries. The World Bank Staff Working Papers, 539. Washington D.C.: The World Bank.

Chenery, H. B., Elkington, H., & Ahluwalia, M. S. (1979): Structural change and development policy. A World Bank research publication. New York: Oxford University Press.

Chenery, H. B., & Watanabe, T. (1958): International Comparisons of the Structure of Production. In: *Econometrica*, *26* (4), 487–521.

Ciobanu, C., Mattas, K., & Psaltopoulos, D. (2004): Structural Changes in Less Developed Areas: An Input- Output Framework. In: *Regional Studies*, *38* (6), 603–614.

Clark, C. (1957): The conditions of economic progress. (3. ed., largely rewritten). London: Macmillan [u.a.].

Coase, R. H. (1937): The Nature of the Firm. In: *Economica*, *4* (16), 386–405.

Cohen, W. M., & Levinthal, D. A. (1990): Absorptive Capacity: A New Perspective on Learning and Innovation. In: *Administrative Science Quarterly*, *35* (1), 128–152.

Collier, P. (2000): Africa's comparative advantage. In: H. Jalilian, M. A. Tribe, & J. Weiss (Eds.), *Industrial development and policy in Africa: Issues of de-industrialization and development strategy* (11-21). Cheltenham: Elgar.

Collier, P. (2008): Growth Strategies for Africa. Commission on Growth and Development Working Paper, 9. Washington D.C.: The International Bank for Reconstruction and Development / The World Bank.

Collier, P., & Dercon, S. (2014): African Agriculture in 50 Years: Smallholders in a Rapidly Changing World? In: *Economic Transformation in Africa* (63), 92–101.

Cornwall, J. (1979): Modern capitalism: Its growth and transformation. (Reprint). Oxford: Robertson.

Cuello, F. A. Mansouri, F., & Hewings, G. J. D. (1992): The Identification of Structure at the Sectoral Level: a Reformulation of the Hirschman–Rasmussen Key Sector Indices. In: *Economic Systems Research*, *4* (4), 285–296.

Cumings, B. (1984): The Origins and Development of the Northeast Asian Political Economy Industrial Sectors, Product Cycles, and Political Consequences. In: *International Organization*, *38* (1), 1–40.

Dabla-Norris, E., Thomas, A., Garcia-Verdu, R., & Chen, Y. (2013): Benchmarking Structural Transformation Across the World. IMF Working Paper, WP/13/176.

Danaher, K. (Ed.) (1994): 50 years is enough: The case against the World Bank and the International Monetary Fund. Boston, Mass: South End Press.

Dasgupta, S., & Singh, A. (2005): Will Services be the new Engine of Economic Growth in India? University of Cambridge, Centre for Business Research, and Faculty of Economics, Working Paper, 310.

De Backer, K., & Miroudot, S. (2013): Mapping Global Value Chains. OECD Trade Policy Papers, 159. OECD Publishing.

Deaton, A. (2009): Commentary: The World Development Report at Thirty: A Birthday Tribute or a Funeral Elegy? In: S. Yusuf (Ed.), *Development economics through the decades: A critical look at 30 years of the world development report* (pp. 105–114). Washington, D.C: The World Bank.

Deraniyagala, S. (2003): From Washington to post-Washington: Does it matter for industrial policy? In: B. Fine, C. Lapavitsas, & J. Pincus (Eds.), *Development policy in the twenty-first century: Beyond the post-Washington consensus* (pp. 80–98). London: Routledge.

Deutsch, J., & Syrquin, M. (1989): Economic Development and the Structure of Production. In: *Economic Systems Research*, *1* (4), 447–464.

Devarajan, S. (2013): Africa's Statistical Tragedy. In: *Review of Income and Wealth* (59), S9-S15.

Devisse, J. (1984): Africa in inter-continental relations. In: D. T. Niane (Ed.), *Africa from the twelfth to the sixteenth century* (pp. 635–672). Paris: UNESCO.

Diagne, P. (1992): African political, economic and social structures during this period. In: B. A. Ogot (Ed.), *Africa from the sixteenth to the eighteenth century* (pp. 23–45).

Dixit, A. (1973): Models of dual economies. New York: Wiley & Sons.

Döhrn, R., & Heilemann, U. (1993): Sectoral Change in Eastern Europe: The Chenery Hypothesis Reconsidered. In: B. Heitger (Ed.), *German Unification And The International Economy* (pp. 83–112). Hoboken: Taylor & Francis.

Dollar, D., & Kraay, A. (2002): Growth is Good for the Poor. In: *Journal of Economic Growth*, *7* (3), 195–225.

Döver, M., & Kappel, R. (2015): Hürden für die Industrialisierung in Afrika. GIGA Focus Africa, 7. Hamburg: German Institute of Global and Area Studies (GIGA).

Drejer, I. (2002): Input-Output based measures of interindustry linkages revisited: A Survey and Discussion. 14th International Conference on Input-Output Techniques: Montreal, Canada.

Duignan, P., & Gann, L. H. (1975): The Pre-Colonial Economies of Sub-Saharan Africa. In: P. Duignan, & L. H. Gann (Eds.), *Colonialism in Africa 1870–1960: Volume 4, The Economics of Colonialism* (pp. 33–67). Cambridge: University Press.

Easterly, W. (2001): The Lost Decades: Developing Countries' Stagnation in Spite of Policy Reform 1980–1998: Journal of Economic Growth, *6* (2), 135–157.

Easterly, W. (2005): What did structural adjustment adjust?: The association of policies and growth with repeated IMF and World Bank adjustment loans. In: *Journal of Development Economics*, *76* (1), 1–22.

Easterly, W., & Levine, R. (1995): Africa's Growth Tragedy: A Retrospective, 1960-89. Policy Research Working Paper, 1503.

Easterly, W., & Levine, R. (1997): Africa's Growth Tragedy: Policies and Ethnic Divisions. In: *The Quarterly Journal of Economics*, *112* (4), 1203–1250.

Economic Commision for Africa (ECA) (1968): Survey of African Economic Conditions in Africa: 1960, 1961, 1962, 1963, 1964. New York: United Nations.

Economic Commision for Africa (ECA) (1971): Survey of economic conditions in Africa, 1970. (part 1). New York: United Nations.

Economic Commision for Africa (ECA) (1989): African Alternative Framework: to Structural Afjustment Programmes for Socio-Economic Recovery and Transformation. New York: United Nations.

Economic Commision for Africa (ECA) (2013): Making the most of Africa's commodities: Industrializing for Growth, Jobs and Economic Transformation. Economic report on Africa. New York: United Nations.

Economic Commision for Africa (ECA) (2014): Dynamic industrial policy in Africa. Economic report on Africa, 2014. Addis Ababa: United Nations.

Economic Commision for Africa (ECA) (2015): Industrializing through Trade. Economic report on Africa. Addis Ababa: United Nations.

Economic Commision for Africa (ECA) (2016): Greening Africa's Industrialization. Economic report on Africa. Addis Ababa: United Nations.

Economic Commision for Africa (ECA), & African Development Bank (AfDB) (2006): The Reference Regional Strategic Framework for Statistical Capacity Building in Africa: Better Statistics for Improved Development Outcomes. Addis Ababa: United Nations.

Economic Commission for Latin America and the Caribbean (ECLAC) (1990): Changing production patterns with social equity: The prime task of Latin American and Caribbean development in the 1990s. (1. ed). Libros de la CEPAL, 25. Santiago, Chile: United Nations.

Economic Commission for Latin America and the Caribbean (ECLAC) (1991): Sustainable development: changing production patterns, social equity and the environment. Libros de la CEPAL, 31. Santiago, Chile: United Nations.

Economic Commission for Latin America and the Caribbean (ECLAC) (2007): Social Cohesion: Inclusion and a Sense of Belonging in Latin America and the Caribbean. Santiago, Chile: United Nations.

Edigheji, O. (Ed.) (2010): Constructing a democratic developmental state in South Africa: Potentials and challenges. Cape Town: HSRC Press.

Eichengreen, B., & Gupta, P. (2009): The Two Waves of Service Sector Growth. NBER Working Paper Series, 14968. Cambridge: National Bureau of Economic Research (NBER).

Engel, E. (1895): Die Lebenskosten belgischer Arbeiter-Familien früher und jetzt. Ermittelt aus Familien-Haushaltrechnungen und vergleichend zusammengestellt. In: *Bulletin de l'Institut International de Statistique*, *9* (1), 1–124.

Englebert, P. (2000): Solving the Mystery of the AFRICA Dummy. In: *World Development*, *28* (10), 1821–1835.

Englebert, P., Tarango, S., & Carter, M. (2002): Dismemberment and Suffocation: A Contribution to the Debate on African Boundaries. In: *Comparative Political Studies*, *35* (10), 1093–1118.

EU SME Centre (2011): Report: Processing Trade in China. Beijing: EU SME Centre.

European Commission (EC) (2010): An Integrated Industrial Policy for the Globalisation Era Putting Competitiveness and Sustainability at Centre Stage: Communication of 28 November 2010 from the Commission to the European Parliament, the Council, the European Economic and Social Committee and the Committee of the Regions. Brussels: European Commission.

European Commission (EC) (2012): A Stronger European Industry for Growth and Economic Recovery: Communication from the Comission to the European Parliament, the Council, the European Economic and Social Committee and the Committee of the Regions. Brussels: European Commission.

European Commission (EC) (2013): European Competitiveness Report 2013: Towards knowledge-driven reindustrialisation. Commission Staff Working Document. Luxembourg: European Union.

European Commission (EC) (2014): For a European Industrial Renaissance: Communication from the Comission to the European Parliament, the Council, the European Economic and Social Committee and the Committee of the Regions. Brussels: European Commission.

Eurostat, & European Commission (EC) (2008): Eurostat manual of supply, use and input-output tables. Methodologies and working papers. Luxembourg: Publications Office.

Evans, P. B. (1995): Embedded autonomy: States and industrial transformation. Princeton NJ [u.a.]: Princeton University Press.

Evans, P. B., Rueschemeyer, D., & Skocpol, T. (Eds.) (1999): Bringing the state back in. Cambridge: Cambridge University Press.

Fabricant, S. (1975): The output of manufacturing industries, 1899-1937. National Bureau of Economic Research publications in reprint, 39. New York: Arno Press.

Fagerberg, J. (2000): Technological progress, structural change and productivity growth: a comparative study. In: *Structural Change and Economic Dynamics*, *11* (4), 393–411.

Falk, M., & Jarocinska, E. (2010): Linkages between Services and Manufacturing in EU countries. SERVICEGAP Review Paper 1.

Fase, M. M. G., & Van Den Heuvel, P. J. (1988): Productivity and growth: Verdoorn's law revisited. In: *Economics Letters*, *28* (2), 135–139.

Fay, C. R. (1940): The Movement Towards Free Trade, 1820-1853. In: J. H. Rose, A. P. Newton, & E. A. Benians (Eds.), *The Cambridge History of the British Empire* (pp. 388–414). Cambridge Mass: University Press.

Faye, M. L., McArthur, J. W., Sachs, J. D., & Snow, T. (2004): The challenges facing landlocked developing countries. In: *Journal of Human Development*, *5* (1), 31–68.

Fei, J. C. H., & Ranis, G. (1963): Innovation, Capital Accumulation, and Economic Development. In: *The American Economic Review*, *53* (3), 283–313.

Fessehaie, J. (2012): What determines the breadth and depth of Zambia's backward linkages to copper mining? The role of public policy and value chain dynamics. In: *Resources Policy - Making the Most of Commodities: The Determinants of Linkages in Africa*, *37* (4), 405–484.

Fieldhouse, D. K. (1981): Colonialism, 1870 - 1945: An introduction. London: Weidenfeld and Nicolson.

Fine, B. (2002): Economics Imperialism and the New Development Economics as Kuhnian Paradigm Shift? In: *World Development*, *30* (12), 2057–2070.

Fine, B. (2010): From the political economy of development to development economics: implications for Africa. In: V. Padayachee (Ed.), *The political economy of Africa* (pp. 60–82). New York: Routledge.

Fine, B. (2010) Zombieeconomics: the Living Death of Dismal Science. In: K. Birch, & V. Mykhnenko (Eds.), *The rise and fall of neoliberalism: The collapse of an economic order?* (pp. 153–170). London, New York: Zed Books.

Fingleton, B., & McCombie, J. S. L. (1998): Increasing Returns and Economic Growth: Some Evidence for Manufacturing from the European Union Regions. In: *Oxford Economic Papers*, *50* (1), 89–105.

Fisher, A. G. B. (1939): Production, Primary, Secondary and Tertiary. In: *Economic Record*, *15* (1), 24–38.

Foellmi, R., & Zweimüller, J. (2008): Structural change, Engel's consumption cycles and Kaldor's facts of economic growth. In: *Journal of Monetary Economics*, *55* (7), 1317–1328.

Fole, A. G. (2003): The Historical Origin of African Debt Crisis. In: *Eastern Africa Social Science Research Review*, *19* (1), 59–89.

Foster-McGregor, N., Kaulich, F., & Stehrer, R. (2015): Global Value Chains in Africa. Inclusive and Sustainable Industrial Development Working Paper Series, 04. Vienna: United Nations Industrial Development Organization (UNIDO).

Fourie, E. (2013): New Maps for Africa?: Contextualising the 'Chinese Model' within Ethiopian and Kenyan Paradigms of Development. PhD thesis. Trento, Italy: University of Trento.

Gann, L. H., & Duignan, P. (1969): Introduction. In: L. H. Gann, & P. Duignan (Eds.), *Volume 1: The History and Politics of Colonialism in Africa 1870–1914* (pp. 1–26). Cambridge: University Press.

Gereffi, G. (1993): The organization of buyer-driven global commodity chains: how US retailers shape overseas production networks. In: G. Gereffi, & M. Korzeniewicz (Eds.), *Commodity Chains and Global Capitalism* (pp. 95–122). Santa Barbara: ABC-CLIO.

Gereffi, G. (1999): A Commodity Chains Framework for Analyzing Global Industries. Durham: Duke University, Institute for Development Studies.

Gereffi, G. (2001): Beyond the Producer-driven/Buyer-driven Dichotomy The Evolution of Global Value Chains in the Internet Era. In: *IDS Bulletin*, *32* (3), 30–40.

Gereffi, G. (2005): The global economy: organization, governance, and development. In: N. J. Smelser (Ed.), *The handbook of economic sociology* (pp. 160–182): Princeton University Press.

Gereffi, G., & Fernandez-Stark, K. (2011): Global Value Chain Analysis: A Primer.

Gereffi, G., Humphrey, J., Kaplinsky, R., & Sturgeon*, T. J. (2001): Introduction: Globalisation, Value Chains and Development. In: *IDS Bulletin*, *32* (3), 1–8.

Gereffi, G., & Korzeniewicz, M. (Eds.) (1993): Commodity Chains and Global Capitalism. Santa Barbara: ABC-CLIO.

Gerschenkron, A. (1966): Economic backwardness in historical perspective: A book of essays. (2nd ed.). Cambridge Mass.: Belknap Press of Harvard University Press.

Ghani, E., & O'Connell, S. D. (2014): Can Service Be a Growth Escalator in Low Income Countries. Policy Research Working Paper, 6971. Washington D.C.: The World Bank.

Ghosh, A. (1958): Input-Output Approach in an Allocation System. In: *Economica*, *25* (97), 58–64.

Gibbon, P., Bair, J., & Ponte, S. (2008): Governing global value chains: an introduction. In: *Economy and Society*, *37* (3), 315–338.

Gibbon, P., & Ponte, S. (2005): Trading down: Africa, value chains, and the global economy. Philadelphia: Temple University Press.

Goldberg, I., & Kuriakose, S. (2011): Fostering technology absorption in Southern African enterprisesa: Document of the World Bank. Washington, D.C.: The World Bank.

Goldstein, M., & Officer, L. H. (1979): New Measures of Prices and Productivity for Tradable and Nontradable Goods. In: *Review of Income and Wealth*, *25* (4), 413–427.

Gore, C. (1996): Methodological nationalism and the misunderstanding of East Asian industrialisation. In: *The European Journal of Development Research*, *8* (1), 77–122.

Gore, C. (2000): The Rise and Fall of the Washington Consensus as a Paradigm for Developing Countries. In: *World Development*, *28* (5), 789–804.

Hahn, H.-W. (2011): Die Industrielle Revolution in Deutschland. (3rd ed.). Enzyklopädie deutscher Geschichte. München: Oldenbourg.

Hanson, K. T., & Leautier, F. (2013): Jobless Economic Growth in Africa: Is There a Role for Agriculture? In: *Journal of African Development*, *15* (2).

Harris, J. R., & Todaro, M. P. (1970): Migration, Unemployment and Development: A Two-Sector Analysis. In: *The American Economic Review*, *60* (1), 126–142.

Harris, R. I. D., & Lau, E. (1998): Verdoorn's law and increasing returns to scale in the UK regions, 1968–91: some new estimates based on the cointegration approach. In: *Oxford Economic Papers*, *50* (2), 201–219.

Harris, R. I. D., & Liu, A. (1999): Verdoorn's law and increasing returns to scale: country estimates based on the cointegration approach. In: *Applied Economics Letters*, *6* (1), 29–33.

Hartzenberg, T. (2011): Regional Integration in Africa. Staff Working Paper ERSD, 14. Geneva: World Trade Organization (WTO).

Hatzichronoglou, T. (1997): Revision of the High-Technology Sector and Product Classification. OECD Science, Technology and Industry Working Papers, 1997/2. Paris: OECD Publishing.

Heckscher, E. F., Ohlin, B., Flam, H., & Flanders, M. J. (1991): Heckscher-Ohlin trade theory. Cambridge, Mass.: MIT Press.

Helpman, E., & Krugman, P. R. (2002): Market structure and foreign trade: Increasing returns, imperfect competition, and the international economy. (8th ed.). Cambridge, Mass: MIT Press.

Herbst, J. (1990): The structural adjustment of politics in Africa. In: *World Development, 18* (7), 949–958.

Hiley, M. (1999): The dynamics of changing comparative advantage in the Asia-Pacific region: Journal of the Asia Pacific Economy. In: *Journal of the Asia Pacific Economy, 4* (3), 446–467.

Hirschman, A. O. (1958): The Strategy of Economic Development. New Haven: Yale University Press.

Hirschman, A. O. (1981): Essays in trespassing: Economics to politics and beyond. Cambridge: Cambridge University Press.

Hirschman, A. O. (2013): A Generalized Linkage Approach to Development. with Special References to Staples. In: *The essential Hirschman* (pp. 155–194): Princeton University Press.

Hobsbawm, E. J. (1990): Industry and empire: From 1750 to the present day. (Reprint). The Penguin economic history of Britain. London: Penguin Books.

Hodgson, G. M. (2012): From Social Theory to Explaining Sickonomics: A Response to Dimitris Milonakis and Ben Fine. In: *Review of Social Economy, 70* (4), 492–507.

Holub, H.-W., & Schnabl, H. (1985): Input-Output-Rechnung: Input-Output-Tabellen. (2., aktualisierte Aufl.). Oldenbourgs Lehr- und Handbücher der Wirtschafts- und Sozialwissenschaften. München, Wien: R. Oldenbourg.

Hopkins, A. G. (1980): An economic history of West Africa. London: Longman.

Hopkins, A. G. (2009): The new economic history of Africa. In: *The Journal of African History, 50* (02), 155.

Hopkins, E. (2000): Industrialisation and Society A Social History, 1830-1951. London: Routledge.

Hopkins, T. K., & Wallerstein, I. (1986): Commodity Chains in the World-Economy Prior to 1800. In: *Review (Fernand Braudel Center), 10* (1), 157–170.

Houghton, D. H. (1976): The South African economy. (3rd ed.). Cape Town: Oxford University Press.

Huff, K., McDougall, R., & Walmsley, T. (2000): Contributing Input-Output Tables to the GTAP Data Base. GTAP Technical Papers, No. 1, Release 4.2. Lafayette: Center for Global Trade Analysis, Purdue University.

Hughes, A. (1992): Marxism's retreat from Africa. London [u.a.]: Psychology Press.

Hummels, D. (2007): Transportation costs and international trade in the second era of globalization In: *The Journal of Economic Perspectives, 21* (3), 131–154.

Hummels, D., Ishii, J., & Yi, K.-M. (2001): The nature and growth of vertical specialization in world trade. In: *Journal of International Economics, 54* (1), 75–96.

Imbs, J., & Wacziarg, R. (2003): Stages of Diversification. In: *The American Economic Review*, *93* (1), 63–86.

Inikori, J. E. (1992): Africa in world history: the export slave trade from Africa and the emergence of the Atlantic economic order. In: B. A. Ogot (Ed.), *Africa from the sixteenth to the eighteenth century* (pp. 74–112).

Inomata, S., & Owen, A. (2014): Comparative Evaluation of MRIO Databases. In: *Economic Systems Research*, *26* (3), 239–244.

International Energy Agency (2013): World Energy Outlook 2013. Paris: OECD Publishing.

International Energy Agency (2014): Africa Engergy Outlook: A Focus on Engery Prospects in Sub-Saharan Africa. World Energy Outlook Special Report. Paris: OECD Publishing.

International Monetary Fund (IMF) (2015a): Regional Economic Outlook, April 2015: Sub-Saharan Africa: Navigating Headwinds. Regional Economic Outlook. Washington D.C.: International Monetary Fund.

International Monetary Fund (IMF) (2015b): Regional Economic Outlook, October 2015: Sub-Saharan Africa. Regional Economic Outlook. Washington D.C.: International Monetary Fund.

International Monetary Fund (IMF) (2016): Regional Economic Outlook, April 2016: Sub-Saharan Africa: Time for a Policy Reset. Regional Economic Outlook. Washington D.C.: International Monetary Fund.

Jack, W., & Suri, T. (2014): Risk Sharing and Transactions Costs: Evidence from Kenya's Mobile Money Revolution. In: *The American Economic Review*, *104* (1), 183–223.

James, J. (2009): Leapfrogging in mobile telephony: A measure for comparing country performance. In: *Technological Forecasting and Social Change*, *76* (7), 991–998.

Jensen, B. S., & Wong, K.-y. (1997): Dynamics, economic growth, and international trade. Studies in international economics. Ann Arbor: University of Michigan Press.

Jerven, M. (2014): African growth miracle or statistical tragedy?: Interpreting trends in the data over the past two decades. WIDER Working Paper, 114. Helsinki: World Institute for Development Economics Research (WIDER).

Johnson, C. (1982): MITI and the Japanese miracle: The growth of industrial policy, 1925 - 1975. Stanford, Calif: Stanford University Press.

Johnson, C. (1999): The Developmental State: Odyssey of a Concept. In: M. Woo-Cumings (Ed.), *The developmental state* (pp. 32–60). Ithaca NY [u.a.]: Cornell University Press.

Jomo, K. S. (2001): Rethinking the Role of Government Policy in Southeast Asia. In: J. E. Stiglitz, & S. Yusuf (Eds.), *Rethinking the East Asia miracle* (pp. 461–508). Washington DC, Oxford [u.a.]: The World Bank; Oxford University Press.

Jomo, K. S., & Reinert, E. S. (2005): Introduction. In: K. S. Jomo (Ed.), *The origins of development economics: How schools of economic thought have addressed development* (pp. vii–xxii). New Delhi: Tulika Books.

Jones, L. P. (1976): The Measurement of Hirschmanian Linkages. In: *The Quarterly Journal of Economics*, *90* (2), 323–333.

Jorgenson, D. W. (1961): The Development of a Dual Economy. In: *The Economic Journal*, *71* (282), 309–334.

Jourdan, P. P (2014): Optimising the development impact of mineral resources extraction in Zimbabwe. Master Thesis. Johannesburg: University of the Witwatersrand.

Ju, J., Lin, J. Y., & Wang, Y. (2009): Endowment Structure, Industrial Dynamics, and Economic Growth. Policy Research Working Paper, 5055. Washington D.C.: The World Bank.

Kaldor, N. (1934): The Equilibrium of the Firm. In: *The Economic Journal*, *44* (173), 60–76.

Kaldor, N. (1966): Causes of the slow rate of economic growth of the United Kingdom: an inaugural lecture. Cambridge: University Press.

Kaldor, N. (1975): Economic Growth and the Verdoorn Law--A Comment on Mr Rowthorn's Article. In: *The Economic Journal*, *85* (340), 891–896.

Kaldor, N. (1977): Capitalism and industrial development: some lessons from Britain's experience. In: *Cambridge Journal of Economics*, *1* (2), 193–204.

Kannan, K. P., & Raveendran, G. (2009): Growth Sans Employment: A Quarter Century of Jobless Growth in India's Organised Manufacturing. In: *Economic and Political Weekly*, *44* (10), 80–91.

Kappel, R. (2014): Africa: Neither Hopeless Nor Rising. GIGA Focus Africa, 1. Hamburg: German Institute of Global and Area Studies (GIGA).

Kayizzi-Mugerwa, S., Anyanwu, J. C., & Conceição, P. (2014): Regional Integration in Africa: An Introduction. In: *African Development Review*, *26* (S1), 1–6.

Kelle, M. (2013): Crossing Industry Borders: German Manufacturers as Services Exporters. In: *The World Economy*, *36* (12), 1494–1515.

Kiely, R. (1998): Industrialization and Development: A Comparative Analysis. London: UCL Press.

Kilby, P. (1975): Manufacturing in colonial Africa. In: P. Duignan, & L. H. Gann (Eds.), *Colonialism in Africa 1870–1960: Volume 4, The Economics of Colonialism* (pp. 470–520). Cambridge: University Press.

King, G., Rosen, O., & Tanner, M. (2008): ecological inference. In: S. N. Durlauf, & L. E. Blume (Eds.), *The New Palgrave Dictionary of Economics*. Basingstoke: Palgrave Macmillan.

Kipré, P. (1993): Industrial development and urban growth, 1935-80. In: A. Mazrui, & C. Wondji (Eds.), *General History of Africa VIII: Africa since 1935* (pp. 357–392).

Knight, G., & Johnson, L. (1997): Tradables: Developing Output and Price Measures for Australia's Tradable and Non-tradable Sectors. ABS Working Paper, 97/1. Canberra: Australian Government Publishing Service.

Kongsamut, P., Rebelo, S., & Xie, D. (1997): Beyond Balanced Growth. NBER Working Paper Series, 6159. Cambridge Mass.: National Bureau of Economic Research (NBER).

Koopman, R., Powers, W., Wang, Z., & Wei, S.-J. (2010): Give Credit Where Credit Is Due: Tracing Value Added in Global Production Chains. NBER Working Paper Series, 16426. Cambridge Mass.: National Bureau of Economic Research (NBER).

Koopman, R., Wang, Z., & Wei, S.-J. (2012): Estimating domestic content in exports when processing trade is pervasive. In: *Journal of Development Economics*, *99* (1), 178–189.

Koopman, R., Wang, Z., & Wei, S.-J. (2014): Tracing Value-Added and Double Counting in Gross Exports †. In: *American Economic Review*, *104* (2), 459–494.

Kortmann, W. (2006): Mikroökonomik: Anwendungsbezogene Grundlagen. (Vierte, durchgesehene Auflage). Physica-Lehrbuch. Heidelberg: Physica-Verlag Heidelberg.

Kowalski, P. (2011): Comparative Advantage and Trade Performance. OECD Trade and Policy Papers, 121. Paris: Organisation for Economic Co-operation and Development (OECD).

Kowalski, P., Gonzalez, J. L., Ragoussis, A., & Ugarte, C. (2015): Participation of Developing Countries in Global Value Chains: Implications for Trade and Trade-Related Policies. OECD Trade Policy Papers, 182. Paris: Organisation for Economic Co-operation and Development (OECD).

Krelle, W. (1989): Jean-Baptiste Say (1976-1832). In: J. Starbatty (Ed.), *Klassiker des ökonomischen Denkens* (pp. 172–187). München: Beck.

Kronenberg, T. (2012): Regional input-output models and the treatment of imports in the European System of Accounts (ESA). In: *Jahrbuch für Regionalwissenschaft*, *32* (2), 175–191.

Krueger, A. O. (1974): The Political Economy of the Rent-Seeking Society. In: *The American Economic Review*, *64* (3), 291–303.

Krueger, A. O. (1985): Import substitution versus export promotion. In: *Finance and Development*, *22* (2), 20–23.

Krueger, A. O. (1986): Aid in the Development Process. In: *The World Bank Research Observer*, *1* (1), 57–78.

Krueger, A. O. (1997): Trade Policy and Economic Development: How We Learn. In: *The American Economic Review*, *87* (1), 1–22.

Krugman, P. R. (1979): Increasing returns, monopolistic competition, and international trade. In: *Journal of International Economics*, *9* (4), 469–479.

Krugman, P. R. (1985): Increasing Returns and the Theory of International Trade. NBER Working Paper Series, 1752. Cambridge Mass.: National Bureau of Economic Research (NBER).

Krugman, P. R. (1993): Toward a counter-counterrevolution in development theory. In: World Bank (Ed.), *Proceedings of the World Bank Annual Conference on Development Economics 1992: Supplement to the World Bank Economic Review and the World Bank Research Observer* (pp. 15–62). Washington D.C.: The World Bank.

Kuznets, S. (1967): Modern Economic Growth: Rate, Structure, and Spread. (2nd ed.). Studies in comparative economics, 7. New Haven and London: Yale University Press.

Kuznets, S. (1973): Modern Economic Growth: Findings and Reflections. In: *The American Economic Review*, *63* (3), 247–258.

Laitner, J. (2000): Structural Change and Economic Growth. In: *The Review of Economic Studies*, *67* (3), 545–561.

Lall, S. (1994): The East Asian miracle: Does the bell toll for industrial strategy? In: *World Development*, *22* (4), 645–654.

Lall, S. (2000): The Technological Structure and Performance of Developing Country Manufactured Exports, 1985-98: Oxford Development Studies. In: *Oxford Development Studies*, *28* (3), 337–369.

Laursen, K. (2015): Revealed comparative advantage and the alternatives as measures of international specialization. In: *Eurasian Business Review*, *2015* (5), 99–115.

Lawrence, P. R. (1986): Introduction. In: P. R. Lawrence (Ed.), *World recession and the food crisis in Africa*. London: Currey.

Leftwich, A. (1995): Bringing Politics Back In: Towards a Model of the Development State. In: *Journal of Development Studies*, *31* (3), 400–427.

Leibenstein, H. (1957): Economic Backwardness and Economic Growth: Studies in the Theory of Economic Development. One of a Series of Books from the Research Program of the Institute of Industrial Relations, University of California. New York: Wiley.

Leiva, F. I. (2008a): Latin American neostructuralism: The contradictions of post-neoliberal developments. Minnesota: University of Minnesota Press.

Leiva, F. I. (2008b): Toward a Critique of Latin American Neostructuralism. In: *Latin American Politics and Society*, *50* (4), 1–25.

Lensink, R. (1996): Structural adjustment in sub-Saharan Africa. London, New York: Longman.

Lenzen, M. (2003): Environmentally important paths, linkages and key sectors in the Australian economy. In: *Structural Change and Economic Dynamics*, *14* (1), 1–34.

Lenzen, M., Kanemoto, K., Moran, D., & Geschke, A. (2012): Mapping the Structure of the World Economy. In: *Environmental Science & Technology*, *46* (15), 8374–8381.

Lenzen, M., Moran, D., Kanemoto, K., & Geschke, A. (2013): Building Eora: A Global Multi-Region Input-Output Database at High Country and Sector Resolution. In: *Economic Systems Research*, *25* (1), 20–49.

Leon-Ledesma, M. A. (2000): Economic Growth and Verdoorn's Law in the Spanish Regions, 1962-91. In: *International Review of Applied Economics*, *14* (1), 55–69.

León-Ledesma, M. A. (2002): Accumulation, innovation and catching-up: an extended cumulative growth model. In: *Cambridge Journal of Economics*, *26* (2), 201–216.

Lewis, W. A. (1954): Economic Development with Unlimited Supplies of Labour. In: *The Manchester School*, *22* (2), 139–191.

Liesner, H. H. (1958): The European Common Market and British Industry. In: *The Economic Journal*, *68* (270), 302–316.

Lin, J. Y. (2011): New Structural Economics: A Framework for Rethinking Development. In: *The World Bank Research Observer*, *26* (2), 193–221.

Lin, J. Y., & Chang, H.-J. (2009): Should Industrial Policy in Developing Countries Conform to Comparative Advantage or Defy it? A Debate Between Justin Lin and Ha-Joon Chang. In: *Development Policy Review*, *27* (5), 483–502.

Lin, J. Y., & Monga, C. (2010): Growth Identification and Facilitation: The Role of the State in the Dynamics of Structural Change. Policy Research Working Paper, 5313. Washington D.C.: The World Bank.

Little, I. M. D., Scitovsky, T., & Scott, M. (1970): Industry and trade in some developing countries. A comparative study. London [u.a.]: Oxford University Press.

Lodefalk, M. (2014): The role of services for manufacturing firm exports. In: *Review of World Economics*, *150* (1), 59–82.

Lodefalk, M. (2015): Servicification of Manufactuirng Firms Makes Divides in Trade Policy-Making Antiquated. Örebro University School of Business Working Paper, 1/2015. Örebro: Örebro University.

Low, P. (2013): The Role of Services in Global Value Chains. Real Sector Working Paper. Hong Kong: Fung Global Institute.

Lucas, R. E. (1988): On the mechanics of economic development. In: *Journal of Monetary Economics*, *22* (1), 3–42.

Ludwig, U. (2010): Aus zwei Volkswirtschaften mach eine: Strukturelle Brüche und Disparitäten im Aufholprozess der ostdeutschen Transformationswirtschaft. In: Institut für Wirtschaftsforschung Halle (IWH) (Ed.), *20 Jahre deutsche Einheit: Von der Transformation zur europäischen Integration; Tagungsband [11. und 12. März 2010]* (pp. 115–132). Halle (Saale), Halle, Saale: Universitäts- und Landesbibliothek Sachsen-Anhalt.

Machlup, F. (1958): Structure and Structural Change: Weaselwords and Jargon. In: *Zeitschrift für Nationalökonomie*, *18* (3), 280–298.

Maddison, A. (1952): Productivity in an Expanding Economy. In: *The Economic Journal*, *62* (247), 584–594.

Maddison, A. (2001): The world economy: A millennial perspective. (Reprinted). Development Centre Seminars. Paris: OECD Publishing.

Magnusson, L. (2015): Political Economy of Mercantilism. Routledge Explorations in Economic History. Florence: Taylor and Francis.

Majluf, L. A., & Zarrilli, S. (2007): Challenging Conventional Wisdom: Development Implications of Trade in Services Liberalization. Geneva: United Nations Conference on Trade and Development (UNCTAD).

Malowist, M. (1992): The struggle for international trade and its implications for Africa. In: B. A. Ogot (Ed.), *Africa from the sixteenth to the eighteenth century* (pp. 1–22).

Manning, P. (1987): The Prospects for African Economic History: Is Today Included in the Long Run? In: *African Studies Review*, *30* (2), 49–62.

Marshall, A. (1920 [1890]): Principles of Economics. (eight edition). London: Macmillan and co.

Mattas, K. A., & Shrestha, C. M. (1991): A new approach to determining sectoral priorities in an economy: input–Output elasticities. In: *Applied Economics*, *23* (1), 247–254.

Maurer, A., & Degain, C. (2010): Globalization and trade flows: what you see is not what you get! In: *World Trade Organization Staff Working Paper ERSD-2010-12* .

Mbayi, L. (2011): Linkages in Botswana's Diamond Cutting and Polishing Industry. MMCP Discussion Paper, 6. Cape Town: University of Cape Town and Open University.

McCombie, J. S. L. (1982): Economic growth, Kaldor's laws and the static–dynamic Verdoorn law paradox. In: *Applied Economics*, *14* (3), 279–294.

McCombie, J. S. L. (2002): Increasing Returns and the Vedoorn Law from a Kaldorian Pespective. In: J. S. L. McCombie, M. Pugno, & B. Soro (Eds.), *Productivity growth and economic performance: Essays on Verdoorn's Law* (pp. 64–114). Basingstoke, Hampshire: Palgrave Macmillan.

McCombie, J. S. L., Pugno, M., & Soro, B. (Eds.) (2002): Productivity growth and economic performance: Essays on Verdoorn's Law. Basingstoke, Hampshire: Palgrave Macmillan.

McCombie, J. S. L., & Roberts, M. (2007): Returns to scale and regional growth: the static-dynamic Verdoorn Law paradox revisited. In: *Journal of Regional Science*, *47* (2), 179–208

McGilvray, J. (1978): Linkages, key sectors and development strategy. In: W. W. Leontief (Ed.), *Structure, system, and economic policy* (pp. 49–56). Cambridge [usw.]: Cambridge University Press.

McMillan, M., Rodrik, D., & Verduzco-Gallo, Í. (2014): Globalization, Structural Change, and Productivity Growth, with an Update on Africa. In: *World Development*, *63* 11–32.

Médard, J.-F. (1991): L'Etats néopatrimonial en Afrique noir. In: J.-F. Médard (Ed.), *Etats d'Afrique noire: formation, mécanismes et crise* (pp. 323–353). Paris: Karthala.

Meier, G. M. (2005): Biography of a subject: an evolution of development economics. Oxford: Oxford University Press.

Melo, J. d., & Tsikata, Y. (2015): Regional integration in Africa: Challenges and Prospects. In C. Monga, & J. Y. Lin (Eds.), *The Oxford handbook of Africa and economics: Volume 2: Policies and practices* (pp. 222–245). Oxford: Oxford University Press.

Menzel, U. (2000): States against Markets: Comments on T.N. Srinivasan. In: W. Schelkle, G. Elwert, & M. Kohli (Eds.), *Paradigms of social change: Modernization, development, transformation, evolution* (pp. 199–217). Frankfurt/Main: Campus-Verlag.

Millemaci, E., & Ofria, F. (2014): Kaldor-Verdoorn's law and increasing returns to scale: A comparison across developed countries. In: *Journal of Economic Studies*, *41* (1), 140–162.

Miller, R. E., & Blair, P. D. (2009): Input-output analysis: Foundations and extensions. (2nd ed.). Cambridge, New York: Cambridge University Press.

Mjimba, V. (2011): The Nature and Determinants of Linkages in Emerging Minerals Commodity Sectors: A Case Study of Gold Mining in Tanzania. MMCP Discussion Paper, 7. Cape Town: University of Cape Town and Open University.

Mkandawire, P. T., & Soludo, C. C. (Eds.) (2003): African voices on structural adjustment: a companion to Our continent, our future. Ottawa: International Development Research Centre.

Mkandawire, T. (2001): Thinking about developmental states in Africa. In: *Cambridge Journal of Economics*, *25* (3), 289–314.

Mkandawire, T. (2015): Neopatrimonialism and the Political Economy of Economic Performance in Africa: Critical Reflections. In: *World Politics*, *67* (03), 563–612.

Mohammadi, H., & Ram, R. (1990): Manufacturing output and labor productivity: Further evidence for the United States. In: *Economics Letters*, *32* (3), 221–224.

Mokyr, J. (1993): The British industrial revolution: An economic perspective. Boulder [u.a.]: Westview Press.

Morris, M., Kaplinsky, R., & Kaplan, D. (2012): One thing leads to another: Promoting industrialisation by making the most of the commodity boom in sub-Saharan Africa. Cape Town: University of Cape Town and Open University.

Morrison, A., Pietrobelli, C., & Rabellotti, R. (2008): Global Value Chains and Technological Capabilities: A Framework to Study Learning and Innovation in Developing Countries. In: *Oxford Development Studies*, *36* (1), 39–58.

Mosley, P., Subasat, T., & Weeks, J. (1995): Assessing adjustment in Africa. In: *World Development*, *23* (9), 1459–1473.

Narayanan, B., Dimaranan, B., & McDougall, R. (2012): Chapter 2: Guide to the GTAP Database. In: Center for Global Trade Analysis (Ed.), *GTAP 8 Data Base Documentation*. Lafayette: Center for Global Trade Analysis, Purdue University.

Naudé, W., & Szirmai, A. (2012): The importance of manufacturing in economic development: Past, present and future perspectives. UNU-Merit Working Papers, 2012-041. Maastricht: United Nations University.

Ndulu, B. J. (2007): The evolution of global development paradigms and their influence on African economic growth. In: B. J. Ndulu, S. A. O'Connell, R. H. Bates, P. Collier, & C. C. Soludo (Eds.), *The Political Economy of Economic Growth in Africa, 1960-2000* (pp. 315–347). Leiden: Cambridge University Press.

Niane, D. T. (1984): Conclusion. In: D. T. Niane (Ed.), *Africa from the twelfth to the sixteenth century* (pp. 673–686). Paris: UNESCO.

Niane, D. T. (1984): Introduction. In: D. T. Niane (Ed.), *Africa from the twelfth to the sixteenth century* (pp. 1–14). Paris: UNESCO.

Nicolini, M. (2011): On the evolution of institutional comparative advantages. In: *Structural Change and Economic Dynamics*, *22* (2), 162–172.

Nurkse, R. (1953): Problems of capital formation in underdeveloped countries. New York: Oxford University Press.

O'Brien, P. (1982): European Economic Development: The Contribution of the Periphery. In: *The Economic History Review*, *35* (1), 1–18.

Okun, A. M. (1962): Potential GDP: its measurement and significance'in Proceedings of the Business and Economics Statistics Section. In: American Statistical Association (Ed.), *Proceedings of the Business and Economics Statistics Section* (pp. 98–104). Washington, D.C.: American Statistical Association.

Oliver, R. A. (1977): Introduction: some interregional themes. In: R. A. Oliver, & J. D. Fage (Eds.), *The Cambridge history of Africa: Volume 3, from c. 1050 to c. 1600* (pp. 1–9). Cambridge: Cambridge University Press.

Öniş, Z. (1991): The Logic of the Developmental State. In: *Comparative Politics*, *24* (1), 109–126.

Oosterhaven, J. (1988): On the Plausibility of the Supply-Driven Input–Output Model. In: *Journal of Regional Science*, *28* (2), 203–217.

Organisation for Economic Co-operation and Development (OECD) (2011): Globalisation, comparative advantage and the changing dynamics of trade. Paris: OECD Publishing.

Organisation for Economic Co-operation and Development (OECD) (2014): African Economic Outlook 2014: Global Value Chains and Africa's Industrialisation. Paris: OECD Publishing.

Organisation for Economic Co-operation and Development (OECD), United Nations Conference on Trade and Development (UNCTAD), & World Trade Organization (WTO) (2013): Implications of Global Value Chains for Trade, Investments, Development and Jobs. Prepared for the G20 Leader Summit Saint Petersburg (Russian Federation) September 2013. Geneva: United Nations Conference on Trade and Development (UNCTAD).

Organisation for Economic Co-operation and Development (OECD), & World Trade Organization (WTO) (2012): Trade in Value-Added: Concepts, Methodologies and Challenges: Joint OECD-WTO Note. Paris: OECD Publishing.

Organisation of African Unity (OAU) (1963): OAU Charter. Addis Ababa: Organisation of African Unity.

Organisation of African Unity (OAU) (1980): Lagos plan of action for the economic development of Africa: 1980-2000. Addis Ababa: Organisation of African Unity.

Ott, A. E., & Winkel, H. (1985): Geschichte der theoretischen Volkswirtschaftslehre: Mit zahlreichen Tabellen. Grundriss der Sozialwissenschaft, 31. Göttingen: Vandenhoeck & Ruprecht.

Owusu, F. (2003): Pragmatism and the Gradual Shift from Dependency to Neoliberalism: The World Bank, African Leaders and Development Policy in Africa. In: *World Development*, *31* (10), 1655–1672.

Oya, C. (2010): Agro-pessimism, capitalism and agrarian change: trajectories and contradictions in Sub-Saharan Africa. In: V. Padayachee (Ed.), *The political economy of Africa* (pp. 85–109). New York: Routledge.

Oyejide, T. A., & Adewuyi, A. O. (2012): Determinants of backward linkages of oil and gas industry in the Nigerian economy. In: *Resources Policy - Making the Most of Commodities: The Determinants of Linkages in Africa*, *37* (4), 452–460.

Pack, H., & Westphal, L. E. (1986): Industrial strategy and technological change: Theory versus reality. In: *Journal of Development Economics*, *22* (1), 87–128.

Page, J. (2011): Should Africa Industrialize? UNU-WIDER Working Paper, 2011/47. Helsinki: United Nations University, World Institute for Development Economics Research.

Page, J. (2012): Can Africa Industrialise? In: *Journal of African Economies*, *21* (suppl 2), ii86-ii124.

Parikh, A. (1978): Differences in Growth Rates and Kaldor's Laws. In: *Economica*, *45* (177), 83–91.

Pasinetti, L. L. (1988): Structural change and economic growth: A theoretical essay on the dynamics of the wealth of nations. (Repr). Cambridge: University Press.

Patterson, M. G. (1991): A note on the formulation of a full-analogue regression model of the shift-share method. In: *Journal of Regional Science*, *31* (2), 211–216.

Perkins, D. H., & Syrquin, M. (1989): Chapter 32 - Large countries: The influence of size. In: Hollis Chenery and T.N. Srinivasan (Ed.), *Handbook of Development Economics* (pp. 1691–1753). London [u.a.]: Elsevier.

Peters, G. P., Andrew, R., & Lennox, J. (2011): Constructing an Environmentally-Extended Multi-Regional Input-Output Table using the GTAP Database. In: *Economic Systems Research*, *23* (2), 131–152.

Pfeiffer, B. (2015): "Upgrading" in Wertschöpfungsketten - Global und Regional. GIGA Focus Global, 08/2015. Hamburg: German Institute of Global and Area Studies (GIGA).

Pieper, U. (2003): Sectoral regularities of productivity growth in developing countries—a Kaldorian interpretation. In: *Cambridge Journal of Economics*, *27* (6), 831–850.

Pons-Novell, J., & Viladecans-Marsal, E. (1999): Kaldor's Laws and Spatial Dependence: Evidence for the European Regions. In: *Regional Studies*, *33* (5), 443–451.

Porter, M. E. (1990): The competitive advantage of nations. New York: Free Press.

Prebisch, R. (1950): The economic development of Latin America and its principal problems. Santiago, Chile: Economic Commission for Latin America, United Nations.

Radelet, S., & Sachs, J. D. (1998): Shipping Costs, Manufactured Exports, and Economic Growth. Columbia University Academic Commons. New York: The Earth Institute, Columbia University.

Raiser, M., Schaffer, M., & Schuchhardt, J. (2004): Benchmarking structural change in transition: The Macroeconomics of Accession: Growth, Convergence and Structural Adjustment. In: *Structural Change and Economic Dynamics*, *15* (1), 47–81.

Rasmussen, P. N. (1956): Studies in inter-sectoral relations. Dissertation. Copenhagen: Einar Harcks.

Ray, D. (2000): What's new in Developing Economics? In: *The American Economist*, *44* (2), 1–16.

Reinert, E. S. (2008): How rich countries got rich … and why poor countries stay poor. London: Constable.

Reinert, S. A., & Reinert, E. S. (2003): An Early National Innovation System: The Case of Antonio Serra's 1613 Breve Trattato. In: *Institutions and Economic Development/Istituzioni e Sviluppo*, *1* (3), 1–33.

Ricardo, D. (1817): On the Principles of Political Economy and Taxation. London: John Murray.

Robbins, L. (1928): The Representative Firm. In: *The Economic Journal*, *38* (151), 387–404.

Rodney, W. (1980): How Europe underdeveloped Africa. (5. impr). London: Bogle-L'Ouverture.

Rodrik, D. (1996): Coordination failures and government policy: A model with applications to East Asia and Eastern Europe. In: *Journal of International Economics*, *40* (1–2), 1–22.

Rodrik, D. (1998): Symposium on Globalization in Perspective: An Introduction. In: *Journal of Economic Perspectives*, *12* (4), 3–8.

Rodrik, D. (2004): Industrial Policy for the Twenty-First Century. C.E.P.R. Discussion Papers, 4767. London: Centre for Economic Policy Research.

Rodrik, D. (2008): Normalizing Industrial Policy. Commission on Growth and Development Working Paper, 3. Washington D.C.: The International Bank for Reconstruction and Development / The World Bank.

Rodrik, D. (2013): Unconditional Convergence in Manufacturing. In: *The Quarterly Journal of Economics*, *128* (1), 165–204.

Rodrik, D. (2015): Premature Deindustrialization. NBER Working Paper Series, 20935. Cambridge Mass.: National Bureau of Economic Research (NBER).

Roider, W. (1971): Zum Stand der Industrialisierung in Tropisch-Afrika. München: Weltforum Verlag.

Romer, P. M. (1990): Endogenous Technological Change. In: *Journal of Political Economy*, *98* (5), S71-S102.

Ros, J. (2001) Development theory and the economics of growth. Development and inequality in the market economy. Ann Arbor: University of Michigan Press.

Rosberg, C. G., & Callaghy, T. M. (1979): Introduction. In: C. G. Rosberg, & T. M. Callaghy (Eds.), *Socialism in Sub-Saharan Africa: A new assessment* (pp. 1–12). Berkeley: Institute of International Studies, University of California.

Rosenstein-Rodan, P. N. (1943): Problems of Industrialisation of Eastern and South-Eastern Europe. In: *The Economic Journal*, *53* (210/211), 202–211.

Rostow, W. W. ([1960] 1997): The stages of economic growth: A non-communist manifesto. (3rd ed.). Cambridge: University Press.

Rowthorn, B., & Wells, J. R. (1987): De-Industrialization Foreign Trade. Cambridge: University Press.

Rowthorn, R. E. (1975a): A Reply to Lord Kaldor's Comment. In: *The Economic Journal*, *85* (340), 897–901.

Rowthorn, R. E. (1975b): What Remains of Kaldor's Law? In: *The Economic Journal*, *85* (337), 10–19.

Roxburgh, C., Dörr, N., Leke, A., Tazi-Riffi, A., van Wamelen, A., Lund, S., Chironga, M., Alatovik, T., Atkins, C., Terfous, N., & Zeino-Mahmalat, T. (2010): Lions on the Move: The progress and potential of African economies. Seoul [u.a.]: McKinsey Global Institute.

Saad-Filho, A. (2005): The Rise and Decline of Latin American Structuralism and Dependency Theory. In: K. S. Jomo (Ed.), *The origins of development economics: How schools of economic thought have addressed development* (pp. 128–145). New Delhi: Tulika Books.

Sala-I-Martin, X. X. (1997): I Just Ran Two Million Regressions. In: *The American Economic Review*, *87* (2), 178–183.

Schefold, B. (1994): Antonio Serra: Der Stifter der Wirtschaftslehre. In: B. Schefold, A. Roncaglia, C. Poni, R. R. Portioli, & A. Heertje (Eds.), *Antonio Serra und sein »Breve Trattato«: Vademecum zu einem unbekannten Klassiker* (pp. 5–38). Düsseldorf: Verlag Wirtschaft und Finanzen.

Schefold, B., & Carstensen, K. (2014): Die klassische politische Ökonomie. In: O. Issing (Ed.), *Geschichte der Nationalökonomie* (pp. 67–92). München: Verlag Franz Vahlen.

Schumpeter, J. A., & Schumpeter, E. B. (2009): Geschichte der ökonomischen Analyse. Göttingen: Vandenhoeck & Ruprecht.

Sender, J., Cramer, C., & Oya, C. (2005): Unequal Prospects: Disparities in the Quantity and Quality of Labour Supply in sub-Saharan Africa. Social Protection Discussion Paper Series, 0525. Washington D.C.: The World Bank.

Sender, J., & Smith, S. (1985): What's right with the Berg Report and what's left of its critics? In: *Capital & Class*, *8* (3), 125–146.

Serra, A., Reinert, S. A., & Hunt, J. (2011): A "short treatise" on the wealth and poverty of nations (1613). London, New York: Anthem Press.

Singer, H. W. (1950): The Distribution of Gains between Investing and Borrowing Countries. In: *The American Economic Review*, *40* (2), 473–485.

Singh, B. (2012): Is the Service-Led Growth of India Sustainable? In: *International Journal of Trade, Economics and Finance, Vol. 3, No. 4, August 2012*, *3* (4).

Smith, A. (2008 [1776]): An inquiry into the nature and causes of the wealth of nations: A selected edition. Oxford world's classics. Oxford, New York: Oxford University Press.

Soludo, C. C., & Ogbu, M. O. (2004): A synthetis of major themes in the political economy of trade and industrialization in Africa. In: C. C. Soludo, H.-J. Chang, & M. O. Ogbu (Eds.), *The politics of trade and industrial policy in Africa: Forced consensus?* (pp. 1–42). Trenton, N.J: Africa World Press.

South Africa - Bureau of Census and Statistics (1960): Union statistics for fifty years Jubilee issue, 1910-1960. Pretoria: Government printer.

Sraffa, P. (1991): Über die Beziehungen zwischen Kosten und produzierter Menge. In: B. Schefold (Ed.), *Ökonomische Klassik im Umbruch: Theoretische Aufsätze* (pp. 137–194). Frankfurt am Main: Suhrkamp.

Srinivasan, T. N. (2000): Evolution of Development Theory and Strategy: Changing Perceptions of the Role of the Market, State and Foreign Trade. In: W. Schelkle, G. Elwert, & M. Kohli (Eds.), *Paradigms of social change: Modernization, development, transformation, evolution* (pp. 171–198). Frankfurt/Main: Campus-Verlag.

Stearns, P. N. (1993): The industrial revolution in world history. Essays in world history. Boulder [u.a.]: Westview Press.

Stein, H. (1998): Japanese aid to Africa: Patterns, motivation and the role of structural adjustment. In: *The Journal of Development Studies*, *35* (2), 27–53.

Steuart, J. (1767): An Inquiry Into the Principles of Political Economy: Being an Essay on the Science of Domestic Policy in Free Nations. in which are particulary considered population, agriculture, trade, industry, money, coin, interest, circulation, banks, exchange, public credit, and taxes. London: A. Miller and T. Cardell.

Stiglitz, J. E. (1986): The new development economics. In: *World Development*, *14* (2), 257–265.

Stiglitz, J. E. (2008): The Post Washington Consensus Consensus. In: N. Serra, & J. E. Stiglitz (Eds.), *The Washington Consensus Reconsidered: Towards a New Global Governance* (pp. 41–56). Oxford, New York: Oxford University Press.

Sturgeon, T. J., & Memedovic, O. Mapping Global Value Chains: Intermediate Goods Trade and Structural Change in the World Economy. Development Policy and Strategic Research Branch Working Paper, 05/2010. Vienna: United Nations Industrial Development Organization (UNIDO).

Su, D., & Yao, Y. (2016): Manufacturing as the Key Engine of Economic Growth for Middle-Income Economies. ADBI Working Paper, 573. Tokyo: Asian Development Bank Institute.

Sutcliffe, B. (1986): Africa and the world economic crisis. In: P. R. Lawrence (Ed.), *World recession and the food crisis in Africa*. London: Currey.

Sy, A. (2015) Are African countries rebasing GDP in 2014 finding evidence of structural transformation? Brookings Institution. https://www.brookings.edu/blog/africa-in-focus/2015/03/03/are-african-countries-rebasing-gdp-in-2014-finding-evidence-of-structural-transformation. Accessed 3 January, 2017.

Syrquin, M. (1988): Productivity Growth and Factor Reallocation. In: H. B. Chenery, S. Robinson, M. Syrquin, & G. Feder (Eds.), *Industrialization and growth: A comparative study* (pp. 229–262). New York: Oxford University Press.

Syrquin, M. (2007): Patterns of Structural Change. In: H. Chenery, & T. N. Srinivasan (Eds.), *Handbook of development economics* (pp. 203–273). Amsterdam: Elsever North Holland.

Syrquin, M. (2008): Structural Change and Development. In: A. K. Dutt, & J. Ros (Eds.), *International handbook of development economics* (pp. 48–67). Cheltenham, UK, Northampton, Mass: Edward Elgar.

Syrquin, M., & Chenery, H. B. (1989): Patterns of Development, 1950 to 1983. World Bank Discussion Papers, 41. Washington D.C.: The World Bank.

Szabó, S., Bódis, K., Huld, T., & Moner-Girona, M. (2013): Sustainable energy planning: Leapfrogging the energy poverty gap in Africa. In: *Renewable and Sustainable Energy Reviews* (28), 500–509.

Szentes, T. (2005): Development in the History of Economics. In: K. S. Jomo (Ed.), *The origins of development economics: How schools of economic thought have addressed development* (pp. 146–158). New Delhi: Tulika Books.

Szirmai, A. (2009): Industrialisation as an engine of growth in developing countries. UNU-MERIT Working Paper Series, 2009-010. Maastricht: United Nations University.

Szirmai, A. (2011): Manufacturing and Economic Development. UNU-WIDER Working Paper, 2011/75. Maastricht: United Nations University.

Szirmai, A., & Verspagen, B. (2015): Manufacturing and economic growth in developing countries, 1950–2005. In: *Structural Change and Economic Dynamics* (34), 46–59.

Tarp, F. (1994): Stabilization and Structural Adjustment: Macroeconomic Frameworks for Analysing the Crisis in Sub-Saharan Africa. London: Routledge.

Temple, J., & Wößmann, L. (2006): Dualism and cross-country growth regressions. In: *Journal of Economic Growth*, *11* (3), 187–228.

Terheggen, A. (2011): The Tropical Timber Industry in Gabon: A Forward Linkages Approach to Industrialisation. MMCP Discussion Paper, 10. Cape Town: University of Cape Town and Open University.

Teubal, M. (1971): Development Strategy for a Medium-Sized Economy. In: *Econometrica*, *39* (5), 773–795.

The Economist (2011): Africa rising: After decades of slow growth, Africa has a real chance to follow in the footsteps of Asia. 3 December, 2011; Issue 12. http://www.economist.com/node/21541015. Accessed 3 January, 2017.

The Economist (2015): African Energy: The leapfrog continent: The falling cost of renewable energy may allow Africa to bypass the carbon-intensive sort up to a point. 6 December, 2015. http://www.economist.com/news/middle-east-and-africa/21653618-falling-cost-renewable-energy-may-allow-africa-bypass. Accessed 3 January, 2017.

Thießen, U., & Gregory, P. R. (2005): Modelling the Structural Change of Transition Countries. DIW Discussion Papers, 519. Berlin: German Institute for Economic Research.

Thomson, A. (2016): An introduction to African politics. New York: Routledge.

Thorbecke, E. (2007): The Evolution of the Development Doctrine, 1950-2005. In: G. Mavrotas, & A. Shorrocks (Eds.), *Advancing Development Core Themes in Global Economics* (pp. 3–36). Basingstoke: Palgrave Macmillan.

Timmer, M., Vries, G. J. de, & Vries, K. de (2016): Patterns of Structural Change in Developing Countries. In: J. Weiss, & M. Tribe (Eds.), *Routledge handbook of industry and development* (pp. 65–83). London: Routledge.

Timmer, M. P., & Szirmai, A. (2000): Productivity growth in Asian manufacturing: the structural bonus hypothesis examined. In: *Structural Change and Economic Dynamics*, *11* (4), 371–392.

Timmer, M. P., Vries, G. J. de, & Vries, K. de (2014): Patterns of Structural Change in Developing Countries. In: *GGDC Research Memorandum 149* .

Tobin, J. (1973): Estimates of Sectoral Capital/Output Ratios for Kenya. Discussion Paper, 171. Nairobi: Institute for Development Studies, University of Nairobi.

Todaro, M. P., & Smith, S. C. (2006): Economic Development. (9th ed.). Harlow: Pearson.

Toye, J. (2006): Changing Perspectives in Development Economics. In: H.-J. Chang (Ed.), *Rethinking development economics* (pp. 21–40). London: Anthem Press.

Tukker, A., & Dietzenbacher, E. (2013): Global Multiregional Input-Output Frameworks: An Introduction and Outlook. In: *Economic Systems Research*, *25* (1), 1–19.

United Nations Conference on Trade and Development (UNCTAD) (1998): Trade and Development Report 1998. New York and Geneva: United Nations.

United Nations Conference on Trade and Development (UNCTAD) (2013): World Investment Report: Global value chains: Investment and trade for development. World investment report, 2013. Genf: United Nations.

United Nations Conference on Trade and Development (UNCTAD) (2015a): Review of maritime transport. Review of maritime transport. New York, Geneva: United Nations.

United Nations Conference on Trade and Development (UNCTAD) (2015b): Unlocking the potential of Africa's services trade for growth and development. Economic development in Africa report, 2015. New York: United Nations.

United Nations Conference on Trade and Development (UNCTAD), & United Nations Industrial Development Organization (UNIDO) (2011): Fostering industrial development in Africa in the new global environment. Economic development in Africa, 2011. New York: UNCTAD.

United Nations Department of Economic and Social Affairs (Ed.) (2007): Industrial Development for the 21th Century. New York: United Nations.

United Nations Department of Economic and Social Affairs (UNDESA) (2015): World Population Prospects: The 2015 Revision. New York: United Nations.

United Nations Industrial Development Organization (UNIDO) (2009): Breaking in and moving up: New industrial challenges for the bottom billion and the middle-income countries. Industrial development report, 2009. Vienna: UNIDO.

United Nations Industrial Development Organization (UNIDO) (2011): Economic Development in Africa Report 2011: Fostering Industrial Development in Africa in the new global environment. Vienna: UNIDO.

United Nations Industrial Development Organization (UNIDO) (2016): International Yearbook of Industrial Statistics. Vienna: UNIDO.

United Nations (UN) (1973): Input-Output Tables and Analysis. Studies in Methods, Series F, 14. New York: United Nations.

United Nations (UN) (1993): International Standard Industrial Classification of All Economic Activities (ISIC). New York: United Nations.

United Nations (UN) (1999): Handbook of input-output table compilation and analysis. Studies in Methods, Series F, No. 74. New York: United Nations.

United Nations (UN) (2008): International Standard Industrial Classification of All Economic Activities (ISIC). (4th ed.). Economic & social affairs, 4, Rev. 4. New York: United Nations.

Uzawa, H. (1961): On a Two-Sector Model of Economic Growth. In: *The Review of Economic Studies*, *29* (1), 40–47.

Vaggi, G., & Groenewegen, P. D. (2006): A concise history of economic thought: From mercantilism to monetarism. Basingstoke, Hampshire: Palgrave Macmillan.

Van de Walle, N. (2008): African economies and the politics of permanent crisis, 1979-1999. (8. pr). Political economy of institutions and decisions. Cambridge: Cambridge University Press.

van Reybrouck, D. (2013): Kongo: Eine Geschichte. Berlin: Suhrkamp.

Vandermerwe, S., & Rada, J. (1988): Servitization of business: Adding value by adding services. In: *European Management Journal*, *6* (4), 314–324.

Varian, H. R., & Buchegger, R. (2011): Grundzüge der Mikroökonomik. (8th ed.). Internationale Standardlehrbücher der Wirtschafts- und Sozialwissenschaften. München: Oldenbourg.

Verdoorn, P. J. (1956): Complementarity and Long-Range Projections. In: *Econometrica*, *24* (4), 429–450.

Verdoorn, P. J. (2002): Factors that Determine the Growth of Labour Productivity. In: J. S. L. McCombie, M. Pugno, & B. Soro (Eds.), *Productivity growth and economic performance: Essays on Verdoorn's Law*. Basingstoke, Hampshire: Palgrave Macmillan.

Vollrath, T. (1991): A theoretical evaluation of alternative trade intensity measures of revealed comparative advantage. In: *Weltwirtschaftliches Archiv*, *127* (2), 265–280.

Vries, G. de, Timmer, M. P., & Vries, K. de (2015): Structural transformation in Africa: Static gains, dynamic losses. In: *The Journal of Development Studies*, *51* (6), 674–688.

Vries, K. de, Vries, G. de, Gouma, R., & Timmer, M. (2013): Africa Sector Database: Contents, sources methods. Groningen: Groningen Growth and Development Center.

Wade, R. (1990): Governing the market: Economic theory and the role of government in East Asian industrialization. Princeton NJ: Princeton University Press.

Wallerstein, I. (1974): The Modern world-system 1: Capitalist Agriculture and the Origins of the European World-Economy in the Sixteenth Century. New York: Academic Press.

Wallerstein, I. (1976): The three stages of African involvement in the world-economy. In: P. C. W. Gutkind, & I. Wallerstein (Eds.), *The political economy of contemporary Africa* (pp. 30–57). Beverly Hills: Sage.

Wallerstein, I. (1983): European Economic Development: A Comment on O'Brien. In: *The Economic History Review*, *36* (4), 580–583.

Wangwe, S. M., & Semboja, H. H. (2003): Impact of Structural Adjustment on Industrialization and Technology in Africa. In: P. T. Mkandawire, & C. C. Soludo (Eds.), *African voices on structural adjustment: a companion to Our continent, our future* (pp. 151–187). Ottawa: International Development Research Centre.

Weiner, M., & Huntington, S. P. (Eds.) (1994): Understanding political development: An analytic study. (Reissued). Prospect Heights, Ill: Waveland Press.

Weiss, J. (2010): The Economics of Industrial Development. Hoboken: Taylor & Francis.

Wells, H., & Thirlwall, A. P. (2003): Testing Kaldor's Growth Laws across the Countries of Africa. In: *African Development Review*, *15* (2-3), 89–105.

Williamson, J. (1990): Latin American adjustment: How much has happened? Washington, D.C: Institute for International Economics.

Woellert, F., & Klingholz, R. (2016): Jobs für Afrika: Wie Nahrungsmittelproduktion und erneuerbare Energien Entwicklung beschleunigen können. Discussion Paper. Berlin: Stiftung Berlin-Institut für Bevölkerung und Entwicklung.

Wolfensohn, J. D. (1999): A Proposal for a Comprehensive Development Framework. Washington, D.C: The World Bank.

Wood, A., & Berge, K. (1997): Exporting Manufactures: Human Resources, Natural Resources, and Trade Policy. In: *Journal of Development Studies*, *34* (1), 35–59.

World Bank (1981): Accelerated Development in Sub-Saharan Africa: An Agenda for Action. Washington, D.C.: The World Bank.

World Bank (1984): World Development Report 1984: Recovery or Relapse in the World Economy? Population Change and Development; Population Data Supplement; World Development Indicators. World development report. Washington, D.C: The World Bank.

World Bank (1991): World Development Report 1991: The Challenge of Development. Oxford [u.a.]: Oxford University Press.

World Bank (1992): Governance and development. Washington, D.C: The World Bank.

World Bank (1994): The East Asian miracle: Economic growth and public policy. (2nd ed.). A World Bank policy research report. Oxford [u.a.]: Oxford University Press.

World Bank (1995): Adjustment in Africa: Reforms, results, and the road ahead. (2. print). A World Bank policy research report. Oxford [u.a.]: Oxford University Press.

World Bank (1997): World Development Report 1997: The State in a Changing World. Washington, D.C: The World Bank.

World Bank (2011): Fostering Technology Absorption in Southern African Enterprises. Directions in Development. Washington D.C.: The World Bank.

Wortzel, L. H., & Wortzel, H. V. (1981): Export Marketing Strategies for NIC and LDC-Based Firms. In: *Columbia Journal of World Business*, *16* (1), 51.

Wright, B. (2004): Africa can leapfrog into 21st century. (cover story). In: *African Business* (298), 12–14.

Yager, R. (2006): The Mineral Industry of Mozambique. U.S. Geological Survey Minerals Yearbook. Reston (Virginia): U.S. Geological Survey.

Yepes, T., Pierce, J., & foster, V. (2009): Making Sense of Africa's Infrastructure Endowment: A Benchmarking Approach. Policy Research Working Paper, 4912. Washington D.C.: The World Bank.

Yotopoulos, P. A., & Nugent, J. B. (1973): A Balanced-Growth Version of the Linkage Hypothesis: A Test. In: *The Quarterly Journal of Economics*, *87* (2), 157–171.

Young, A. (2012): The African Growth Miracle. In: *Journal of Political Economy*, *120* (4), 696–739.

Young, A. A. (1928): Increasing Returns and Economic Progress. In: *The Economic Journal*, *38* (152), 527–542.

Young, C. (1970): Decolonization in Africa. In: P. Duignan, & L. H. Gann (Eds.), *Colonialism in Africa 1870–1960: Volume 2. The History and Politics of Colonialism 1914–1960* (pp. 450–502). Cambridge: University Press.

Young, C. (1982): Ideology and development in Africa. Council on Foreign Relations Book. New Haven: Yale University Press.

Yusuf, S. (Ed.) (2009): Development economics through the decades: A critical look at 30 years of the world development report. Washington, D.C: The World Bank.

Zarembka, P. (1970): Marketable surplus and growth in the dual economy. In: *Journal of Economic Theory*, *2* (2), 107–121.

Zhang, L.-Y. (2011): Is industrialization still a viable development strategy for developing countries under climate change? In: *Climate Policy*, *11* (4), 1159–1176.